The King *of* Orchard Street

Vincent Palmieri

ISBN 979-8-89243-015-9 (paperback)
ISBN 979-8-89243-016-6 (digital)

Copyright © 2024 by Vincent Palmieri

All rights reserved. No part of this publication may be reproduced, distributed, or transmitted in any form or by any means, including photocopying, recording, or other electronic or mechanical methods without the prior written permission of the publisher. For permission requests, solicit the publisher via the address below.

Christian Faith Publishing
832 Park Avenue
Meadville, PA 16335
www.christianfaithpublishing.com

Printed in the United States of America

The King of Orchard Street is dedicated to my grandparents, mother, father, sister, aunts, uncles, cousins and all the residents of Orchard Street in Frankfort, NY that inhabited those five small blocks from the early 1900's through to the 1970's.

A marked dedication also goes to Robb Marchione M.D. in light of the brief discussion we had in the summer of 2020 that allowed the premise of the King of Orchard Street to crystalize in my consciousness and develop into the end product.

❦

Every kingdom, regardless of its size, must have a king. Throughout the prodigious history of mankind on this planet, the size of the numerous kingdoms that have existed has varied immensely. From tribes of primitive people wandering together in small bands searching for food and protection from the elements to Genghis Khan ruling, who, except for Jesus of Nazareth, controlled the largest swath of territory in history, mankind has always gathered purposely to achieve common goals. The Khan's reach stretched from China across two continents to Eastern Europe. A single person maintaining a large degree of authority over a huge piece of the Earth and millions or perhaps even a billion people. That person goes by many names through the ages such as emperor, king, president, czar, chief, maharajah, or other monikers. As time has passed, like with many situations in the world, size matters. Yet in the case of kings and kingdoms, size in the context of square miles and people has no relevancy. The Khan's kingdom covered millions of square miles, and he ruled over perhaps a billion people. On the other hand, the Duchy of Luxembourg is ruled up to today by the Grand Duke who controls less than a million people spread out over 998 square miles. Obviously a massive discrepancy in terms of Jesus, Genghis Khan, and the Grand Duke of Luxembourg, the as-of-yet undetermined King of Orchard Street reigned over possibly the smallest kingdom that ever existed. The kingdom only covered three to five small blocks and encompassed perhaps two hundred to three hundred people. Still, for all intents and purposes, it met the criterion of a kingdom, that criterion being a singular area encompassing a singular group of people all adhering to the same manner of dress, language, mores, and a specific code of conduct.

  There are numerous contenders for the coveted title of the King of Orchard Street. There's John-John Tubia, Uncle John Iocovozzi,

Donnie Ruffalo, and others. Each of the listed and more will get a chance to make their case as to who will ultimately be crowned the King of Orchard Street.

That choice in the end will be up to you, the reader.

Donnie gets the first attempt.

Donnie

The first words out of his mouth were, "I love the idea. I could tell stories for hours. We had a good life there, safe, happy, content. What else could you ask for? I must say, though, for the first few years after I left, it was a little tough for me. That was as an adult. As a child, there was nothing else I could have asked for.

"Tough? Obviously, we both knew a nerve had been struck," Donnie continued.

"The reason was I spent a lot of time worrying about my mom and dad. There were times when I was confused about it.

"I wondered if I did the right thing by leaving. Maybe I should have stayed and helped my mother and father. By the time I got back to them and finally did get them to Rochester, it was too late. There was nothing I could do. They had gotten too old. I wondered if I should have stayed in Frankfort and helped them. That's what I spent hours of time wondering about. I'm not quite sure how I could have helped, but at least I could have been there to try. Thank God I don't spend much thinking about it anymore. In certain situations, I did feel leaving them was the biggest mistake of my life."

The angst in his face and eyes from the other side of the table was evident. Donnie was still asking himself questions and wondering.

I tried to provide him with some perspective. I carried on. "Donnie, you did what you thought was right. You did what you thought was best. You did what you thought was going to help you the most. We all make choices that we think are best at the time, and as the years pass, sometimes we conclude that it wasn't the best choice. Way back then you thought it was fine. Life could be strange like that. I live fifteen miles from my parents' house. My sister lived five blocks from them, and we found ourselves in the same situation. It's a fact of life. We will all get our chance. Someday my kids and my kids' kids will be facing the same dilemma. No one gets away."

"I know that's the case," he said to me. "And at the time I did what was best for me, but I still feel that it wasn't the best for them. I wasn't there when they needed me. I wasn't there when I could have helped. When I finally did get to them, it was too late. There was no human help for them anymore. By then only God could help them."

We left it there for the time being and returned to Labor Day 2020 cookout. We both vowed to get back to the topic as soon as possible. Donnie had a good, positive story to tell to secure his chance in contention for the King of Orchard Street title. He was as primed to tell it as I was to hear it.

I called Donnie on Wednesday, September 15, 2020, during a powerful rainstorm. He and his wife, Joanne, were at Mount Rushmore National Memorial on their way to Yellowstone National Park and then proceeding from there to Las Vegas to visit his stepdaughter and all his wife Joanne's family. I told him I had begun working on *The King of Orchard Street* and wanted to know if he was still interested in being involved. Donnie told me that he was and would be back in Rochester on approximately October 2. I explained to him that oddly, that was the weekend I had intended to meet him in Rochester if we attended the Buffalo Bills versus Houston Texans football game in Orchard Park on Sunday, October 3. If he were home by October 2 and if the football game worked out, it would be convenient for all of us. Yet if the game didn't work out, Carol and I can make an overnight trip to Rochester to start working on our project. In any case, Donnie was still interested in the King of Orchard Street title, and I was thrilled that he was.

As in the iconic Marlon Brando and Rod Steiger scene from *On the Waterfront*, "I coulda' had class. I coulda' been a contender. I coulda' been somebody, instead of a bum which is exactly what I am," Donnie is a contender for the title of the King of Orchard Street.

As we continued to talk, I was reminded of our conversation on Labor Day 2020 as described above. I continued that I was sorry he felt that way, and I hoped that he still didn't because, again, it happens to us all. I suggested that he start taking notes and laying out his time line so that he could figure out where he wanted to start. With the Labor Day 2020 conversation as a given, Donnie and I agreed to wait until his return from Las Vegas about October 1 to begin full-scale on his narrative.

Donnie and Joanne returned from Las Vegas on October 2 as planned. Carol and I never made it to the Bills' game but instead went to Rochester on October 5. When we arrived at Donnie's home, he was relaxing in his living room. After hellos, a hug, and some small talk, we began to discuss *The King of Orchard Street*. We started from last Labor Day weekend when Donnie and Joanne came to Whitesboro for the holiday.

Donnie picked up with how he felt when he drove north on Cemetery Street in Frankfort the first time after moving and likely every time since.

He began. "I knew how difficult it would be for me to come back to Frankfort because of the emotion of the memories. I knew everything had changed. It was difficult because all the memories that I had growing up were not the same anymore. The home I grew up in was no longer ours. The street, the entire village changed. Most of the people were gone. Most of the landmarks were gone. The police station was demolished. The only bakery in the village, Latella's, was now owned by the Vitis. The North Side School was no longer a school; it was now the village office. On the other hand, all the great memories swelled up also. The playground on Orchard Street that the fire department used to flood in the winter to be used as an ice-skating rink was now a parking lot. It was emotional for me to come home and see that the reality of it all existed in my mind, but it was really gone. The on the ground reality was that it would never be the same again. It was hard for me to come to grips with that fact, both good and bad, but factual. The good certainly overpowered the bad, but still the fact remained that everything had changed. I got emotional every time I would come home. When I said it was hard for me, I wasn't kidding, not then not now."

"Prioritize," I suggested. "What do you think you missed the most? What do you think right away changed the most?"

Instantly, Donnie replied, "My house was not ours anymore. The house that my father toiled over and worked so hard for was no longer my house. It was no longer my security. It was no longer my family's security. My family, friends, and the neighbors were all gone. The memories of my youth are enthralling to me even though I had long ago moved on. I realized nothing had stayed the same. I had great expectations of finding the same scenario that was there when I left. I was very wrong. I was immediately confronted with a complete change, and it shook me. In 1977 my decision to leave after I graduated from college was very difficult. I knew I had to go because there was really no opportunity for me there. It was very difficult. Traumatic doesn't describe it. I remember driving down Cemetery Hill the first time I came back in 1978 and seeing the telephone pole down at the bottom of the hill that I hit with my sled head-on when I was nine. The impact put me in the hospital with a concussion and a fracture. The telephone pole is still there with the dent at the bottom where I hit it. I remember thinking to myself, 'This is going to be a tough one.' What an emotional experience. That split second in 1963 could have changed my entire life. Luckily, it didn't. Again, the whole village had changed, but that dent remained. When we were kids, we all thought Frankfort was huge. Then when we returned as an adult, it seemed so small. As an adult after all these years, I only want to maintain those exact memories."

It struck me unquestionably as an admirable goal. We collectively decided to take a break for a minute, get a drink of water, use the bathroom, and so on. When we resumed, we started with someone we both knew well on Orchard Street, a longtime resident by the name of Joffery Scalise.

"I heard you mention earlier a perfect King of Orchard Street–type story concerning Joffery Scalise. Tell me again your recollection of the Fourth of July each year and Joffrey's part in it," I said. I knew intuitively this would be good. There had to be loads of love in this tale of police and illegal fireworks, all covered up by the powers that be on Orchard Street.

Donnie smirked broadly and began the story of an annual Fourth of July exposé.

"Joffery was the lookout. He allowed us to keep evading the police all night. At that time fireworks were illegal any time of the year. Now certain types of fireworks are legal at specific times of the year. Way back then they were illegal all year long. Joffery Scalise was one of the key characters in our neighborhood. He was always sharply dressed in a starched white shirt, clean and pressed, every day. I can still see him sitting on the porch with a can of beer in his hand.

"Every Fourth of July we would stock up with fireworks beginning about two weeks prior. When the night came, we would paint our faces with black cork we made by burning the end of a real cork. We would paint our faces black with the cork, put on black clothes, and run recklessly all over Orchard Street, Litchfield Street, and Tisdale Avenue, really throughout the entire area, lighting fireworks everywhere. We had a group of about six to eight of us.

"When the police, with the station only a block away, heard the commotion, the officer on patrol straightaway headed for Orchard Street. Whether the police witnessed the ruckus themselves or were dispatched we will never know. They got there quick. This is where Joffery became a prime player in the process. From his porch he could look south and see past Main Street where the police station was located. As soon as he saw the patrol car move north on Litchfield Street, he would let out this loud, piercing whistle that we could hear all over the block. That was our signal. We would run north across the railroad tracks and hide in the tall weeds until we got a second all-clear whistle from Joffery, which meant the police had driven away. We would then proceed again creating havoc in the neighborhood with more fireworks. We could go again for about thirty minutes without fear of being caught before the police would drive down Litchfield Street again. Then Joffery and the rest of us would repeat the same cycle over and over until usually well past ten o'clock or until we ran out of fireworks, whichever came first.

"We did it every Fourth of July without fail for I bet ten years. Mike, Eddie and Ronnie Scalise, John Tubia, Johnny Kipper, and I. We loved and looked forward to it every year, and I think Joffery, at probably forty years old, did too. A full-grown man looking out for a group of minors so that those minors could do something illegal. Granted small scale, minor, harmless illegal but a ton of fun at the same time. It doesn't get more mischievous than that. What makes it even more funny is that we were hiding in plain sight right on the other side of the railroad tracks in the weeds. Perhaps the officer on patrol did see us in the weeds and really didn't care about something as inconsequential as fireworks. He just had to make certain that at least he appeared to be doing his job. We will never know, but it is possible.

"At sixty-seven years old now, I realize, by just being a kid, I could have gotten my father in trouble many times. Nothing serious, just doing what, at least then, I thought was fun, never aware that as I was a minor, my father was accountable for my actions. There was an incident that now I think was very funny, but I didn't think so when it happened. Johnny Kipper and I were probably twelve years old and very bored on a rainy day. We took it upon ourselves to walk to Corrado's Mill to climb on the bags of feed in that they were covered by a roof on the loading dock and dry. We would climb up on the piles of bags and jump from one stack over to the other, then to the other, and so on. An unofficial 1960s version of a version of a jungle gym.

"We were jumping and climbing all over the feed bags for probably thirty minutes when we decided to take out our pocket knives and split a few of the bags open. We cut open about four of them, and of course, the grain started to pour out all over the dock. When we realized what we had done, we both got scared and ran home, Johnny to his house and me to mine. I remember being home for about an hour and thinking that we must have gotten away with it. I soon found out how wrong I was. Unbeknownst to us, someone must have seen us do it. I was sure we got away with it until the manager of the mill was at our door telling my father what we had done. The manager was insistent that someone pay for the wasted grain. My dad's counteroffer was that if he and Frank Kipper Sr. went over to the mill, put the grain back in the bags, and sewed them up, would that resolve the issue?

"Thank goodness, the manager reluctantly agreed. My dad then called Frank Kipper Sr. and explained to him what we had done and what the mill manager agreed to. Frank Sr. and my father then met at the mill and proceeded to shovel the grain back into the bags we had cut open. After my dad left the house, I waited about fifteen minutes and walked toward the mill slowly. I could see from a distance my father shoveling the grain back into the bags and Frank Kipper meticulously sewing them together.

"I found out from Johnny after that when his dad got home, he wasn't very angry, but I thought my father was going to kill me as soon as he came in the door. He really didn't say anything. He must have understood we weren't being malicious. We were just being kids. Still, my father and Frank had to face the music for Johnny and me. We didn't mean anything by it, but we inadvertently had gotten both of our dads involved. It wasn't funny then, but I do get a chuckle out of it now."

I explained to Donnie that those are the archetype of accounts that the world needs to hear to accurately assess and determine who the real King of Orchard Street is.

That being the unabridged purpose of our collective efforts. A seemingly uncomplicated postulation.

Nevertheless, I suspect there is more to it than meets the eye.

I questioned Donnie if he had ever heard of the Great Schism. Which he had not.

I explained, "It happened about a thousand years ago in the Catholic Church, whereby two separate men backed by two separate factions of the Church both laid claim to being the real pope for a variety of reasons. I am not certain what each group's reasons were, but each of them had approximately half of Europe's total population in their respective camps. A papal selection process that had moved along effortlessly for about one thousand years prior to the Great Schism now became an immense controversy that literally tore the Catholic Church in two. I am not exactly sure how it happened, but two people along with their followers both creditably claimed to be the real Catholic Church with one group and pope centered in Rome, Italy. The other pope and group centered in Constantinople, Turkey. The entire dilemma eventually caused a split in the Catholic Church into the two churches that exist today. The Roman Catholic Church and Orthodox Catholic Church. It seems at that time two factions in the Catholic Church had different opinion as to the power of the pope, the type of bread used in Communion, the canonical territories, and a number of other church precepts.

"Consider the possibility that the same scenario develops with this book. For example, if ten thousand people read *The King of Orchard Street*, and two thousand five hundred of them conclude you are the king, two thousand five hundred think John Tubia is, two thousand five hundred think I am, and so on. It will make it hard to precisely determine the king because the premise is for the reader to crown the king. The same conditions as the Great Schism but on a lesser scale. In our case, we can name it the Minor Schism. I think you get my point. We would then have to proceed to a run-off of the top four vote getters to sooner or later determine the bona fide King of Orchard Street. We will have to see how it plays out over the long term, but I suspect there is another book in there somewhere. Maybe even a franchise. I question, is there a message in this bottle? For now, I suggest we get back to the proposition at hand. Who is the King of Orchard Street?"

So we did.

Donnie wanted to know if I remembered what happened with Malinda Murtaugh, him, and a bunch of firecrackers. I told him that

I had a vague recollection, and somehow, I knew that he would fill me in.

He continued. "Malinda's father, George, was a justice of the peace in Frankfort, and from a case the state police had confiscated a lot of firecrackers in a bust. I convinced her to steal them from her father and give them to me, which she did. My father had an enclosed sunporch on the front of the second floor of his house. Near the floor of the porch, there were four equally spaced out, about eight-inch-long by four-inch-high vents to let air in. My father had screened off the vents to keep the birds from getting in and building nests.

"I was in my room sleeping. I think it was a Saturday morning. I remember it being very warm, so it must have been in the summer. The birds had gotten almost through the screens and in the porch through the vents. They were making a lot of noise, squawking, screeching, and scratching. I took some of the firecrackers that I had gotten from Malinda, stuffed them in one vent, lit them, and then went back to my room to get more firecrackers. Needless to say, the burning firecrackers caught the insulation, the walls, and almost the entire porch on fire. I could hear Mrs. Caruso screaming from across the street in half English and half Italian to my mother, who was downstairs cooking, that the house was on fire. There I was in my underwear, literally watching my house burn down. Next thing I know, the fire department is with the police, and the whole porch is burning. Luckily, no one got hurt, but the fire did some damage.

"Now, I had to wait for my father to come home. I spent the whole time waiting in my room, practicing being hysterical in the hope that would make my father go easy on me. When he did finally come home, I tried the hysterical thing, but it didn't work. I could hear him yelling from the minute he came in the door. I don't think I ever saw him that angry. There was insulation, glass, and whatever else all over the street and the sidewalk. My brother went so far as to tell my dad that I wasn't hysterical and had been practicing in my room, waiting for my father to get home so I could make a scene and get off easy. Again, then not funny, now a little funny but sad for my father too. Then and now."

I told Donnie what an excellent man George Murtaugh was. How we had both belonged to Frankfort Kiwanis for many years and how we worked together at Frankfort High School. How George let me off the hook once for a traffic problem and how his father H. Frank Murtaugh always allowed my grandmother Mary to spread her heating bills out over the whole year because the poor woman didn't have enough money to pay the entire bill at once during the winter heating months. I always thought the world of him and still do. George passed away many years ago while living in South Carolina. I believe his wife, Marty, is deceased too, and their children are scattered all over the country. George was always a fine man and a great American.

I could see it in his eyes that Donnie now had what athletes call "the flow" and was ready to talk.

"How much of the activity at the North Side School playground do you remember?" Donnie asked.

My reply was quick. "Mostly I remember the ice-skating rink and how much fun it was to skate outside, which kids have no idea of now. When Carol and I used to take our kids ice-skating, it was usually at the indoor Whitestown Rec Center or the Clinton Arena, which was fun but not the same as outside. I still spot ponds in the winter and think that would be a great outdoor ice rink, but nobody does that anymore. The basketball court, which in the winter was the flooded ice rink, was always fun and full of kids. My best story or recollection of that playground is funny. I usually tell it in the presence of Tony Acquaviva.

"I start by asking, 'Do you know what they used to call me when I was a kid?' Usually their reply is 'No.' Unless I have told them the story twenty times. To which I reply, 'The Jesus of the playground.' To which Tony, not being able get the words out his mouth fast enough, adds, 'That's true because when people saw him coming down the street, all you could hear was doors slamming shut and people saying, "Jesus, here he comes again."' Always good for a laugh. I have told that story so many times now that I don't even need Tony there for the straight man anymore, although the effect is better when he is there. Mostly, I just tell the story. Still, always good for a laugh. I think I'll keep telling it. Tell me what you remember," I suggested.

Donnie began. "Mostly the school parking lot. It was actually a parking lot, but we used it as a playground. At some point the school put up baskets, then it became a parking lot, a playground, a basketball court, and in the winter an ice rink. In the winter the DPW used to drag a little shed to the side of the ice that had benches to sit on so that you could change your skates. We used to spend the entire winter there ice-skating. There were really no open or close hours. There was no one really in charge, so we stayed there 24-7. I mean we just about froze, but we never went home. It was so cold, almost excruciating, but we still stayed. When the summer came, the same area was used for basketball, football, baseball, or whatever. It had to be one of the busiest spots in Frankfort.

"I've got myself in whole lot of trouble there once. We decided to go down by the corner of the playground that would be that eastern corner of the schoolyard by the GLF and play baseball. My aunt Theresa lived across the street from that corner. At the time my grandmother was old and was living there with my aunt too. My aunt came out a couple times and told us to move away from the corner because someone was going to hit a ball through her front window. I got smart with her and told her we were just playing baseball and she should mind her own business. My grandmother was sitting in her wheelchair in the living room looking out the window at us playing baseball. Naturally, someone hit a foul ball that went through the window and almost hit my grandmother. I don't think it was me, but I really can't remember who it was. My eyes just locked on my grandmother. The look on her face was shocking. She was scared to the point of bewilderment. I can still see the poor old woman.

"My aunt Theresa came running out of the house like a crazy person screaming and yelling at all of us, telling us that we needed to leave, that we were dangerous, that she was going to call the police, and so on. Everybody ran but me. I had to stand there and argue with her. Finally, I ran too and went home. As soon as I got home, my aunt Theresa called and told my father what happened. That I was being a wiseass and that she never wanted to see us in the field playing baseball again. I tried to explain to my father that it was a playground, and we could go there any time we wanted, but he was having none of it. He insisted that I go to my aunt's house and apologize to her and my grandmother. I was going pay to fix the window and that was the end of it. I hated the idea, but my aunt was 100 percent right, and I was 100 percent wrong.

"Thinking back, if I had just kept my mouth shut and listened to my aunt, we could have moved our game to the other corner of the playground so that none of this would have happened. I didn't have enough sense to do that. I insisted that we had to stay where we were because it was our right, which in the end it was. After all, the area was a playground. Yet I had to argue with her just to be a wise guy. Sure enough, it got me in trouble. My father told me to never hit baseballs in that corner again and to stop being a smart-ass with people. He told me if we had gone to play in the other corner, we wouldn't be talking about any of this. Not Donnie, though. I had to do it my way, to a fault. Man, what was I thinking of?"

I next asked him, "Wasn't there a little chapel at the other end of Orchard Street near Corrado's Mill?"

Before I could even get my question out, Donnie said, "Do you remember that?"

My reply was, "I remember it being there, but I don't remember who it belonged to."

Donnie replied, "I believe that it belonged to the Addolorata Society. Don't you remember, every year they would have the festival at the end of Sheldon Avenue? They would start a little parade from their chapel on Orchard Street, proceed east to the corner of Orchard and Railroad Street, turn left to go north on Railroad Street until they got to Sheldon Avenue, then proceed east to the end of Sheldon Avenue where they would have their festival."

I asked, "Are you sure it belonged to the Addolorata? The reason I ask is because of the Sicilian-Calabrian thing. Historically, in Frankfort, the Sicilian population lived mostly "below the tracks" or on the north side of town. Tibber used to say that he resented the "below the tracks" concept because which way is north? Tibber felt he actually lived above the tracks because he was on the north side of town, and I lived "below the tracks" because Orchard Street and where we moved to, Fourth Avenue, was on south side of town, the Calabrian side. He was also convinced that he lived on Sheldon Boulevard, not Sheldon Avenue. Be that as it may. The reason I say this Sicilian-Calabrian thing is because to have their chapel on Orchard Street, the north side of Frankfort, and their festival location on Sheldon Avenue, the south side of Frankfort, goes against the idea of "above the tracks or below the tracks," which tended to be the separation line, the railroad tracks, between the north side and the south side of Frankfort. The line between the Sicilian and the Calabrian if you will. To go even farther, that's why you find the Saint Francis Club on the south side of Frankfort and the Addolorata on the north side of Frankfort. The Addolorata was named after Saint Maria who I believe was from Sicily. The Saint Francis Club was named after Saint Francis DiPaola, which I believe is in northern Italy, near Venice. Again, the Saint Francis Club was historically a Calabrian organization and the Addolorata was historically a Sicilian organization. At least that's my understanding of it. In any case, I remember the chapel and parade vaguely but the festival a lot. Tell me what you recall about it."

Donnie said, "It was a typical Italian festival and parade. They would march on Orchard Street with the banner with their patron saint on it. Everyone would line the street and make the sign of the cross as the saint went by and then pin money on the banner of the saint. That's the way you contributed to the society and got the benefit of the saint protecting you or helping you."

"Funny the way that works," I said, "in that I can remember my cousin Damian Iocovozzi saying if you pin a dollar on the saint, you go to heaven. If you pin five, your whole family goes. Leave it to Damian to make a statement like that, but ironically, whether he knew it or not, at a time in the history of the Catholic Church those, I suppose you could call them payments, were the main issue that caused the Protestant Reformation. The kings and nobles in Europe were doing horrible things, then paying the church to forgive them, whether God felt that way or not, only to go back out and do worse things. Then pay again and be forgiven again until their eventual death and eternal admittance into heaven. The Church and the Church's officials bought the idea for centuries. The Church gladly took the money, and who knows who did what with it? They made themselves rich and not much more than that, especially for the poor and sick.

"The list of 95 Theses that Martin Luther nailed on the door of the Wittenberg Castle Church in Germany in 1517 listed the payments, I think they were termed indulgences, as the number one issue. The Reformation also had a lot to do with the Bible and faith in God along with a very strong interpretation of using the Bible only as a guideline on how to live. It had to do with reforming the churches laws in general, but the indulgences were the driving force of it all. It was a whole big thing, and it really made the Catholic Church break off into four or five different Protestant churches. A huge moment in western history, but again that's where his idea of donating money to the church and certainly particular saints comes from. Martin Luther believed that you got into heaven not by doing good deeds but only by faith in God. Your good deeds helped, but you got in to heaven by strict faith in God. There was a lot of even bigger effects too.

"The Reformation led to the ideas of capitalism, democracy, and civil rights. It changed music, art, and literature. It really changed the whole world. It started to affect people and the concept of an education. People began to get an education on their own. They came to the conclusion that the Catholic Church was not the only place to learn. That you didn't have to learn only the way the Catholic Church said you had to and what the Church wanted you to learn. Education changed because it became more of a cultural thing based on where you lived, what you saw, and what you did. The whole idea of going against the grain of the Church really was a watershed moment in history. It happened, and it changed the world, and five or six hundred years later, you and I are still talking about it. Amazing stuff really."

Donnie said, "I have a lot of the same recollections of that festival and parade. We would go to the festival and run around the grounds all day and night. We would eat fried dough, sausage and peppers, hamburgers, hot dogs, and of course, when we got older, check out the girls. It really was wonderful. Sadly, it is all gone now. How about when they used to climb the greased pole? It was like a big thing. I think they did it on both Friday and Saturday night. It was the highlight of the entire event.

"The festival would take about a fifteen-foot pole and grease it with motor oil or cooking oil. I'm not sure exactly what, but obviously, it was very slippery. Then they would stand up the pole and put a staple on probably a $20 bill to the top of it. People would put teams together and try to hold on to the pole while their teammates climbed over them to stand on the next highest person's shoulders to get up to the top of the pole and grab the money. Once your team fell, you had to let another team try. They would keep going until one team got the money. Whatever team got up there first would keep the prize. People really went crazy over this. They'd be trying to hold on, with guys trying to climb over their backs to get above them and the people below trying to hold everyone up who was standing on their shoulders. All the while covered with some kind of grease for a twenty-dollar prize. I am not certain if the prize was $20. Remember, it was the 1960s, and $20 was a lot of money then, but I can't imagine it being much more than that. I would think $100 at the most, but that seems like far too much money for, again, the 1960s.

"They would get halfway up there, and sure enough, somebody would slip or couldn't hold the guy above them, and down they would all come. Thank goodness I never saw anyone get hurt, but it was hysterical to watch these people try to get up to the top of this pole when it was covered with grease. I have even seen people take motor oil, cooking oil, or whatever and put it on the pole of a bird feeder so that when squirrels try to climb to get at the bird seed, they slip down and never get to the feeder. If you think it is funny to watch a squirrel do it, it was even funnier to watch full-grown men do it. Those days will live with me forever because they were so funny. How could I ever forget something like that?

"They would have someone in the parade carrying a bell. The person would ring the bell, and everybody would come running down with their money to pin it on the saint. We really looked forward to it. Years later they tore down the chapel and built a new one on their property on Sheldon, so that was the end of the parade. It was something we looked forward to every summer. Then we had the Saint Francis Festival next, which had the same type of atmosphere.

"There's another situation that breaks my heart. I understand the Addolorata hasn't had a festival in over forty years. I guess they still have their property on Sheldon Avenue, but there's not much to it. The Saint Francis Festival is still going strong at almost one hundred years old. They probably haven't had their festival in the past couple of years mostly because of COVID, so that one will come back. It's a shame because those are the things that we looked forward to literally all year. We waited for the summer to come so that we could go to those festivals. They were great. I never had such strong positive feelings about anything in my life. I am glad the Saint Francis is going strong, but the Addolorata is long gone, and that makes me regretful." He paused.

I continued. "Do you remember during the Saint Francis Festival they would send up those aerial depth charges? They were loud and could be heard all over the village. If you looked up quick after the boom, you could see a little puff of smoke against a clear blue sky. That was the signal the festival was going, and we would all head that way. Recently, the village started to do a Harbor Fest in the harbor behind my grandmother's old house, and they use those same aerial depth charges. When I hear those explosions, it really makes the memories in my brain light up. Do you know, Donnie, that that harbor is only like one of two natural harbors on the entire Mohawk River? You should go check it out. They really did an excellent job with it. They have a microbrewery, boat slips, fishing dock, and the like. Pretty nice.

"The Saint Francis Club has more members than ever. You're right they haven't had their festival in two years due to COVID, but hopefully it will be back next year. They still have the parade from the chapel to Saint Mary's Church, sorry, I mean Our Lady Queen of the Apostles, then mass, and back to their grounds to continue the festival. The two buildings on their property are constantly booked for grad parties, stag parties, and birthday parties. The bar does a great business. The club will be one hundred years old in, I believe, 2026. The whole thing is a Frankfort institution. The Saint Francis and Frankfort Kiwanis are about the same age. Other than the Frankfort Fire Department, which is from about 1865, the Saint Francis and Frankfort Kiwanis are the two oldest nongovernmental institutions left. Consider this too. I am the second longest living member of Frankfort Kiwanis, and if you check the membership board at the Saint Francis with over one hundred members, I am about tenth from the top there too. Man, I mut be getting old. I am not certain what that means other than I am older than dirt, but by the grace of God, I'm still here. Real eye-opener, don't you think?

"Donnie, do you remember the Mr. Softee ice cream truck coming down Orchard Street?"

"I sure do. The truck would come down the street playing a little jingle with bells. Everybody would hear it, and all the kids would come running with their money. That bell ringing was like a magnet. We would order our ice cream and walk away as happy as hell. My mother would give me $0.25 to get a cone. It was okay, but I would rather have a sundae or a banana split, something of that sort. John-John Tubia would always come to the truck, and he would have a dollar or whatever the case may be, and he would buy a hot fudge or pineapple sundae. Whatever it was, it more expensive than my ice cream cone. I'd eat my cone, and I really enjoyed it, but I'd see Johnny eating his sundae, and it would kind of make me jealous. I would go in the house almost every time, and I would say to my mother, 'How come John-John could get a sundae and I only get a $0.25 ice cream cone?' She would tell me, 'You're not John Tubia, are you? Eat your ice cream cone, and that's the end of it. When you're John Tubia, you can get the ice cream that you want. For right now you're Donnie Ruffalo, and you're getting a $0.25 cone. Take it or leave it.'

"I didn't like it. I would rather have the sundae, but that's the best I could do. Now I think back how fortunate I was to even get an ice cream because there were kids on the street and kids all over the village of Frankfort who didn't get any ice cream. At least I got an ice cream cone, and now looking back, I'm very grateful for that. John-

John's looked good, though. Every day it was a milkshake, a pineapple sundae, a chocolate fondue, or whatever, and it sure looked good. I just ate my cone and kept my mouth shut for once."

I pointed out to Donnie, saying, "Do you know these days those trucks don't have soft ice cream on them? All they have is popsicles, Nutty Buddy, ice cream sandwiches, that sort of thing. I went out one day to get ice cream for my kids and asked the vendor why he didn't have soft ice cream on the truck any longer? He told me that the machines for soft ice cream were too expensive and too hard to maintain, so it wasn't worth it. To show you how people have changed, in the Town of Whitestown, someone was running a small ice cream route. The guy I asked about the soft ice cream had the theme song from the movie *The Sting* playing. Someone in the Town of Whitestown complained and made such an issue out of the fact that this song was playing that the town board ordered the guy first to turn the volume down, which he did. That wasn't sufficient. People still complained. Then the town board ordered him to turn it off, which then made no signal that he was coming. Obviously, very few kids came out to buy ice cream because they didn't know the truck was coming. Then I think eventually it wasn't even worth it for the owner anymore, and he just dropped the route. Again, talk about regretful.

"The thing I remember most about that ice cream truck was Michelle Reina Caiola being four to five years younger than me, hearing that bell and running out, like the rest of us, calling out Mr. Saucy, Mr. Saucy. I thought that was the funniest thing I had ever heard. To this day, when I see Michelle, I often remind her of that Mr. Saucy, Mr. Saucy name. Every time I hear one of those trucks, I think of Michelle running down the street after Mr. Saucy. Great ideas. Great memories. I agree with you 100 percent it's something that's irreplaceable." I explained this to Donnie while getting a little misty myself. "Let's talk about the sled accident. You almost got yourself killed as I recall. Am I correct?"

I got an instantaneous reply from Donnie. "Killed? You're not kidding. I can't remember the exact date, but it was December 1963. I had served mass at Saint Mary's that morning. In the early afternoon, I was supposed to meet my father at my grandmother Ruffalo's house on Orchard Street. When I came home from church, there was a few new inches of snow on the ground, and the snow was starting to pick up. I got in the house and started to put my snowsuit on. My mother asked me where I was going. I told her that with the fresh snow I wanted to go sledding for a little while. She reminded me that I had to meet my father later. I told her that I knew, but I didn't want to go to my grandmother's, and that was all to it. She was livid. She told me that my father was going to be very upset because I did 't show up. I told her that I didn't care, and with all this fresh snow, I was going to go sledding on Cemetery Hill. My mom was angry, but I insisted I was going to go, and I did.

"We went down the hill a couple of times. There was no problem. Nice, fast, good snow. I was enjoying it. The third time that I went down the hill, there was a couple of NYS Colony girls walking up the hill in the road. Being kids playing in the snow, we were riding double on one sled, jumping on and off of moving sleds at any time, jumping on another sled with someone already on it while it was moving, all in all just enjoying ourselves. We always rode down the hill on the sidewalk. I think I must have looked over at the girls walking up the hill in the road and lost control of my sled. I ran head-on into a telephone pole. No one wore helmets or anything like that in those days. I remember looking at my sled all kind of mangled up. I remember hitting the pole and seeing my sled. All but everything else was bewildering to me, especially in light of sixty years ago. I think Johnny Kipper picked me up and brought me to my house. On the way we ran into Charlie Giambrone who also helped Johnny get me to my house. I vaguely remember going in my house, but I was pretty much in and out of consciousness. About two hours after arriving home, I vomited. At that point my dad, mom, Phyliss, and Rossi Caruso put me in the car and took me to the hospital. I remember Phyllis telling me all the way to the hospital, 'Don't fall asleep, Donnie.' I was still slipping in and out of consciousness the entire time. I must have been in the hospital for three or four days.

"Apparently, while I was unconscious, the nuns from school had been coming to the hospital every day, praying for me. When I woke up, there was one of those tables that hospitals use to feed people over my waist with a gold crucifix and a votive candle on it. Being mid-December, about the eleventh I think, and in the late afternoon, my room was getting dark, and I was restrained. I thought for sure I was dead and started to freak out. As I looked about the room, there was a whole bunch of prayer cards, Christmas cards, get-well cards, and more votive candles scattered around. There were many homemade cards from all the kids in my class and probably from kids in other classes too. The nurse told me that the nuns came there almost every day with cards and stayed for a while to pray for me. I don't remember a whole lot about it other than I was diagnosed with a pin fracture of my skull, a long thin crack like a pin, resulting in a concussion. There was a possibility of some permanent damage, but thank goodness nothing ever came of that. That's why when I saw that telephone pole, some fifty years later, still sitting there on Cemetery Hill, I was shocked. It was the one that I had hit. I went so far as to take a closer look and I think I even located the spot on the pole where my head or my sled or both made contact. It was very scary for me then and now. Looking back, I really don't even know how I survived without there having been some kind of permanent brain injury. Frightening to say the least."

I continued. "You could have suffered what is called TBI, traumatic brain injury, like a few kids I had in my class did. It is often a devastating lifelong injury. NFL players, football players, from the constant hits in the head over decades can sustain an injury called CTE, chronic traumatic encephalopathy, which is permanent injury too. Yours could have been TBI, which is from one hard, severe impact. Affected NFL players committed suicide, killed, and hurt others. Do you remember Junior Seau from the Chargers and Eric Hernandez from the Patriots? There is a whole bunch of them and probably many more that we don't even know about for many years.

"I remember the nuns talking about you in school. They told us that you had a concussion and that you were in the hospital. There was a possibility that you could have some type of permanent injury. Sight or walking or whatever, but your doctors were hopeful there would be nothing long term. They wanted us all to pray for you, and I think we actually did in unison a few times. We all made get-well cards and sent them to you. It was a pretty big thing in school. When you recovered and came back to school, it was actually very nice. We were all happy to see you again and happy that you made a full recovery. Everything was back to normal pretty fast. You are very lucky that you didn't develop a long-term brain injury. At least that we are aware of."

We both chuckled at that statement.

"How about the Herkimer County Fair? That was the biggest party of the summer," I said.

Donnie replied, "You are absolutely right. There was food, candies, rides, clown shows, and more. It went on for a week, just one big party. Every year without fail the weather would always be good. There were years when it rained a little bit, but for the most part, the weather cooperated. They used to put a plastic owl on top of the flagpole, which was supposed to be on the lookout for the good weather. Even if it did rain a little bit, it didn't make any difference. We still went every day. We ran around that place like we were out of our minds. The best part, at times, was watching the fair employees. Those poor people. I'm not sure where many of them came from, but they always seemed to be struggling, and they were wild. There were beer tents all over the place. I think there were four or five. There would be fights and arguments all the time. It was wild, really wild. The games were almost impossible to win, but that didn't stop us. We kept playing and playing and playing all day and night long. I used to get so mad when I didn't win, but I would come back with more money and lose again. It was terrible, but it was a lot of fun.

"The parade was great. It was a pretty good size. It started out by Reese Road School. They would line up the divisions of the parade starting on Fifth Avenue. The next division would line up on Fourth Avenue by your house, then Third Avenue, and so on. The first division would start moving north from Fifth Avenue on Reese Road. Each section would leave from their respective avenue and follow the one before it until the whole parade was moving north on Reese Road. When the first division got to Main Street, it would turn west and proceed probably about two miles, then turn south on Cemetery

Street with six or seven good-sized divisions. I bet from one end to the other it covered from Reese Road to almost Frankfort Street. The left on Cemetery Hill would take the parade all the way to the fairgrounds. Then they would have an opening ceremony and would put that plastic owl up on a flagpole. I think they had fireworks that night too.

"We ran all over the place for a week. When we finally went home, we were cold and tired and hungry but it didn't stop us one bit. The only bad part about it was once the fair was over, school was right around the corner, and we all knew it. School started probably two weeks after the fair ended. When it was all over, after they took all the rides and concessions down to be moved to the next site, a whole bunch of us used to go to the fairgrounds and search through the grass for coins that people had dropped. Once in a while, someone might even find a bill. We found a lot of strange things. Even if we didn't find a penny, it was still a lot of fun. I really think that the only time that there was any traffic in Frankfort was the week of the fair. For that one week there would be cars, trucks, farm tractors, music acts, and demo cars in and out of the village all day long until close to midnight. Usually around six at night, traffic would actually back up on Main Street if you could believe that. It was a lot of fun. Once in a while, there would be a little rain, which would slow it down for maybe a day but not very often. It just kept going.

"We waited for it every year. There wasn't a week that went by that somebody didn't mention the county fair was opening soon. All week long, if the wind was right, you could smell that greasy fair food cooking, you could hear the bands playing until ten or eleven at night, you could see the light from the rides, and in that light the dust rising up from the demo derby and the tractor pulls. The smell of gasoline was everywhere. I can still see it and smell it now some sixty years later. It's burned in my brain."

"You know, Donnie," I picked up. "Fairs and carnivals trace their roots to biblical times. There's evidence that fairs are more than two thousand years old and are mentioned prior to the Bible. It seems they were held for mostly commerce being a good place for merchants to buy and sell products. As the centuries passed, they turned into entertainment occasions more than anything else. Think of the minstrels with the kings in England, and so on. They have been around forever. Small county fairs, big state fairs, world expositions, and all sort of festivals happen constantly. I still go to Herkimer County Fair every year. I've been going since I was probably five years old. I've started over the past fifteen or twenty years going to the New York State Fair every year again. Still a lot of fun and a lot of people.

"I've been to the World's Fair in 1964 in New York City. On one of the trips we used to take to New York City, my mother and I attended the World's Fair. We stayed with my uncle Rocky and his family on Fourteenth Street in Queens. The day we went to the fair, my mother and I walked about three blocks west on Fourteenth Street to Broadway in Queens. On the corner, we turned left and walked about five blocks south on Broadway to purchase tickets and board the elevated train or "L" that would take us over to Flushing Meadows, the site of the fair. Our pickup and drop-off point on Broadway was at the famous Steinway Piano Company, which I believe is still in business at the same location. The train disembarked to attend the fair near the site of what was Shea Stadium, at that time the new home of one of the latest expansion teams in baseball, the New York Mets. When we got off the train, the first thing I spotted was Shea Stadium. Shea opened up April 17, 1964, and my mother and I were there in July of 1964, making the stadium about three months old. It was very space-age with many multicolored squares attached to the building to the extent I thought for sure that it was part of the World's Fair, which it was not.

"My mom and I continued to walk across a footbridge to what was the actual entrance to the fair indicated by the famous Unisphere sculpture. The Unisphere is a stainless-steel spherical representation of the Earth built for the fair. Originally conceived by Gilmore D. Clarke, it turned out to be one of the biggest draws of the fair. The sculpture is 140 feet high and 120 feet wide, a globe depicting the continents of the Earth to indicate the interconnectedness of the whole planet along with orbits of space vehicles circling the Earth to indicate the dawning of the Space Age. Today the Unisphere still sits in Flushing Meadows, which is now also the site of the United States

Tennis Center, home of the US Tennis Open, and continues to be a large attraction for tourists.

"We were very fortunate to see Michelangelo's *Pieta*. The line was long, but my mother and I decided to wait. The wait was certainly worth it. The line ushered in on a long, darkened catwalk that eventually lead to a completely blackened room with a wall of glass about twenty feet in front of the *Pieta*. To see that unpigmented, polished marble monolith, at least life-size or more, from twenty feet away, bathed in a stark white light, the sculpture glistening in the darkness is a scene that will never escape my memory. *Staggering* does not do the experience justice. When the *Pieta* was shipped from the Vatican to Flushing Meadows by boat, it was packed in a large waterproof crate and set on the deck of the ship with hot air balloons attached to the crate so that in the event the ship sank, the balloons could be inflated and the *Pieta* would float into the air to be picked up safely. The risk was too large that the ship would sink and the *Pieta* would end up on the bottom of the ocean. Truly an indication of the reverence the world, art, and otherwise has for this age-old sculpture and its creator, Michelangelo. The sculpture in and of itself is stunning, and the method in which it was put on view combined to make the experience staggering. I will never forget it.

"Many of the attractions at Disney World in Florida today were originally displayed at the 1964 fair. The General Electric Carousel of Progress, It's a Small World, Pirates of the Caribbean, The Hall of Presidents, and more were all originally at New York World's Fair. My mom and I were extremely fortunate to see, in the context of the time, such world-class exhibits whereas nothing comparable had yet risen to the level of entertainment that those early attractions provided.

"Fairs of any size anywhere are great, and the same ideas color all of them. Greasy food, animals, exhibits, sales pitches, getting a little dusty, getting a little sweaty, drinking some beer, and enjoying yourself. The first steak sandwiches at a fair were served by a Jaycees Club in the 1950s, and baked potato bars became popular about then too. To this day the most popular food and the biggest seller is the cotton candy. It was first sold around 1897, and of all people, it was invented by a dentist and a confectioner. I think they both saw a market there but on two completely different levels. It is also called fairy floss and candy floss. Clear evidence of a dentist's involvement. Amazing info on different levels.

"My experience with fairs, which is quite a bit, is that is where the real people congregate. That's where the real people hang out. Not in mansions or on yachts or in two-million-dollar apartments in Atlanta. Those people are good. If that is the life they want for themselves, great for them. Yet my experience is different. Real people, down-to-earth people, "salt of the Earth" people, I guess you could say, hang out at county fairs, state fairs, and the like. Always have and always will. That is why politicians love them. Fairs make the politicians seem real, down-to-earth, common, like you and me. Those down-to-earth, common people are the ones who will get them in office, give them power, and in the end, that is all they are looking for—power. Big game, big ploy, but it works.

"The first known permanent all-purpose bazaar, the Grand Bazaar in Istanbul started in 1459 and still operates today. From there they spread all the way through Europe, Africa, the Middle East, India, and all over the world. Early evidence indicates the first ones were in the Tigris and Euphrates Valley in Mesopotamia held by the Persians prior to the time of Hammurabi. Remember Hammurabi from high school social studies? He was the Persian king who developed Hammurabi's Code. Really the first written laws. Prebiblical times were the start of fairs and bazaars. They show up in Europe around the 1500s, generally, with the Druids and their festivals. From there it seems the various kingdoms picked up the idea with the jousting, food, marionettes, and plays—all activities that became very popular. From there they spread to the New World and the colonies.

"The first fair that shows up on record is the York Fair, which I believe is in York, Pennsylvania, beginning 1765, which is eleven years before the American Revolution. It is the first operating fair in America, and I believe it still stands to this day. In the American colonies they began as agricultural affairs, but with the Industrial Revolution in the beginning of the nineteenth century morphed into mostly farm equipment and produce shows. The oldest state fair in in the United States on record is the Great New York State Fair in Syracuse originally held in 1841 and has been going strong ever since. I went a number of times when I was a child up to the age of maybe twelve or thirteen years old, and then I stopped going for whatever reason. I usually went with my aunt Grace, uncle Bill, Mary Lynne, and Willie Petrilli. I didn't go back again till probably fifteen years ago when my kids got a little older and wanted to go.

"New York State put a lot of money into the fairgrounds in the past five or six years. I think it was about $250 million. They put a new entranceway facade. They knocked down the old racetrack and grandstand in the back where they used to have concerts and Standardbred horse racing along with stock-car racing. That's where I saw the Doobie Brothers, the Beach Boys, and I think it was Carlos Santana way back in 1975. The crowd got wild, and the state police used tear gas to calm the situation down, not pretty for sure. Across Route 690 West by Onondaga Lake is now a concert venue called Lakeview that is owned by Saint Joseph's Hospital where they have concerts with famous performers. When the old grandstand came down, they built a new midway with grass, benches, picnic tables, and of course, rides, shows, and games. It still has some of the old buildings like the horse and cow barns, the show ring, and the like, but little by little, it is all coming down. They have a new building called the Cuomo Convention Center, which must be 150 yards long and 50 yards wide. Car shows, outdoor shows, and the like, are held there. They also have not the Syracuse Crunch but another hockey team that's playing there. They host high school and college graduations. Really a nice asset if they use it the way it is intended and don't misuse it. Should be a moneymaker.

"I noticed when I started going there, maybe fifteen years ago, that they were still smoking cigarettes and allowing beer and wine consumption all over the grounds, not in designated areas only. I was shocked to see that because every place you go nowadays, those practices are only in designated areas. This year with the legalization of marijuana in New York State, they were smoking weed all over the grounds also. Legal but it is inappropriate, with families and kids around, for marijuana, cigarettes, and alcohol consumption to be allowed everywhere, not in designated areas. Apparently, the fair got many complaints and has decided they will allow those practices only in designated areas, which should have been that way long before marijuana legalization. What were they thinking of? You can still smoke marijuana and cigarettes, you can still drink alcohol, but it's going to be in designated areas only at best or worst depending on your personal proclivities. That decision was a no-brainer.

"The Boonville Oneida County Fair is still going strong, which was originally organized as the Boonville Fair Association. Then it changed to the Boonville Union Agricultural Society in 1871. At some point after that, it became the Boonville Oneida County Fair. In 1888 the association purchased the grounds where it still stands. President Howard Taft gave an address there. Thomas R. Proctor and Fred Proctor were once presidents. Carrie Nation, also known as Hatchet Granny, of saloon destruction fame, gave a speech there rallying against the evils of alcohol I bet. Thomas E. Dewey and Nelson Rockefeller, former governors of New York State, have attended. Country stars from all over the United States such as Crystal Gayle, Jeannie C. Riley, Barbara Mandrell, and Dolly Parton have appeared at one time or another.

"I think it gets less of a crowd than the Herkimer County Fair because it's in Boonville, and people have to drive there, which is twenty-five to thirty miles each way from here, whereas the Herkimer County Fair from Utica is eight miles east in Frankfort. Both continue to go strong but again a lot more restrictions now. A lot less alcohol and smoking only in designated areas. Nowhere as wild as it used to be for certain. The Herkimer County Fair began in 1861 as the Herkimer County Agricultural Society in Herkimer at the spot where the NYS Thruway exit is located. It too had a racetrack and grandstand just like many of these fairs. It was destroyed by a fire in 1950. From there it moved to the Cemetery Hill site in Frankfort, which was Slocum's Farm, allowing it to continue to grow. There are about ten buildings now, a horse corral, display buildings, food, all the good stuff.

"There have been numerous groups using the grounds all year long like the NYS Trappers Association, Good Sam Club, the Mohawk Valley Blues Society Festival, and a good-sized country show called Frog Fest sponsored for twenty years by a local radio station called Big Frog 104. The Frog Fest may no longer be there, but it was big for many years. Indeed, a busy place all year long. In the winter they store boats and trailers. All that plus their fair for a week.

"There is the irony of it all for me. No matter how this thing plays out, always about seventy-five thousand people attend the fair each year. It can rain for four out of six days or be sunny all six days, and seventy-five thousand people still attend. Directly, that is iffy for me because in my experience, and I've been dealing with the Herkimer County Fair since I was about ten years old, obviously, weather is a factor. I have parked cars in downpours, in ninety degrees and 95 percent humidity, perfect sunny days, whatever conditions, and the attendance never fluctuates. Really? Come on now. The biggest issue is "too many hands in the in the pot." A pot full of cash for that matter. There was one guy in Frankfort that was on the fair board of directors for years, and the standing joke was the only time he had any money was the week of the fair, which seemed to be the truth. Loads of cash flowing in with little or no oversight. The kind of situation Tony Soprano and the guys loved. I'm not sure about the money that comes in. I'm not exactly sure where it all goes, but it does seem to disappear. The Fair Association has made some improvements, and it looks pretty good, but really not much has changed.

"I started parking cars when I was a Key Club member at Frankfort High with Kiwanians like Rudy Egnazyak and Joe Kiszka in 1968. Frankfort Kiwanis parked cars there until about the year 2000. Every year was a battle. We had to go and negotiate with the fair board as to how much they were going to pay us, usually about $2,500. We had to be there from noon to midnight for Tuesday, Wednesday, Thursday, Friday, Saturday, and Sunday. A big number of hours and bigger number of man-hours. In about 2000, the whole deal fell apart, but luckily, right across the street, the Herkimer County Area Development Corporation built a business park, and a company called Fiberdyne Labs, owned by a guy from Herkimer, allowed us to park cars on their property.

"Fiberdyne was the first in the park and kept a big chunk of the land empty for them to expand if they felt they should someday. Through the efforts of Jimmy "Coots" Accattao, who passed away recently, we got access to the empty piece of land, probably six or seven acres. We have to provide them with a certificate of insurance, and they let us use the lot. The certificate of insurance comes through Kiwanis International. Approximately five hundred cars fit in there at $5 a car. We can do about $2,500 in one night if we fill it up. We rarely do that, but it has happened before. We open it from Tuesday, Wednesday, Thursday, and Friday from 5:00 p.m. to about 9:00 p.m. Being open approximately sixteen hours over the course of four days. Saturday from noon to about nine. That's another nine hours and then Sunday from noon to six. Total thirty to thirty-five hours depending on the weather. We cancel at anytime if the weather doesn't cooperate. It usually works out well for us. Then every penny goes back to the community in the form of youth programs. We do it pretty much at our convenience, and it works out great. The whole area is called the Frankfort Industrial Park South.

"Again, some of the tenants are Fiberdyne Labs, a fuel company named Harbor Fuel, another company named Hale Manufacturing that is moving out soon to their other factory in Schuyler. Believe it or not, Amazon has purchased the Hale Building for one of their 'last mile centers,' which is the final stop for a package before delivery to the customer's door. If you go across the bridge on Route 5S over to where Frank Paratore had his pumpkin and strawberry patch when we were kids, Tractor Supply Company came in and built a huge thirty-five- to forty-truck-bay distribution center. Of course, with that sprang up ADK company with showers, food, fuel, and places to park the tractor trailers. Exactly what truckers need. Another company moved in that makes mostly stainless steel and any type of tank up to three stories high. They put up a four-story building so they could assemble the tanks standing up. Recently they made four or five new stainless-steel tanks for Genesee Beer, put them on barges, and floated west on the Erie Canal to Rochester. Imagine that canal, almost two hundred years later, is still being used for transportation and commerce as when it was when it was opened in 1825. I also hear that across the street David Russell's farm has been purchased by Motel 6 where they're going to build a location for the truckers to sleep and shower instead of sleeping in their trucks or showering in ADK. A good thing for business, a good thing for commerce, and a good thing for taxes.

"I must admit the first time I drove west on Route 5S from by the Frankfort Gorge toward where the Herkimer County Fair is and I saw that distribution center sitting on the left-hand side of the road, with green or red flashing lights to indicate which bays were open or closed, and the three-story building there, I was aghast. I was so shocked I had to look twice. As if Martians had landed. Instead of Frank Paratore's pumpkin patch and a field of strawberries, there is now fifteen- to eighteen-acre industrial park. Shocked isn't a strong enough word, and neither is aghast. Great site for jobs, commerce, and business, but it's certainly not sleepy, little hole in the wall, Frankfort stuff. Like you said one hundred times, 'That's what shocks me when I go there.' I'm appalled to see what has happened also, and I still live in the area. Go ahead, Donnie. I'm sorry I got you way offtrack there. This is supposed to be your story."

We both smiled, and he started again.

"Litchfield Street being a one-way street going north only had parking on one side only, the side father's house was on. On the other side of the street was Puzze's Restaurant. Cars would park on my side for Puzze's. My brother and I would sit on the curb, blocked from the sight of the customers in Puzze's, and pry the chrome off the parked cars. We would get off bits and pieces and then use them to put on his bike. My brother was really doing it, and I was the lookout. A coconspirator if you will. My brother really did it all, and I just happened to be there watching. I bet you're thinking that's a likely story or that's what they all say. We did it for a lot of years until a guy named Fred LaVeck finally caught us taking chrome from his car and began chasing us down the street. The jig was up. Fred then spread the word to the customers in Puzze's, which put an end to our little enterprise or at least my brother's little enterprise. I don't think

I actually ever got any chrome for my bike because my brother took it all.

"On Sunday I would walk across the street to Puzze's with my father. He would sit in the bar and read the newspaper. My dad would buy me a Coke and some smoked herring to eat. The Yankee game was always on the radio. I would eat a lot of herring. That salty taste was so good. At times I would switch to Orange Crush from Coke. Wonderful, simple experiences. Priceless. What is going on at Puzze's now?" Donnie wanted to know.

Wonderful, simple, and priceless don't give those Sundays full credit as verified by the fact that sixty years later Donnie still remembers them vividly.

"Closed up," I said. "It has been made into apartments. Doesn't look like a real positive crowd living in there. Same old story absentee landlords and not the best tenants, you know the routine. Remember Johnnie Puz standing behind the bar with his white apron on, pouring the drafts, then with a tongue depressor skimming the foam off the top, and refilling the glass until you got a full draft? All the while with the picture of John F. Kennedy above the bar watching him. I can recall sitting on your steps watching Johnnie Puz working away. Priceless is not the word for it. Simple. Sweet. Timeless. Gone now. Ironically."

"How about my other fireworks incident?" Donnie asked.

I replied, "There was another one? Wasn't one enough? Did the house incident happen first? What is it with you and fireworks?"

He replied, "I think it was some of the same fireworks I got from Malinda Murtaugh that she stole from her father and gave to me, but it was about a year later, after I almost burned down our house. Remember, Malinda's father was a village justice and would keep all the confiscated fireworks at his house, so there was a big variety and an almost constant supply. Malinda would steal them from her father and give them to me. One day she showed up at school with a big bag of cherry bombs, depth charges, and so on. Nice ones, the more powerful ones. I didn't want just firecrackers anymore. I had moved up to more dangerous things. She asked me if I wanted them, which of course, I did. I took the whole bag home and put it behind the dresser in my room. Every now and then I would take out three or four and go to the creek behind the Corrado's Mill and light them.

"One day I told my father I was going fishing with Richard Nicastro. We had no intention of fishing. We went to light a bunch of the fireworks I had gotten from Malinda. Richard and I were lighting them one after the other and having a grand time. For whatever reason, we had about three or four cherry bombs that wouldn't detonate. I decided to break them all open and light the gunpowder thinking it would just fizzle out. I then proceeded to do just that. We quickly learned that the loose gunpowder wouldn't explode, probably due to the lack of it being compressed, but it sure did catch on fire fast. It flared up so quick with such a flash that for about a minute I was blinded. The flare-up was hot, I mean, white-hot. When the pile of gunpowder ignited, so did the fingers on my right hand. I ended up with third-degree burns on three of my fingers. They were burned black and real ugly. Richard and I were debating whether or not I should go home because, again, I knew I was going to get it from my father. I really didn't know which choice was worse, my father or the burns. Classic devil-and-the-deep-blue-sea scenario. All I was supposed to be doing was fishing, and here I was coming home with an injury again.

"Richard got the idea to put my hands in the cool creek to kill the pain and save my skin. It really didn't help, and the pain was getting worse as I was getting more frightened by the second. I had no choice now but to go home. As we were walking back to my house, I could see my father standing on the corner of Orchard Street and Litchfield Street. He was watching me walk toward him crying with my hands up in the air covered in black soot. He's yelling out to everybody in the neighborhood that he sent me fishing, and I came back home with my hand burned. In any event, I ended up in a doctor's office with third-degree burns. Naturally, I must get a tetanus shot. Dr. Enzien Sr. lived in Frankfort at the time and had an office attached to his house. My dad brought me to his office where Dr. Enzien examined my hand and diagnosed third-degree burns. He put my whole hand in an alcohol wrap, which sent my pain level through the roof. He then bandaged my hand very carefully and sent me home.

"When I got home, my father naturally wanted to know where I got the fireworks. I wasn't about to blow Malinda in for the second time, but I had to. There was no other choice. My father then called Mr. Murtaugh to tell him what had happened and that the fireworks came from Malinda. Poor Mr. Murtaugh felt terrible for a second time. He apologized to my father and told him that he would straighten it out with Malinda once and for all. At some point in the next day or so, Mr. Murtaugh came to my house with a gift. It was a blue shirt with a matching blue tie, very nice actually. I also remember how nice the gift was wrapped up and how apologetic he was, so much so that I felt sorry for him.

"Malinda must have gotten in a whole lot of trouble because she didn't talk to me for over a month. Although they caused a lot of trouble for me when I was young, I still love fireworks—cherry bombs and all that stuff—and always will."

All this talk about fireworks really gets my memory ignited, so to speak. I never knew where the fireworks came from in Frankfort, but I knew who had them to purchase and that they were illegal. There was always three or four people in town who would sell them. The sellers also knew full well that they were dangerous too, but that did not deter them one bit from selling them to children and adults. About two weeks before the Fourth of July, suddenly, they would be available in several places. Not in public locations but mostly in the homes and garages of these three or four individuals. Many years later did I find out where they came from and how they got into Frankfort. I don't remember anyone seriously getting in trouble for selling and possessing fireworks, but they were illegal. Most times if you were caught with fireworks, the police would just confiscate them, soak them in a tub of water to render them not ignitable, then dispose of them in the garbage. One person did at one point get into some serious trouble for possessing and distributing fireworks, but that was only the tip of the iceberg. He was breaking so many laws that I think the police had to do something about it. Most of the violations were street level, but he was extremely blatant about it.

He was promoting gambling, booking bets, selling stolen goods, and among other things, selling and distributing illegal cable television boxes. The problem was not so much that other people weren't doing the same things. The problem was he was so flagrant about what he was doing. He got so wide open and so accessible that the police had to put a stop to it. Finally, he was arrested for several different charges all put together under what I think was a racketeering charge under New York State's RICO laws. This individual may have done a short period of time in jail and paid some fines, but I don't think anything ever became more than that. If my memory serves me correctly, soon after that arrest, for whatever reason, he passed away.

New York State has now made it legal to possess and use fireworks for the two weeks prior to July 4 and for the period between Christmas and January 1 but only certain types of fireworks distributed by licensed merchants. The legal type are the ones that are ground-based and not aerial displays. That really doesn't stop people from using whatever type of fireworks they please, but the laws are on the books, making only certain varieties of fireworks legal for a specific period of time. I had no idea where the fireworks came from when I was a child, but at about twenty-eight years old, I found out. The same individual who was eventually arrested for fireworks and a variety of other charges asked me one summer day if I wanted to take a ride with him for a few hours. It being on the weekend in the beginning of June, I agreed. I really wasn't sure where we were going or what we were going to do, but since I'd known him my whole life, I went along for the ride. We made a whole day out of it. We stopped and had lunch, did the business we set out to do, and returned to Frankfort probably about four o'clock in the afternoon. We drove about two hours south on Route 12 through the Southern Tier of New York State to the Spectacular Fireworks store in Gibson Pennsylvania about ten miles across the New York–Pennsylvania border. Fireworks even way back then in approximately 1980s were legal in Pennsylvania and still are, which I did not know until the day I walked into the store way back then. We went in the store, and the person who invited me to come along bought probably $500 worth of fireworks, which in 1980s was a huge amount. We loaded the legally purchased fireworks into the car and started our trip back to Frankfort. After the two-hour ride back, we unloaded the fireworks into his garage where he then proceeded two separate the large packages of various types into many smaller individual packages to sell at the street level. Right from purchasing them as a teenager beginning in about 1965 to seeing the purchases made in Pennsylvania and the distribution set up in about 1980s, I had no idea how the fireworks got into the Mohawk Valley or how they were distributed. I would bet that, that wasn't the only purchase and distribution network in the area. There were probably many people doing the same thing, but evidently, that was how it was done. It started with a legal process in one state but ended up being an illegal process in another state.

All of this brings me to the most dangerous situation I ever encountered with fireworks, which is really quite similar to one of Donnie's experiences.

After about two weeks prior to the Fourth of July, running all over the village of Frankfort igniting fireworks, some of my friends and I still had a good amount of them leftover after the fourth. We recognized that at some point, soon, we were going to have to dispose of the rest of them. Dennis and Michael Fiorentino, Johnny Chard, Alex and Frank "Foof" Palumbo, Frank Bianchi, Joey Bellino, and I put together a plan to dispose of those remaining fireworks. The entire group of us walked from Fourth Avenue to the Frankfort-Schuyler football field behind Reese Road School. We all agreed the best method of disposal would be to light all our remaining fireworks at once. On a warm, dry summer day, we piled them all up at the fifty-yard line of the football field to light the whole pile. In the pile we had firecrackers, cherry bombs, depth charges, bottle rockets, Roman candles, and others. Certainly a good assortment of very dangerous fireworks. As we were standing around the pile in a circle, we tried to light them. For whatever reason, none of them would ignite right away. The seven or eight of us were down on our hands and knees, wondering out loud why the pile would not ignite. The whole group had our faces not more than twelve inches away from this pile of fireworks while blowing on it to get the flames to start. We very soon realized they were actually ignited. In a flash, in a real flash of less than five seconds, the whole pile ignited, shooting out flames, projectiles, and strong detonations directly into all of our faces being not more than a foot away. The eruption briefly stunned us all, but we were still able to get back on our feet and run away from the pile of still exploding fireworks. The group of us must have sat on the ground a hundred feet away from that pile for probably ten minutes before we came back to our collective senses. To this day, I recall it starkly and still wonder how none of us lost an eye, severely burned our faces or even the rest of our bodies by catching our clothes on fire.

Only by the grace of God in that situation and in many others did all of us not get severely injured or even killed.

Count your blessings, both big and small every day.

"Tell me more, Donnie," I urged.

Donnie continued. "Do you remember when Rossi Caruso had the strip bar?"

"I certainly do, and I bet I know what you're about to say. Before you do, Jimmy DeRollo suggested the other night when I was at his house that this whole King of Orchard Street project may be a waste of time in that the king is a forgone conclusion. As Jimmy suggests, whenever you think of Orchard Street, the first person that comes to mind is Rossi Caruso, and he maybe right. Only issue with that is Rossi has been dead for twenty years. Obviously, he can't tell his story. Again, I bet I know what you're about to say, but please go on. Jimmy does raise a good point, though."

"The bar was originally Zito's, but at one point, Rossi bought it, renamed it the Grand Prix, and converted it to a strip place. Do you remember when you and I used to sneak through the alley between your aunt Josie's house and Jimmy Kipper's house and duck behind the hedges in your aunt's front yard to get a glimpse of the strippers by looking through the picture window that was on one end of the bar?" Donnie queried.

"I remember it like it was yesterday. Really got my attention. We did it for so long that eventually, when Rossi gave up on the strippers and went to go-go nightclub sort of bar, we were still doing it. We used to do the same thing but watch the go-go dancers in the cages instead of the strippers. Do you remember the TV show *Hullabaloo*? I was just watching it the other night. It was on NBC for about a year in the mid 1960s. ABC also ran a similar show named *Shindig*. Both shows were big hits with big stars making appearances. Cher, Woody Allen, Simon and Garfunkel, Chuck Berry, among others all did appearances. The episode I watched the other night was with Chuck Berry and Trini Lopez. It had the Hullabaloo Dancers in the cages with the white go-go boots and the frilly dresses, really risky stuff for those days. *Shindig* was pretty much the same thing at the same time. A Los Angles disc jockey named Jimmy O'Neal was the host with his wife Sharon Sheely. Both series were really the result of the British Invasion. *Shindig* had appearances by the Beatles, the Who, and the Rolling Stones. They were the first no-holds-barred rock-and-roll shows seen in America. They are all available on YouTube, which is where I watch them. Again, I am offtrack. This is your story. Sorry, go ahead."

Donnie restarted. "Rossi, Chico Sanders, Johnny Caruso, Philly Caruso, the whole clan was there every night. I still can see them through the window all lined up, sitting at the bar. That went on for probably ten years until Rossi closed it down, or it burned down. I can't remember. That whole scene was entertainment in and of itself.

"The Frankfort Pool and the Hilltop Park were also big spots for entertainment in the summer especially. We spent literally all day at that pool from ten or eleven in the morning to six or seven at night. Swim, run around in the woods, swing on vines hanging from the trees like we were Tarzan, running up and down Dead Man's Trail, and on and on. In the winter we were sledding down the road when the village closed it to cars, and sledding down Dead Man's Trail. Our energy was limitless. What in the world has happened in the past sixty-five years? I swear I missed it all."

"I think the same way. I ask myself the same question every day, and honestly, I don't have an answer."

That brief interaction made me weary and sad for a split second but not enough to quit. So we continued.

Donnie started again. "How about the Frankfort Pool? Hanging out on that ledge by the spring with the ice-cold water flowing out of there about a gallon a minute. Checking out all the girls wandering back and forth. Nice, warm summer days. Honestly, at that time I didn't think it was ever going to end. Wasn't that like one of the biggest freshwater pools in New York State or maybe in the entire United States? You said it was built during the Great Depression by the Works Projects Administration to keep masons and concrete plants working?"

I replied, "Yes, as I said, along with thousands of other public facilities all across the United States. What about all the fun we had in the winter, sledding down from the Hilltop? It was a lot safer than sledding on Cemetery Hill, as you can personally attest. The road from Litchfield Street up the Hilltop Road was blocked for traffic. Usually the rider and sled would stop before getting to the bridge or at least the very bottom of the hill. After that you ran into Litchfield Street. That was not good. We had a lot of fun in the winter. We'd start way up at the top of the hill, running with the sled in our hands. When we got some momentum, we would drop the sled on the ground and jump on it to start traveling down to the bottom of the hill, probably moving fifteen to twenty miles per hour. Still dangerous but again a lot safer than Cemetery Road with traffic moving up and down that road while you were too, but only on a sled. During the course of a day, there would probably be twenty to thirty kids on the Hilltop, all sliding, jumping in the snow banks, racing each other down the hill on sleds, and really enjoying ourselves. In the summer, at least you had brakes on a bike and could slow yourself down, but there was still some nasty spills that I recall. One was another student at Saint Mary's School by the name of Tommy Collins. If I remember correctly, Tommy fell off his bike one summer day, got really scrapped up. In the winter on a sled, there was really no way of stopping. You just hoped the sled ran out of speed before you and it slid on to Litchfield Street with cars moving north and south all the time. We were all very fortunate to have never gotten really hurt. At least on the Hilltop Road."

I could tell by the expression on his face the memories of both the winter and summer at the Frankfort Pool and Lehman Park or, as we called it, the Hilltop, really thrilled Donnie.

Donnie continued. "Do you remember how they used to pump water right out of the creek? What is the name of it? Moyer Creek? Fish and all would get sucked into the pool. Then they had that big chlorine pit where they would dump in gallons of chlorine to try to kill the germs. I don't think it killed one germ. I think it may have even multiplied them. How about when you used to go down and touch your feet on the bottom in about eight feet of water? You could feel your feet slide from the moss that was literally covering the bottom of the entire pool. You could never see the bottom. Was the water ever cold? It never warmed up. We were always swimming in freezing water. If you didn't swim there, we went to the Drops and swam or went south in the Frankfort Gorge to swim. In the end, I think those spots were even cleaner than the pool because at least the water was running, whereas in the pool they could put all the chlorine in the world in there, but their water was pretty much stagnant. Except for that one pump on the kiddie end and a small outlet on the other end by the diving board, which was gravity-fed. The rest of the water just sat there. How much could it have really moved in and out? Not much, I bet. That's why it turned green all the time, that's why it was never clear because the water hardly moved. At times it would get so bad that they would close the pool for a couple days, drain it out, and then try to clean it up with the mold in the slime growing all over the place, only to pump the water right back in from the creek. It might have stayed somewhat clean for that week, and then it was right back into the same condition."

I asked Donnie, "Have you gone by there lately?"

"I have, as a matter of fact, and I see it's been all flattened out and made into a basketball court. The spring is still running, and water is coming out faster and colder than ever. I see people filling up gallons with water at the spring. Seemed like something is going on there because kids were running around. It's a pretty big playground. Nothing like the pool area used to be, though. I see that the buildings have all been knocked down, even the one on the other side of the street, and the rock ledge was removed."

I responded, "Unfortunately, it got to the point that the whole area was so dilapidated there was nothing you could do to save it.

The village got some money wherever they could, at least enough to fill it in, as you say, flatten it out, and make a playground. The village put up a basketball court and swings. They made the fountain still functional, and you're right. The water pours out of that thing just like it did fifty years ago. I think the kiddie pool in the back of the lot is still there, and that's about all it's become now. The village had closed down the bridge to go to the Hilltop a number of years ago because New York State DOT deemed it unsafe, which it was for about twenty years before they declared it to be. To get to the old pool area, you had to go around from Cemetery Road and down the hill.

"Finally, they put together the money to tear the old bridge down, hell, that thing was unsafe when we started to drive, and are putting up a new bridge. I am amazed by the amount of work, people, and equipment required for such a small bridge. It must have taken a month to tear down the old bridge, remove the parts, and grade the area before they even started to build a new one. It seems small to me, but evidently, it is much bigger than I understood it to be. I am not a civil engineer, but my daughter Alaina's fiancé, Noah, is. Clearly, I am naive concerning the scope of such an endeavor. The magnitude of the work required is shocking to me. That is an indication of how little I understand of such things. What does it take to build something like the Sunshine Skyway Bridge that connects Tampa to St Petersburg? Thank God for smart people like Michael Palmieri and Noah Bushey, a construction manager and a civil engineer, respectively. I bet it was a historic bridge, built most likely by the WPA as was the Frankfort Town Hall and the Frankfort Fire Department. In most of these villages and towns that you drive through in the United States, you will see municipal buildings, fire departments, pools, and the like with probably 75 percent of them built by the WPA.

"Again, you're right. It was Roosevelt putting people to work because the Depression had put so many people out of work. The government paid them to build municipal projects. Then they even went so far as to I hire artists and sculptors to put them to work painting full wall-size pictures on the inside of the buildings and creating sculptures to be placed in the lobbies. In the Frankfort Post

Office, I believe it's still there, is a painting by I don't know who, that is likely a WPA painting. There is also a statue, I believe it's still there also, on the wall to the right as you walk in, that is probably a sculpture by a WPA sculptor.

"My wife and I have friends who live in Kingsport, Tennessee, where another Depression program, the Tennessee Valley Authority, built dams all along the Tennessee River to produce hydroelectricity to distribute to the rural areas of Tennessee that never had electricity up to that point. One of the plants that Jim Wright worked at, a TVA plant, has a massive painting on the wall, has to be fifty feet long and twenty feet high. I imagine it's still there. The type of things that those artists painted were farms, cattle, mountains, industries, big city skylines, and so on. The WPA had them paint those kinds of pictures to give people confidence in America. To give people confidence that the American way of capitalism would eventually find its way out of the Great Depression. That everything would be all right. That we would work through it, and in the end, capitalism would play out the right way.

"Franklin Roosevelt used to give the famous fireside chats, I believe they were on Saturday night, that people would listen to on the radio. Roosevelt's only purpose was to inspire confidence in the typical American. That it would all work out, that he and the American government were working on it, and in the end, everything would be fine. We just had to stick together and work our way through it. The same idea was exemplified by those paintings, those pools, those municipal buildings, fire departments, town halls, and so on. The concept was that in the end the Great Depression was a temporary thing, and it would all work out. It would take time, but it would eventually all work out. As Roosevelt said, "We have nothing to fear but fear itself." Take a good look at those buildings sometime. Usually red brick, very colonial-looking, tall Roman classic columns meant to generate confidence, stoicism, and permanence. Those buildings and America were not going anywhere. Next time you come to Whitesboro, remind me we will drive by the middle school, perfect example of what I am talking about. The building is probably one hundred years old, and I have said from when my kids went there to school that it is the best building they have in the entire district. A lot of bases were covered by all those dramatic policies of the federal government during the Great Depression. Really not that long ago and yet, in my opinion, humbling and inspiring, to say the least.

"Have you checked out the actual Hilltop lately? It has changed a lot too. About ten years ago, Frankfort Pop Warner and the village of Frankfort together built a small football field for the team to play. It's a funny story how it got named. There was no name for it at the time, and there was a game being played on a Sunday afternoon. Fred Pumilio was at the game, you remember Potter, watching his son Anthony play who played on the team. A newspaper reporter was covering the story about the new field opening and asked Potter what the name of the field was. He told him he didn't know, but he thought it was Potter's Field. Fred just said that name because Potter was his nickname. Lo and behold, the reporter called the new field by that name in his article, and it stuck. People now refer to it the Potter's Field. Potter, not knowing what else to say, just happened to tell the reporter that name. He took it as the truth, put it in the newspaper article, and the facility got tagged with the name Potter's Field. That's how it's referred to now. A true story and the stuff Frankfort legends are made of. A century from now, it will still be referred to as Potter's Field, and maybe someone might know why.

"You must remember Dominic "Smokey" Lille? He was a justice of the peace in Frankfort for many years. Truly another great guy. About fifteen years ago, after Dominic died, his family put together a bunch of money and gathered a bunch of donations to build a small covered pavilion area in his honor. They named it "Smokey" Lille Grille. It gets used quite a bit, and it makes me happy when I go to the Hilltop and see it. Between "Smokey" and George Murtaugh, town and village of Frankfort justices of the peace, we were in good hands. They were both such honorable and sincere men but also well aware of when someone just needed a break. God knows how many times they waved, dismissed, or reduced whatever the case may be— parking tickets, speeding tickets, running stop sign tickets, or whatever it may be for me. Both were fine people. The village and town were both full of people like them, which made it such a safe, fun place to grow up. We probably got away with more than we should have, but most incidents were harmless. There was no sense making big issues out of situations when it was easier and smarter to just keep the peace.

"The term *justice of the peace* comes from the thirteenth century and the reign of King Edward III in England. It seems Edward felt minor infractions could be handled in a low-intensity way by someone who had little if any education and minimal training in the law. The purpose was to keep small issues just that, small. Edward appointed people to do that, and the idea of a JP was born. It kept everyone happy, and in the end, that was the point. Some seven hundred years after Edward, I couldn't think of two other people, other than George and "Smokey," that could have met the criteria of Edward's idea better than them, although Joey Bellino, not Joey F. or C. Bellino, the other one, has been doing a good job at it too for the past thirty years. Others, I understand, not so good. With a little leeway "Smokey," George, and Joey made Frankfort safe and fun to live in."

"Let's go on. Tell me what you remember about you and me meeting up with Dominic "Ming" Bianchi on weekday nights to go to Loiacano's bar and drink beer when we were both probably sixteen years old. Tell me your story and see if it matches up with my mine."

Donnie took right off on cue. "It was the funniest thing. All true, you and I had a great time with that, didn't we? I would call you, and you would walk from your house on Fourth Avenue to Main Street. We usually met up on the bank corner intersection of Litchfield Street and Main. We would walk to Ming's storefront, I guess you could say that was a storefront, on the east end of that block on Main Street. It started when Ming would be sitting out in front, and we'd stop and talk to him. After a number of nights doing the same thing, we asked him if he wanted to go to George Loiacano's bar and have a beer. Were we fifteen or sixteen years old? He told us that he really didn't drink but that he would go with us for one beer. I think more than anything else, Ming lent us both some credibility since we were both well below the drinking age.

"That went on for probably two months. How we both knew that we would get served in the bar, I still have no idea. Well, before you know it, he would be looking for me or looking for you if we didn't walk past his store. Here was a guy probably thirty years older than us, looking for two minors to go drink beer with. Again, similar situation to Joffery Scalise covering for us with the fireworks. Before you know it, he was in the bar every night of the week whether he met up with us or not. When we walked in the bar, he was often in there before us. What gumption we had, two minors walking into a bar like we owned the place. Huge chutzpah, for sure. Then he really started to drink. Every time I walk into a bar, he would be there and usually drunk at that. He started blaming us for it. Ming would say, 'I never drank until I got into it with you guys. You both ruined me.'

I picked the story up. "All true, Ming would tell me the same thing over and over. You're absolutely right about that. After you moved out of Frankfort and I returned to Frankfort from college, Ming got worse. I'd go into Club Royale, and he would be sleeping in a booth at seven or eight at night, completely drunk. Every time he would have an argument with his wife or his girlfriend or his kids, which was pretty much every night, he'd be in the bar, getting more wasted by the minute. I'd see him there all the time, and I bet that went on until I was twenty-five or twenty-six years old.

"At some point he decided that he was not going to drink anymore and quit. Ming would tell me that he was out every night drinking, and you and I were at fault. His famous line was, 'I never drank before I got going with you guys. Winnie, you, and Freddy ruined me.' Isn't it funny how Ming always called me Winnie when he knew my name was Vinny, and he always called you Freddy, like your father and brother, when he knew full well your name was Donnie? He must have blamed us one hundred times for his drinking. Ming always claimed he never had a problem before. 'You guys got me started,' he would say again and again as he got more and more tipsy. What did we do to him? Years later, when you and I were probably twenty-five or twenty-six years old, he was still drinking a lot, and it's our fault? I don't remember us ever holding a gun to his head. Did we drag him into the bar every night? It really became a problem because he was drinking way too much. Thank goodness, after many years, he quit, which was a good thing. Once in a while he would have a beer, but for quite a few years, there he was flipping out with booze regularly. Imagine, he was blaming you and me. Us being about fifteen years old at the time when Ming started. Amusingly Ming all the way.

"While we are on the topic of Ming, tell me the story about Tommy Dovi filling his car up with diesel fuel and the one about digging worms for fishing. You must have told Ming both stories fifty times, and we laughed about both of them every single time, especially Ming."

Donnie started to laugh just thinking about it.

He said, "Tommy had this huge Chevy that he just loved, and so did we because he was the only one who had a car. We were driving through the streets of Frankfort one night, and the car was low on gas. Tommy said to me, 'Buddy, we need gas.' He didn't have any money, and neither did I. Tommy was always a very funny guy. His body language, facial expressions, and tone of voice always made me laugh. He had a low-pitched voice that was amusing. It's an asset to be funny, and Tommy was always funny. I told him at the milk station there was a gas pump that was never locked. In those days with the price of gasoline probably thirty 30¢ a gallon, nobody paid much attention to it.

"As we pulled into the lot, I suggested we move behind the pump so that no one would see us. Tommy turned his lights off, and we slowly pulled the car in. Sure enough, the pump was there with no lock on it. I am not sure if they just forgot to lock it that night or if there was ever a lock on it. I really don't think it was ever locked. Tommy turned on the pump and started putting in the gas. I could still hear the bell on the pump ding each time a gallon went in. After probably ten dings, I said to Tommy that was enough, but he didn't care. He told me, 'No, buddy, we might as well fill it up.' The way he said it was comical. He must have put twenty gallons in. Those were big gas tanks in cars that long ago. He was thanking me up and down, telling me how he was good for probably a week with gas, that we could keep coming back, and on and on he went.

"He finished filling the car, and we drove away. I bet we didn't get one hundred yards, and the car started bucking, banging, dinging, spitting, and sputtering. Neither of us had any idea what was going on. We were just looking at each other blankly. The car then died. We walked back to the pump because we weren't a hundred yards away. We looked at the pump, and we both came to the quick realization it's pumping diesel fuel. In the dark, and the car behind the pump, we never saw the sign or even looked up at the pump. We go back to the car, and it was dead. It wouldn't turn over. Nothing.

He looked at me and said, "Donnie, we have to get the diesel out of the tank. We are going to have to suck it out by a siphon.'

I stayed with the car, and he walked home to get a hose or something to use as a siphon. When he got back, he snaked the tube into the tank and started sucking on it to siphon the fuel out. He got two or three big mouthfuls of diesel fuel to the point it was coming out of his nose, but he couldn't get a siphon going. I was watching and laughing while he was getting angrier by the second.

He looked over at me laughing and again in that low, dry tone of voice said, 'Come on, buddy, you suck.'

I said to him through my laughter, "I am not sucking anything."

I turned around and started to walk home. Tommy continued to curse me with just about every word you could imagine. I was halfway down the block and could still hear him swearing. When I got home, I went to bed and forgot about the entire incident. If my memory serves me correctly, he did get the car repaired but got rid of it soon after that. It was likely dead anyway. I never mentioned it to him again. Watching Tommy getting huge mouthfuls of diesel, with it coming out of his nose, is one of the funniest things I have ever seen in my life. Ming loved that story and laughed every single time I told it. Whether he, I, you or all three of us were drunk or sober."

I had to add, "I agree with you. Tommy is very funny. He was always combing his hair and making sure his clothes looked just right. The guy was really way ahead of his time. Some people in this world are just funny. I always think of Jamie Farr as Corporal Klinger on *M*A*S*H*, Carol Burnett on her own television show, and many others over the past sixty years. A more modern actor Steve Carell on

The Office comes to mind. I also think of many of our friends who were just funny. Frank "Bongo" Bianchi, Ricky Palumbo, and the recently deceased Don Roberts Jr. The look on their faces, their body language, the tone of their voice, even the way they walked across the room just all lent itself to being funny. That is certainly not a bad thing. People with good sense of humor are usually perceived by others more approachable, considerate, and successful. They tend to think outside the box in the sense that they see funny situations that someone without a good sense of humor might not even notice. A good sense of humor is also an indication of a higher performing IQ. There is no question people tend to like others who demonstrate a sense of humor and make them laugh. Most people will say one of the things that attracts them to their spouse or significant other is that they make them laugh. It is an asset, and anyone with that asset available to them should use it to its maximum to make better lives for themselves and for anyone they come in contact with. I agree with you. Tommy was always funny."

Donnie kept going. "The other story that cracked Ming up was digging worms for fishing. Tommy's grandfather had a big garden. When we wanted to go fishing, we would go into his garden with a spade and dig for worms. Worms at that time were sold three for a penny. Nice big, fat night crawlers. If you buy them now, they are about ten for three or four dollars, and they are terrible. I never dreamed worms to catch a fish would cost that much.

"Looking back, we probably were not even doing it for the worms. What we were actually doing was spading Tommy's grandfather's garden for him. Marvelous experience to say the least. It was inadvertent, and I wasn't aware of it. Maybe Tommy was, but in the end, that is what we were doing, spading the garden. That is what I miss, the fact that we were helping Tommy's grandfather and getting the worms we needed to fish. We would dig them the day before we went fishing so we could leave the house to fish about 5:00 a.m. If we didn't dig them the day before, we would be out in the garden at 4:00 a.m., digging. If my memory serves me correctly, in one case we forgot to get worms the day before, so Tommy and I were out in the garden at 4:00 a.m. I was still half-asleep, and Tommy was working away digging for worms. I kept talking to him to keep him distracted while he dug so I didn't have to. Finally, after about a half hour, he said to me in that tone of voice of his, 'Donnie, you dig.' He handed me the spade, and I started, still talking a mile a minute now to distract myself because I didn't want to dig. I didn't want to work for those blasted worms. I would've been happier to buy them. Tommy kept saying to me, 'Donnie, shaddup and dig. Donnie, shaddup and dig.' Every time he said it, I laughed and talked more. He was getting madder and madder with each passing second. Finally, he just grabbed the spade out of my hand and spaded practically the entire garden himself. I don't think I even collected the worms.

"Ming wanted to hear that story repeatedly. I must have told it to him a hundred times, no exaggeration, and he hysterically laughed every single time. What experiences, the diesel fuel tale and digging worms. Situations so impetuous and hysterical at the same time. We did them day in and day out, never once considering how farcical they were.

"Where is Tommy now? Do you ever see him?"

"I really haven't seen him in probably twenty years," I replied. "He worked for the post office for a long time, then retired. I bet he has been retired fifteen to twenty years now. I used to go with Tibber occasionally to see him. He bought a house on William Street, right around the corner from where he grew up on Sheldon Avenue. A small raised ranch but perfect for him. He never got married or had kids, I don' think. He lives by himself, mostly stays home, and minds his own business. Next time you come to Frankfort, let's make it a point to go visit him. I would like to see him myself, and I bet he would get a kick out of seeing you."

"That is a good idea," Donnie confirmed, and then I could see another story pop into Donnie's head.

Then Donnie continued. "What about the time when your cousin Cos was supposed to trim the tree branches of my father's pine tree that were rubbing up against your aunt Josie DiCamillo's house? I don't know if my father contacted Cos or Mrs. DiCamillo did, but somehow Cos got the job of trimming the tree. I think my father was the one who called Cos, but I can't be sure. My dad wanted him to trim the branches off a forty-foot pine on the north side of the tree to get them back from your aunt's house to let sun and wind in and keep the shingles on her house dry. My dad didn't want him to touch any other part of the tree. Only trim those north side branches back maybe two feet or so from the bottom branch up to the roof of your aunt Josie's house and leave the rest of the tree the way it was.

"We had gone to Boston to visit my mother's family. When we returned and drove into our driveway, my father couldn't believe his eyes. Cos had trimmed the entire tree from the bottom branches all the way up to probably the last five or six feet of the tree around the whole trunk so that all that was left was probably six feet from the top up with full branches all the way around the trunk. The rest of the branches, all the way around the trunk of the tree, had been trimmed right back to the trunk. The tree looked like a well-manicured palm tree does in Las Vegas with only the top branches growing out from the trunk. I don't know how old the tree was, but I believe it was planted by my aunt Lena thirty years before Cos got to it.

"When we turned right into our driveway, my dad was stunned. He stared at the tree through the driver's window silently for about two minutes. When he finally opened the car door, he walked to Puzze's to ask Johnny and the guys in the bar what they had seen. Johnny told him Cos trimmed the tree, and he didn't think anything of it because he thought that was the way my dad wanted it. Stunned does accurately describe my father's appearance at the time.

"Next, he went in the house and called Cos. I don't know what he told him about the tree. In less than five minutes, Cos and his brother Vinny were at my father's house. I think Cos immediately knew my father wasn't happy when he saw the look on his face. I think Cos also knew that my father was very hurt by what he had done to the tree, and Cos felt bad also. Cos tried to keep it light and explained to my father that he thought that was the way he wanted it trimmed. To keep my father from feeling worse, Cos continued that it was just a tree and my dad could plant another one, this time where he wanted it. In a few years the new tree would grow and look just as good or even better than what was left of the existing one. My father agreed, at least to some extent, and let it go mostly, I think, to keep there from being more problems. Eventually, he had the tree cut down because it no longer looked the way a pine tree is supposed to look. I don't think he'd ever planted another one, but I'd really have to drive by and see. My father didn't like the idea, but there was really nothing he could do. I guess he took the approach that it was a misunderstanding and left it at that."

I had to add, "I think, in a nutshell, that was the code we all lived by on Orchard Street, and it worked flawlessly for almost forty years over the three generations that this book documents."

We both thought about that statement for a few seconds and quickly came to the realization that…as Jesus said, "You shall know the truth, and the truth shall make you free" (John 8:32).

"How about Duke Muldoon? Do you remember him?" Donnie asked.

"I can't say I do," I replied.

"You must remember him. He had the TV repair shop next door to my father," Donnie said.

I thought for a minute. "It was a small building with a beauty shop as I remember it."

Donnie told me I was right, but the beauty shop was there years later. The building was owned by two of my dad's cousins Carmen and Tommy Ruffalo. Prior to the beauty shop, for years the building housed Duke Muldoon's TV repair shop. Now he had stirred up my memories.

I told Donnie that I did vaguely remember the TV repair shop, and off he went.

"Duke had the shop there for years. He was such a good guy. When we were playing, he would call us all over and give us soda and sometimes a quarter too. I think there were days that he gave away more in quarters than he did making money on repairs. Duke always had such compassion for all the kids in the neighborhood. The guy loved us. He was so happy when we stopped over to see him. Duke was always smiling and would always shake every one of our hands. We would go over there at times looking for him, and at other times we didn't even have to because he would come looking for us if he hadn't seen anyone for a while. Duke was always willing to give us something to drink or eat. A kid could accept things like that in those days, especially in Frankfort on Orchard Street. Duke took better care of some of the kids in the neighborhood than their parents did. He always told us all to be safe, stay out of trouble, don't go in the road, and so on. Just a super person. His shop was there for a long time. As the years went by, he got older and was by himself. I don't think he was ever married or had kids. I never saw anyone there, only customers and all the kids from the neighborhood that congregated at his store.

"I don't remember who I was with, but we went over one day and knocked on the door to see what Duke was doing, and he didn't answer. We kept knocking again and again but no answer. We all started to worry because he usually came right to the door. I can't remember if I told my mother or somebody else went and told their mother, but someone informed the police that Duke wasn't answering the door. In any case, someone had called the police for what is now considered a welfare check. The officer went around behind his store where Duke had a little apartment. When the officer knocked and got no response, I can't remember if they contacted his family or if they just went in. Sadly, the officer found Duke dead. Evidently, he had passed away in his sleep. Needless to say, we were all shocked. Duke gave Orchard Street such a homey atmosphere. There was never anybody on the street, I don't think, that treated us as well as Duke. Our parents had to have more responsibility for us than he did, but in the end, he was just so good to every single one of us as our parents. To this day I'm amazed by him. I don't even think people like that exist anymore. Duke was a huge part of our neighborhood.

"After Duke, you're right, someone opened up a beauty shop. I believe it was called the Beauty Hut. Long before that, it was Duke Muldoon's TV repair shop. When I think of stores in the neighborhood and little shops on Orchard Street, I think it was a mini business district. Toward the east end of the street by Railroad Street, Tommy and Carmen Ruffalo, same guys who owned Duke's building, opened up a small hardware store and years later a grocery store. There were times my father would want me to walk over with him to visit Carmen and Tommy. I think he just wanted to talk and visit with his cousins, so he brought me along too.

"One afternoon, while my dad and I were in the store, I noticed what I thought was candy sealed in a bubble pack for freshness. I wasn't sure what was inside, but whatever it was looked enticing. I really thought it was candy. While my dad wasn't looking, I popped one of them in my mouth and bit down, which naturally popped the bulb pack open. I don't know if it was Carmen or Tommy who saw me do it, but one of them quickly called my father and told him that I had a broken light bulb in my mouth. My father scooped me up and looked in my mouth. He could see the broken glass from the light bulb, the filament, and the packaging sticking out of my mouth from where I had bit everything into small pieces. I had a mouthful of glass, filament, wire, and bubble wrap. My dad had me spit it out on the floor. My father had that same look in his eyes as when he saw what Cos had done when he trimmed our pine tree. I was scared witless that I had hurt myself again. To be safe, my Dad took me to the emergency room at Ilion Hospital. The doctor who examined me told me that there was no damage but that I shouldn't do things like that, and the next time I might not be so fortunate. Again, I panicked my father and myself nearly to death. In the end, it didn't prove to be anything other than Donnie being mischievous Donnie for the hundredth time.

"You also mentioned John Peach living under the old milk plant on Mill Street. I remember him too. I remember when we used to go there in the summer, and we'd go a little bit past the Drops and try to build a stone dam so that the spot where the Drops pooled would get deeper. Then we had somewhere to swim before the pool opened and even while the pool was open. We would swim there in the morning before the pool opened for the day and even go back at night to swim after the pool closed. We built that dam every summer. It usually lasted for a week or two, then we got a rainstorm, and the water would move fast and break up our dam. The next day we'd go back and build it again, and it probably last another week or so, and then the water would eventually wear it out, and over it went. We did it back and forth, went on from probably June through the end of

September. We would build it, and the creek would destroy it again. I don't think we ever came to the conclusion that we were fighting a losing battle, but we kept right on doing it. I don't think kids do much of that stuff anymore. They have pools in their backyards. They belong to golf clubs, yacht clubs, and that kind of thing. Yet for us there was nothing like it. Certainly the place to be for the summer. It was such a good experience for all of us being together like that. I think kids now, because they miss a lot of those sort of experiences, just don't have the kind of childhood we were lucky enough to have. They are way overscheduled. Time gets compressed. When time gets compressed like that, a lot goes awry. We had all the time in the world, and in the end, it benefited us immensely. Right up to this day, I am so grateful for it. What a blessing day after day. As you said earlier, humbling and inspiring at the same time."

Now that over a course of two days we have collaborated for close to ten hours, it was time to wrap it up and have a few beers. That was our collective decision. We continued to jibber-jabber for probably another hour over three Coronas each. Donnie's with lime, mine without.

"Look how fast the time has gone by, Donnie. Do you realize for the past two days we've done about eight to nine hours, almost twenty man-hours together? That's pretty good. We covered about fifteen years of your life and about ten of mine in that I was in some of your situations, with you up to my eyeballs. Impressive, don't you think? After a while it just rolls out of your consciousness. James Joyce, an influential Irish writer around the 1900s, along with others like Virginia Woolf and more after them, formulated a writing style called stream of consciousness, in which the written word mimics the immediate flow of thoughts and feelings from the character, generating a higher sense of realism for the reader. That is what we are doing here. All we have to do is think about it a little, do some research, and there it is. Keep thinking about it, take a few notes, and we can add almost anything later in a continuing stream of consciousness style."

Donnie felt he was good for now, but we could actively pursue more info if warranted and see how it played out in the long run.

I told him how he really jogged my memory with Duke Muldoon in the TV repair shop, Malinda Murtaugh with the firecrackers, the Addolorata Chapel at the west end of Orchard Street, and the go-go girls dancing in the cages at the Grand Prix. I told him I was glad he had stirred up those memories in my head over the past forty-eight hours, how I thought we were off to a good start, and how we would certainly continue with this project.

Paul Anka summed up the past forty-eight hours best:

> The seasons are passing one by one
> So gather moments while you may
> Collect the dreams you dream today
> Remember, will you remember
> The times of your life?

I didn't think those Coronas ever tasted better. With the lime, like Donnie's, or without, like mine.

Johnny

I first mentioned to Johnny Kipper about getting involved in the King of Orchard Street project on Labor Day 2020 when he was at my house for a cookout. He immediately told me he was interested and wanted to start right then in the middle of the cookout. We briefly discussed the premise of the King of Orchard Street, which served to only deepen his interest, and we talked a little about a time line. I explained to him that Ruthie Deeply had just gotten published and that it would take up to a year to line up the other people potentially involved in the King of Orchard Street project. Then I would start the writing with him being the second or third person to make his case as the potential king. Having discussed a time line to make his case, he was likely to be on the schedule for late fall 2021. Johnny told me to make sure I didn't forget him and that he would be waiting impatiently.

In November 2021 a mutual friend of Johnny Kipper's and mine, Jimmy DeRollo, called and invited Carol and me to come to his house for a small Thanksgiving party. Of course, I responded immediately that we would attend in that Jimmy and Diane's parties are always excellent. I would go even if the parties were terrible because Jimmy is a lifelong friend, but the parties are certainly not terrible. As a matter of fact, they are very good. Jimmy's wife, Diane, runs a small restaurant, Roso's Café, open for breakfast and lunch in downtown Utica, for probably the past seven or eight years. She has been very successful. Diane is a good cook/chef. The food at Roso's is always good, the portions are big, and the price is reasonable. What else could you ask for in a restaurant? I naturally jump at every chance to go to a party at Jimmy and Diane's house because I know what I am in for before I walk in the door.

When I got to the party, Jimmy greeted me, shook my hand, hugged me, and told me that Johnny Kipper was coming too. I was glad because I wanted to reconfirm with Johnny his commitment to the King of Orchard Street project in that I hadn't seen him in probably three months. Again, when he arrived, Johnny told me he was still interested and again wanted to know if we could start right then. I told him that for obvious reasons we couldn't, but it would soon be his turn. I was still working on Donnie's account at that time, and when that was done, John would be next.

After about two weeks since that night at Jimmy's, Donnie was finished. I called Johnny Kipper Friday night, November 19, to find out when he was available. He told me he would talk to his wife to check her schedule and that the week being Thanksgiving week, he thought they were pretty much booked up, but he would let me know. Johnny called me back the next day to inform me that he had checked with his wife, and with Thanksgiving, grandchildren, and so on, they were booked until the following Sunday. We agreed that next Sunday was fine, if that was convenient for him, and did he want come to my house or me come to his. We both agreed to his house, Sunday, November 27, at 4:00 p.m. Johnny wanted to know what we would eat and drink so he could go to the store and buy whatever we needed. I told him that anything was fine, and at this point the biggest issue was to keep the process of the King of Orchard Street project moving forward. Johnny confirmed that he had a lot of ideas in his head, but he wasn't sure how exactly to get them out. Yet the ideas were there. I stressed to him not to worry, and we discussed, as with Donnie, the James Joyce, Virginia Woolf "stream of consciousness" format. We also discussed the process that we could go through whereby he could say exactly what he wanted to say just as he wanted to say it. Then by him and me editing together, we could confirm the wording and format he wanted. Our work then would get reviewed by a professional editor at my publisher as many times as we saw fit. Again, until it was exactly the way we wanted it. We were currently at the level of preliminary efforts, and we could tweak until we got it right at least from our perspective. I gave him some general time lines, and hopefully, by the middle of January, we could finish up with his end of the story because in mid-January Carol and I are scheduled to go to Georgia. Johnny reconfirmed his interest and told me that he would call me during the week to make sure everything was still on schedule. Next Sunday, I knew we would have some fun and be productive at the same time.

We ended our call to wait until the next Sunday to meet and hopefully get a good start on what he wanted the world to know concerning his take as to why he should be, in perpetuity, the King of Orchard Street. I am certain Johnny Kipper will mount a full-scale effort.

Johnny Kipper, Carol, Emily, and I met on Sunday, November 28, to begin discussing Johnny's claim to the title of the King of Orchard Street. The weather was cold, wet, and snowy, typical for the end of November. Johnny Kipper's house on Oneida Street in Chadwicks was warm and cozy once we got inside. Johnny and Emily greeted us with hugs and handshakes, COVID be damned. We decided to have something to eat before we began discussing *The King of Orchard Street*. Emily had good, sharp provolone, the kind that makes the roof of your mouth itch. We had crackers, potato chips, tomato pie, Italian soppressata, black and green olives, all the good stuff, the very kind of Italian specialties that Johnny and I grew up on. Johnny had two martinis with a dash of olive extract, and I had two white labels on the rocks. Even Carol indulged with an orange juice and peach schnapps as did Emily.

Then we decided to start our discussion. Johnny and I went into his den, with Carol and Emily going into the living room to watch television.

We connected to Johnny's Wi-Fi, set the dictate mode on my computer, and off he went.

"I remember growing up as a kid, we all spent a lot of time at my grandmother Frances Caruso's house. My mother, my cousins, my thirteen aunts and uncles, a whole group of us flowing in and out all day long. Every Sunday we got out of church, and all met at my grandmother's. She would have a huge bowl of fried meatballs on the kitchen table, and we would all help ourselves. The meatballs were just fried fresh that morning, and did they ever smell good the minute I walked in the door. I really enjoyed every Sunday morning. With my grandmother having been born in Italy, everything was made fresh and by hand. There was no substituting for that. It seemed like her kitchen table was always covered with flour because every time I walked in her house, she was baking or cooking something. It really was nonstop. Remember, she had fourteen children. I always went to my grandmother's house to find either macaroni, her own sausage bread, rolls, or something being made. Many times when I walked in her kitchen, she had run out of an ingredient, usually yeast, so she would give me money to go buy yeast or whatever she had run out of. Getting yeast was the best deal in that I would go to the bakery to buy it. I think all along she knew the yeast was only 15¢, but she would give me a quarter, which would leave me 10¢ to keep. She would tell me if there was any money left, which she knew there would be, I could keep but not to tell my other cousins. Being in Viti's Bakery to buy the yeast, most times I bought a doughnut with the dime. I think I could actually buy two. At other times I went to Lucy Dades's store or wherever. With that whole dime in my pocket, I knew I had the potential to be the King of Orchard Street way back then. I felt like I was already.

"Another situation I recall vividly many times happened when someone in the family had a newborn, and with fourteen children of her own, there was always a newborn grandchild. I remember walking into my grandmother's bedroom, and there she would be with whoever the newborn was, the baby lying on her chest asleep. I am not certain why she did that, but it sure worked because the baby was always sound asleep.

As we grew up, she would always speak Italian because she wanted us to speak Italian along with English. Unfortunately, I never got to the point where I knew that much Italian, but I do remember her trying to teach it to all of us."

"Funny you should say that," I said to Johnny, "because I remember her sitting in her screened-in porch jibber-jabbering with whoever in Italian. Classic little old Italian lady with the bun on the back of her head and all. That is the way I remember her exactly."

Johnny smiled and continued, "I never knew my grandfather growing up, but as I got older, I found out he was in a nursing home quite young. His name was Philip. He would come home on weekends and holidays to spend time with his family but during the week was in a nursing home. I remember my father and me picking him up at my grandmother's and bringing him back to the nursing home. At Christmas my grandfather would wait for all of us in the living room. All the grandchildren would go to see him. He would hug and kiss us all and give each of us a dollar. I later learned that he suffered from what was back then known as "hardening of the arteries" and today known as dementia or Alzheimer's disease. I didn't know him for very long or very well, but I always remember him as very kind and a gentleman. Even having known him for that little bit of time, I still miss him dearly and wish he was around a lot longer than he was.

"I don't know if he spoke Italian or English. I would think, as a result of the dementia, he was always very quiet. I would think also at some point he must have had conversations with my grandmother, aunts, and uncles, but I never really had a conversation with him. I have no clue how old my grandfather was when he died, but my grandmother died long after him when she was eighty-six years old. Isn't it funny how you know one grandparent well, but you really don't know the other? He was in a nursing home all those years. In that I only saw him on weekends and holidays, it was difficult to get to know him, but I really wish I could have. In probably the last year before he died, he did stay more at my grandmother's house, I think, mostly because the family didn't want him to pass away in a nursing home but rather in his own home. At least near the end, he had some extended time with his family without being in a nursing home or hospital. I don't know for a fact, but I bet prior to becoming ill, his life was full and happy with his wife and fourteen children. After all, he lived on Orchard Street in Frankfort.

"My uncles all hunted deer, pheasant, rabbit, or whatever was in season at the time. Whatever they shot and brought home my grandmother would prepare for us. My uncles would field-dress the game and bring it home. My grandmother would fillet the meat, make roasts, and grind the meat to make sausage and meatballs. Half the time we didn't know what we were eating, but it was always good. Usually spicy but good. I remember as a child walking in her bedroom and seeing pillowcases on the floor moving and squiggling all over the room. I didn't know what was going on, but it scared me. After seeing those moving pillowcases a number of times, I worked up the nerve to ask my grandmother why the pillowcases moved. She had a very simple explanation. There was no room for a chicken coop in her backyard, like my father had and the Hotalings had in their backyards, thus there was no place to keep the live chickens she had bought. In true Great Depression mindset, she had a plan to make it work. She would buy chickens three or four at a time, put them live in pillowcases, and place the pillowcases in her room. When the time came, she would wring their necks, cut the heads off, clean them, pluck them, and that night have them for dinner."

I asked, "Johnny, did she get chicken plucking lessons from Mr. Hotaling who lived on the other end of Orchard Street? I will get to it later, but I have a chicken plucking story from the Hotalings that I remember like it happened this morning. Now I wonder if the chicken I always smelled cooking after Mr. Hotaling got done with his chickens on any given day was coming from his house or your grandmother's or both. That chicken story about your grandmother opens the Hotaling chicken story for me. You tell me your memory, and it opens mine. The same thing happened with Ruth, or after a discussion with Bob Reina, or after meeting Thelma Richardson's daughter while all the while writing *Ruthie Deeply*. Certainly a vigorous dynamic that functions well and creates memory after memory on numerous levels for anyone involved in this process. That seemed like a good place to stop, poor weather and all, so we did."

A few days later, after working on Johnny Kipper's chronicle for about two hours, Carol and I decided to break for lunch. We chose a local health food store named Peter's Cornucopia in the New Hartford Shopping Center. Peter's is a business we frequent due to a large array of health food products supplements and, of course, gluten-free products for my son Michael. When we arrived at Peter's, we found that his menu has changed and that they no longer serve sandwiches but have moved to healthier wraps and bowls. It was unexpected, but Carol and I still were able to order lunch that we liked and shared. After lunch, we proceeded to walk to Joann Fabrics where Carol was in search of a specific material and then to Ollie's Bargain Outlet to continue our search for a package of Jobe's fertilizer sticks for trees and shrubs. I prefer my landscaping to appear bright and colorful, and the Jobe's sticks certainly help to that end.

While proceeding through Ollie's, Carol and I coincidentally meet my lifelong friends Rosemary and Chuck Coppola. Rosemary happens to be one of Johnny Kipper's few last living biological aunts, and Chuck is her husband. As I approached the couple, Chuck looked at me, a little confused as to who I was because I hadn't seen him in a while. I understand Chuck has had some health problems recently, and I was pleasantly surprised as to how healthy he looked. When I took my glasses off and told them that it was me, he and Rosemary were thrilled to see Carol and me. Chuck is a cousin of Carol, and Rosemary I have known since the day I was born. Needless to say, a group of four elderly Italian Americans who hadn't seen each other in a while were certain to make a commotion in the store. I was happy to see Chuck healthy because I had every intention to stop at his house and visit him, but I just hadn't gotten to it yet. When I told him that I've been meaning to come to his house, I got the usual response, "And when are you coming? I'm going to keep waiting for you and see how long it takes for you to show up." I definitely still will go to visit, but I knew what his response automatically would be. He looked good, better than I expected, and I was happy for that. As for Rosemary, she never changes. I then proceeded to tell her what I had been doing before I came to Ollie's, which was writing her nephew Johnny Kipper's story, specifically concerning Rosemary's mother Frances, all her brothers and sisters, and of course, the many children, nieces, and nephews who were sure to be at her mother's on Sunday morning. Chuck continued to explain how when he had first moved to Frankfort from East Utica, he would go to his mother-in-law's house on Sunday morning, and there would be so many people at her house you couldn't tell who belonged to who or even if they belonged there. I told Chuck, as Johnny Kipper said, there were so many people that whether Johnny showed up or didn't, they probably would have never noticed because the crowd was big. It could be fifty to sixty people and on holidays perhaps one hundred. Chuck absolutely agreed and told me how he used to invite coworkers from Univac who were not from this area but found themselves living here due to their job, or were just in the area for maybe three weeks to work on a specific project, then return home. Chuck would take it upon himself to invite them to his mother-in-law's house on Sunday morning, give them directions so that they could get there—a GPS didn't exist way back then—and sure enough, many times they would come. Nobody knew who they were but Chuck or cared for that matter, and there were so many people there that the outsiders just blended in. They helped themselves to the fried meatballs or sausages and even had a glass or two of wine. When Chuck went back to work on Monday, they would all tell him how much they enjoyed themselves, how welcome they felt, and asked if could they come back again sometime. Naturally, Chuck was happy about their experience and invited them back anytime they wanted to come. They often told Chuck how when they went home to Oklahoma, California, or wherever and told their family and friends about Sunday mornings at the Carusos, they wanted to come with them the next time.

That was the life, in a nutshell, we all led on Orchard Street. Whether they were your child, grandchild, niece, nephew, your niece's or nephew's friend, or somebody you never saw in your life, everyone was welcome. Everyone had a seat at the table. It was the way of life, and it never failed to bring even the remotest stranger into the fold to completely absorb anyone into the warmth of family and home.

I thank you, God, for that blessing from all those involved, whether we knew who they were or not.

After lunch, I returned home to continue with Johnny Kipper's take on the King of Orchard Street just as he had dictated it to my computer.

*****

"The memory of that wild game food is etched in my mind, my senses, my taste as if I had it for dinner last night. It was always such a good time with my grandmother, thirteen aunts and uncles, their spouses, and so many cousins I couldn't keep count. I loved my grandmother because at the end of the day, that is what it is all about," Johnny Kipper said.

I nodded my head in 110 percent agreement. Johnny Kipper did too. Both of us with tears in our eyes.

"Keep talking, Johnny. Please," I said.

Thank goodness he did.

"Every Saturday morning, until I was probably thirteen or fourteen years old, I would have to get up and go to George Corrado's Feed Mill, pick up a twenty-five-pound bag of sheep manure for my grandmother to fertilize her garden. My grandmother and Joe Papa's grandmother shared a garden, or maybe they were side by side. I don't remember exactly, but we had to go fertilize their gardens because they were both afraid of dogs, and people let their dogs wander around without a leash. The job then fell to me, but what neither one of them realized was I was more afraid of the dogs than they were. Nevertheless, my grandmother, Mrs. Green, and I would go ahead to fertilize their gardens. I would spread the manure, and they would keep an eye open the entire time for dogs, waiting for one to sneak up on one of us. Thank goodness none of us ever got bit, and the payoff was I got to spend a lot of time with my grandmother. Really very nice. I will never forget it."

Misty eyes again.

Unprompted, Johnny moved on to Christmas.

"Christmas was the same as any other day with fourteen aunts and uncles and too many cousins to keep track of, but it was special on a lot of other levels too. When the holidays came around, we all gathered in my grandmother's house. My uncle Ross would buy every niece and nephew a present, and I mean everyone. There must have been seventy-five presents. They weren't huge presents, maybe a pair of gloves, a puzzle, or earmuffs, usually something simple, but every single one of us got something. My grandmother, mother, and aunts cooked and made cookies for a week straight before Christmas. We would have fish, ham, maybe some of the game my uncles hunted, and it was all delicious. My grandmother's kitchen was very small, so I honestly think they worked in shifts. When they were all finished, they would distribute the cookies throughout the family. It was amazingly fun to see the aunts, uncles, and cousins together in one place. There were so many people in that small house it left hardly any room to move. As the family got bigger, there was less and less room, and it made us feel more as one than ever before. It is impossible to go wrong with such a strong family setup, yet some people still do. How? I don't understand. We never missed a Christmas, New Year, Thanksgiving, Fourth of July, or anything. What a blessing. It could never be recreated. An immense blessing for all of us for sure.

"As we got older, we played any kind of ball you could think of. Contact football, kickball, baseball, basketball, anything. Soccer hadn't hit America yet, so I think that is the only thing we missed. Hide-and-seek was huge, and we played for hours. We had a tomato basket nailed to the telephone pole on the corner of Litchfield Street and Orchard across from Mrs. Dee's house, and that was our court. Something as simple as that was worth a million dollars to us. We all used it every day to the extent that after a week or two, the basket would wear out, so someone would have to take it down and put up a new one. It just happened almost magically. A new bushel would appear. Cars would come by, and the drivers would yell at us to get out of the street. We would yell back to them that we couldn't afford a playground so that is where we had to play. What were they going to do? Call the police on a bunch of kids playing basketball in the street. Nobody got hurt, and it was a ton of fun."

I asked Johnny, "Did you ever check out the origins of hide-and-seek?"

He told me that he had not. A perfect time for some research.

We discovered the original game was different from the way we played. It started in the second century and was called *apodidraskinda*. A Greek scholar named Julius Pollux was the first to describe it. The rules were different in that one player hid, and after a minute or two, the other players would spread out to find the hidden player. As each seeker found the hider, the seekers would then join the hider in the hider's spot, and all would remain quiet. The last seeker to find the group would be the hider for the next game. As I remember it, we changed the rules quite a bit. There would be one seeker and four or five hiders. After a minute or so, the seeker would go out to pursue the hiders and tag each one as they were found. When hiders were all found, we would start another game. Really, it turned into a large game of tag. I would bet the rules varied from group to group, but we always had so much fun with it for hours. Like Johnny said, fertilizing his grandmother's garden was somewhat pointless, yet the most important aspect of it was the time you had interacting with your grandmother. There are four things in this world that once they are gone, you never get back: time, money, opportunity, and your words. Rarely, once out there, do you get them back. That time we spent playing hide-and-seek and Johnny spent with his grandmother fertilizing her garden is priceless, but it will never come back. The time together is the grace we get.

Johnny resumed. "Honestly, what we did back then was a lot of fun. Everybody enjoyed themselves, there were no problems, nobody got in serious trouble. We did a few little things we weren't supposed to, but no one was hurt. There was no penalty. No harm, no foul. For example, the tomato basket on the telephone pole near you're aunt Josie's house, all the time playing together in the street, and we got pretty rough too. Do you ever remember there being an argument or a fight? I sure don't. We were competitive. We had fun; it was exercise, but there was never an issue that I recall. Mr. DiCamillo, we called him Mr. D, used to sit on his porch and watch us, but he never said a word to anyone because there was never a problem. We ran all over the entire area. Orchard Street, Tisdale Avenue, Sheldon Avenue, by the canal, by the Drops, and Litchfield Street. I mean everywhere. Never a single problem with any of us, the neighbors, no one. Now everywhere you go, there is a problem. There are fights at Walmart, at football games, at baseball games, in parking lots, in office buildings, everywhere, all the time. We had none of that."

"Funny that you should mention running together all over those blocks. Back another generation, to my mother's age, both mine and your aunts' and uncles' age, my mom told me the name of the whole group was the TOL Gang. The Tisdale, Orchard, and Litchfield Street Gang, and they all did the same thing up and down every block, in groups, all day long. After I told your cousin Johnnie Caruso that, every time he saw me, he would yell out "TOL." My point is from our parents' generation to our generation, nothing really changed, but for the generation after ours, it is an entirely different world," I explained.

Johnny went on. "Don't misunderstand me. There were a few small problems, but not anything we didn't handle ourselves, for example, Donnie hitting a telephone pole on his sled head-on. He was lucky he didn't get killed. Donnie was coming down that hill at full speed, lost control of the sled, and hit a telephone pole directly. Guess what? The pole didn't give an inch. He had a severe concussion. If my memory serves me correctly, he was in a coma for a few days. How he got out of that without a permanent injury or even got killed I will never know. My point is, the whole of Orchard Street rallied around the family as did the entire village. All the old Italian women started to pray the rosary. Others brought food to the house and visited in the hospital. Luckily, he walked away from the whole thing without any permanent injury. We, everyone on Orchard Street together, handled it. That is the sweetness of the story. We were all in the same boat, and we rowed it together to get where we had to go. Together, never alone.

"Fishing in Moyer Creek was a huge part of our day. I fished every day right behind my house. I loved it, and the fishing was great too. I don't think I ever left the bank of that creek without catching at least one or two fish. I was there all the time. I loved fishing. I still love it. I can't imagine how many hours I spent fishing in that creek as a kid and as an adult.

"The dairy next door to my house always had a lot of activity. At one point they had a milk strike. I don't know if it was over prices or what. A whole bunch of trucks came down my street and started dumping pails, I mean big pails, of milk in the street. The people working in the milk station came out of the building and started dumping even bigger containers than the farmers themselves dumped in the street. It must have happened eight or nine times over the course of two or three days. I remember thinking what a terrible waste. There were people who couldn't afford a gallon of milk and here were these farmers dumping it in a sewer. I guess they were trying to create a shortage so that the price would go up. I am not sure what their motivation was, but I was appalled at seeing all that milk wasted. I still am appalled when I see it happening now, which at times, it still does. If there is anything that would make a farmer cry, that must be it.

"I don't know if Donnie ever told you this story, but he and I were playing on the sacks of grain at Corrado's Feed Mill. One of us had a jackknife, and we cut two or three of the grain sacks open with the knife, which clearly, we should not have done. When we cut them open, the grain ran out all over the ground. Floyd Hotaling, who lived on the corner of Orchard Street and Tisdale Avenue, unbeknownst to Donnie and me, saw us do it. At some point he went over to Corrado's office and informed them that Donnie and I had cut open the sacks of grain that was spilled out all over the loading dock. I am not certain if it was George Corrado or one of his employees, but someone from the mill went over to Donnie's house and mine to tell both our fathers what we had done. Rather than pay for the sacks of grain we cut open, both Donnie's father and mine went over to the mill, put the grain back in the sacks, and then with a needle and twine sewed the sacks back together. Again, nothing terrible, just childhood shenanigans, but the point is, we handled it. No one got hurt. There was no real financial damage, and it was all over. I don't remember how my father punished me, probably just made me stay in the house for the rest of the day but nothing big. A few bruised egos maybe but nothing else."

I explained to Johnnie that Donnie told the same story, but his father was really angry, and Donnie's punishment was pretty severe. I agreed with Johnnie; it was a small-scale mischief by two boys, no real harm done to anybody, and all initiated by two candidates for the King of Orchard Street. The issue was resolved quickly by those same two King of Orchard Street candidates as would be expected, with both their father's help.

Johnnie asked me what names come into my head first when I think of Orchard Street. My reply was quick and effortless.

"Usually, I think of my cousin Joe Favat, you, Donnie, John-John Tubia, and Santo Falcone. Next comes Terry Stone, Larry Stone, Tommy Stone, Sharon Stone, Ruth and Thelma Richardson, Ronnie and Richard Sassone all are on top of the list along with Joe Ingro, Joe Tubia, and Philly Caruso," I said.

Johnny agreed with my list.

"I think about almost the same people too. They were all older than us, but we hung around with them," he replied.

I explained further that when I tell my kids stories about Orchard Street, they are always amazed that here were seven-, eight-, nine-year-olds spending a lot of time with fifteen-, sixteen-, or seventeen-year-olds. They always want to know why our parents let us do that. I try to paint the picture for them that there was no separation of age, color, or nationality. We were all the same, and the code we all adhered to was to look out for each other all day, every day, from one end of the block to the other.

My kids are truly astonished. They tell me that is the way the world should be, and they wish it still was. I agree with them without reservation.

While the tears welled up again, Johnny continued the discussion. "Most of those people were older than us, but I remember them well. Tommy Stone was tall and muscular. Terry and Larry were twins. Terry was born with cerebral palsy or something of that nature and walked with a pretty bad limp. I have no idea where Tommy is, but I know Terry lives on Vickerman Hill in Mohawk, and Larry lives in Florida. I found out recently that Ronnie Sassone has died, and Richard lives in Florida. I also looked up to Joe Smizzi because he was a police officer, and he was probably older than my father. If we got in any trouble, Joe would talk to us about not causing problems in the village, not to annoy people, and to stay out of the road. Joe was never nasty to any of us, just a little lecture and slap on the wrist, then he would get back in the car and drive away. He really was a very good guy and police officer. We need a lot more Joe Smizzis in law enforcement these days.

"How about my cousins Georgie and Johnny Caruso? I know they didn't live on Orchard Street, so they cannot, in the end, be the king, but they spent enough time there that some of their stories are worth being told. What about my uncle Shep? He would be a good candidate for king, but he's dead, so clearly, he can't tell his story. My cousin Philly Caruso was hysterical too. You should get in touch with him. He has great stories, and he lived on Orchard Street, which would make him a possible king. They were all good guys, never really bothered anyone. Maybe got drunk at times and talked a little crazy, but for the most part, they were harmless. George and Johnny Caruso were different in their own way, but they were the same too."

I asked Johnny what he remembers about his uncle Shep, whose real name was Joseph, singing the infamous "Douche Bag Blues?"

Johnny responded in a millisecond, "Do you remember that? Wasn't it the funniest thing you ever heard in your life?"

Now, we were both smiling from ear to ear.

He went on. "My uncle was gay before anyone even heard the word. At one point after World War II, once he had been released from the military, he got married. I don't even know to whom. Obviously, the marriage was short-lived, and then he went to a completely gay lifestyle. Again, long before anyone mentioned it, he was full-scale gay and told the whole world right up front with no remorse. When he would get drunk, in one or two of the bars, there would be a guitar that belonged to the owner, someone had left, or God only knows how it got there. Someone in the bar at the time would consistently bring up "The Douche Bag Blues," and off my uncle would go. He would strum the guitar he had no idea how to play and make up the lyrics as he went along. The lyrics generally began:

> I married that f——— b———.
> She left me after a year.
> I don't know where she is now.
> And I don't want to know.

"And so on and so on, making up the lyrics and strumming as he went along. Until he got to the last line, which was always the same:

> That's why I sing these douche bag blues…

"On a few occasions he would then smash the guitar on the floor and step on it until it was in pieces. The problem was that with no guitar he couldn't do it again until somehow another guitar turned up in the bar. If you saw him do the entire routine, you would never forget it. Talk about hysterical. That story must live in perpetuity."

I had to comment on that story line and said, "Cos and I were lucky enough to witness it live on two separate occasions, and you're correct. It was hysterical. The second time was even funnier than the first. Shep was in such an uproar that his false teeth flew out of his mouth and went flapping across the bar, like that old windup toy set of teeth that used to bounce across the table in a chewing motion. Then the conclusion was Sheppy smashing the guitar. Unfortunately, cell phones didn't exist in those days because a video would have gotten big hits across the world. I used to crack up when Shep would tell me, 'I know you're not gay, but if you ever decide to jump the fence, let me be the first to welcome you over.' Or when we would go with him to the only gay bar in the area called the Hub on Bleecker Street and he would tell all of his buddies, 'None of these guys with me are gay, but I am the biggest fag around, and I want everybody in the bar to be aware of that.'

"You can't make this stuff up. It is too real. Someone just opened the old Hub up with the same name, but I gather it is a legitimate restaurant now."

I wanted to continue with more Shep Caruso stories now. So I did.

"How about Sheppy's famous Rock Hudson story?" I asked.

"I know it word for word, but go ahead. You tell it," Johnny replied.

"We used to hang out in the Argonne Grill on Litchfield Street, which had been there since World War I, thus the name. Most of us minors at the time with Sheppy, Georgie and Johnny Caruso, Joe Sportello, and whoever else happened to be there. Sheppy would tell the story of how when he was being discharged from the navy at the end of World War II, the navy brought him to Los Angeles, put him to work on one of the naval bases there. The navy told him to go to work every day, that it might take a month or so, but eventually, he would be discharged and sent home. Sheppy, along with many other young men saw the stay in LA as an opportunity to have some fun and as long as the navy continued to pay them, why not stick around for a while? I say along with many other young men because my father used to tell a similar story about his discharge from the navy at the end of World War II, only he was waiting in San Francisco, and my dad's stories had nothing to do with being gay.

"Anyway, Sheppy used to tell us that he spent his off-work hours partying in Los Angeles with a good-sized crowd of gay men and women. One of the guys he associated with in this gay group was a young, very handsome aspiring actor named Rock Hudson. You have to understand this story in context. Sheppy was in LA about 1945, right after World War II. He was telling us the story about 1945 in approximately 1972 or 1973. By 1972, Rock Hudson was a huge, macho Hollywood leading man, whose real name was Roy Harold Scherer Jr. Rock was of the biggest names in movies in the 1950s and 1960s, was nominated for Academy Award as Best Actor for *Giant* in 1956, found great success in a series of romantic comedies such as *Pillow Talk*, *Lover Come Back*, and others with his costar Doris Day. Hudson also made some macho man movies such as *Tobruk* and

Ice Station Zebra. *Ice Station Zebra* was a movie with Hudson as the captain of a submarine stuck under the polar ice cap. As an aside, *Ice Station Zebra* was the famous billionaire, recluse, and germophobe Howard Hughes's favorite movie. Hughes would watch it for hours in his penthouse on top of the Desert Inn in Las Vegas naked, his hair down to his shoulders, his fingernails about five inches long, with mason jars full of his urine scattered all over the place. You get the picture: recluse, germophobe, and the like with all the money in the world, watching the *Ice Station Zebra* play again and again. Alone, frozen, isolated submarine under the polar ice cap, no way to escape just like the lifestyle Howard Hughes was leading. All fits together. Hudson was even on television into the 1980s with a cute show I used to watch called *McMillan & Wife*. In public he was extremely discreet about his sexual orientation, but in the movie industry, it was a well-known fact that he was gay. Then, in the early 1980s the AIDS epidemic burst on to the world stage beginning in San Francisco with Hudson being one of the first public figures to be diagnosed.

"See whole continuum here, starting with Sheppy in Los Angeles right after World War II with a bunch of young gays partying away, moving to the mid-1970s with a bunch of straight young men in the Argonne Grill in Frankfort partying away while the AIDS epidemic spread throughout the world a decade later in a matter of a few years, and ending with the death of one of Hollywood's leading men, Rock Hudson, in 1985, of AIDS-related illness at the age of fifty-nine. Who would have thought, when Sheppy was telling us in the 1970s that Hudson was gay, it was the truth? And Sheppy knew it in the 1940s. Shep also claimed another actor, Tab Hunter, a tall blond Hollywood leading man in the 1950s was gay, along with Roman Gabriel, the star quarterback of the Los Angeles Rams. Shep claimed to be friends with all of them. I don't think Tab Hunter and Roman Gabriel being gay ever proved true. Yet in the case of Rock Hudson, Shep was 100 percent correct.

"When Shep would tell the story, we would all typically reply, 'Come on, Shep, Rock Hudson of all people. You say everyone is gay. You probably tell people I am gay.'

"Your uncle would swear up and down that it was the truth. Then we would all laugh, order another round of drinks, and move on to whoever's turn it was to tell the next story."

Every single word of Sheppy's Rock Hudson story was true, and it took a horrible disease like AIDs to prove it.

No matter, that Hudson never publicly revealed anything about his sexuality. Sheppy and some in the movie industry knew the truth about Rock Hudson some fifty years before the world.

Poor Rock Hudson, stuck in an era when he wasn't free to lead the life he wanted. God bless Sheppy for openly leading the life he wanted at the same time most gays like Rock Hudson did not.

The biblical verse, "Ye shall know the truth and the truth shall make you free" (John 8:32 KJV) was never more valid than in Sheppy's and Rock Hudson's case.

Sheppy made the choice to be free. Rock Hudson did not.

Poor Rock Hudson.

Johnny Kipper continued after my Sheppy story with another story about his uncle George, his uncle Shep's brother.

"I don't remember how the conversations would start, but when someone would ask my uncle George if he had any pets, which he did not, he would always tell them that he had two dogs. He would continue about what good dogs they were and how he was happy that he had them. Uncle George would really lay it on thick about his dogs. I think he did have one for a short period of time, but I am not certain. In any case, when he told the story, he wasn't talking about his dogs. He was talking about his sons George and Johnny Caruso. After a few minutes of painting this beautiful picture of his dogs, he would start talking about how hard they were to feed, that they were very picky eaters and were far overweight. The person he was telling would buy it all. After a while, my uncle would tell the listener that he really didn't have any dogs. All along he was talking about his adult sons. The look on the listeners face when my uncle told them the truth about his sons was comical. Usually, the listener didn't know what to say. Uncle George could tell that story like a professional comedian. By the time my uncle told the truth, the people who knew the truth were about to burst at the seams after hearing him tell the story so many times, then waiting for the reaction of the unknowing person when my uncle told them the truth. Did you ever hear him tell it? That story was just as funny as Uncle Shep's 'The Douche Bag Blues' story."

I replied, "I can't say I did, but I did hear him tell another story about when he was single that was unbelievable, which I won't repeat now but will tell you later off the record. George was a very funny guy." I agreed with Johnny 100 percent. George Sr. was a born comic, and Sheppy wasn't bad either.

I asked Johnny to tell me about his cousin Johnny Caruso. His face lit up.

"My cousin Johnny Caruso was a beautiful guy. He had the gift of gab. You just couldn't say no to him. He talked me into taking him to Syracuse once. When we got there, he rented a room to stay overnight. I thought we were going for the day, but he had other plans. Johnny Caruso wanted to stay overnight because he knew all the spots to go, and he wanted to hit all of them. I lost track, but I think we must have gone to ten bars. He flimflammed his way through everyone. By the time we got back to our room, it was about three in the morning. After an all-night drinking, I was drunk and passed right out. About twenty-five minutes after I fell asleep, I could hear someone in the room talking to the extent it woke me up. I looked over to the other bed, and there he was talking on the phone. He was talking away like it was the middle of the afternoon. When I asked him who he was talking to, he told me that he had gotten some phone numbers in a bar and was calling "hookers" for both of us. I told him not me and went back to sleep. I don't think he ever found anyone, but you could never be sure with him. That's just the way he was, always some sort of turmoil going on."

Too bad Sheppy wasn't alive and Johnny Caruso never lived on Orchard Street because those two could tell some genuine King of Orchard Street stories. Yet they certainly do add "street cred" to Johnny Kipper's claim to the title.

We rolled on.

"Did I ever tell you the incident with Johnny Caruso's dad, my uncle George's snowblower?" asked Johnny Kipper.

I replied, "No, tell me more."

"Johnny Caruso liked to bet the NFL like we all did. On one weekend he bet $100 on four different games and lost them all. He owed the bookie $400, which naturally he did not have. The bookie, whom I will not name, wanted the payment. Johnny told him that he didn't have the money to cover the bets, but he just bought a new snowblower that was over $400. The bookie could go to his house and remove the snowblower off his porch as payment. The bookie agreed and left to go to Johnny's house, actually his dad's house, my uncle George, to get the snowblower. My uncle was sitting in the house minding his business when he heard noise on the porch. When he went out to look, the bookie was loading the snowblower on a truck. As you might expect, my uncle had no idea what was happening and wanted an explanation. The bookie explained to him that Johnny owed him 400 from losing bets on the NFL. Johnny Caruso told him to take the snowblower in lieu of payment and that was what he was going to do. My uncle heard that and went ballistic, not so much for the bookie but for his son gambling with money he didn't have and then giving away his father's property to pay gambling debts. Unbelievable, but that was Johnny Caruso 100 percent. I am not certain how it ever got resolved, but I know my uncle would have strangled his son on the spot if he were standing there. Leave it to him to make a big problem out of something as simple as a snowblower."

Without as much as even catching his breath, Johnny Kipper started up with another Johnny Caruso story.

"One weekend Johnny Caruso decided that he wanted to go to Albany for a few days to mostly drink in the bars and see what situations he would encounter. Johnny got on the train in Herkimer so that he could drink the whole time he was in Albany and not have to worry about driving. Naturally he got on the train half-drunk and continued to drink on his way to Albany. Along the way, he was acting ridiculous on the train, really out of control. By the time the train got to Amsterdam, the conductor had had enough and wanted to throw Johnny off. He's sober enough to realize that if he got thrown off in Amsterdam, he had to somehow get a ride back to Frankfort.

He convinced the conductor to call a cousin of ours Sammy, who was a professional firefighter in Amsterdam. The conductor agreed and called the fire station. As his luck would have it, Sammy was working. The conductor asked Sam to vouch for Johnny Caruso. Otherwise, he's going to throw him off the train. Sammy vouched that Johnny was his cousin and really was not a bad guy. Johnny just had too much to drink, and Sam convinced him not to throw Johnny off the train. Looking back, it was probably Sam's best move because likely, if Johnny got bounced off the train, Sam was going to have to babysit Johnny while he was in Amsterdam and get him back to Frankfort also. Johnny didn't get thrown off and did get to Albany. Who knows what kind of mischief he made in Albany, but two or three days later, he came back to Frankfort on the train, telling us the story about how he practically got thrown off in Amsterdam. That guy could BS with the best of them. There is no doubt."

Johnny Kipper talking about riding on a train all the way across upstate New York lends itself to more research.

The research indicates that those train routes made the population of upstate New York from around the 1900s to the 1930s almost tripled. The New York Central Railroad was the original train that ran upstate. The company was in business from 1853 to the mid-1960s. New York Central was first built by Cornelius Vanderbilt, which he then sold to Erastus Corning. Corning was a businessman from Troy, New York, who started as a clerk in his uncle's hardware store in Albany. He eventually became the partner of James Spencer in a retail store, which he combined with the business he inherited from his uncle to create Erastus Corning and Company. The company's products included tools, farm implements, nails, stoves, and parts for railroad cars and rails. He eventually became the owner of New York Central Railroad. Erastus was also the mayor of Albany, a New Yok State senator, and a member of the House of Representatives. Corning played a big role in the Peace Conference of 1860, which unsuccessfully tried to prevent the Civil War. The headquarters of his railroad was Grand Central Terminal in New York City, which is still in use today. The company started out as the Mid-Atlantic Great Lakes train. As the years went by, New York Central absorbed many small rail lines like the Lake Shore, the Michigan, Pennsylvania Railroad, Utica–Schenectady line, Buffalo–Rochester line, Boston and New York line, Cleveland–Chicago line, eventually extending into Canada as the Ontario and Quebec Train Corporation. New York Central developed some of the most famous trains themselves such as the 20th Century Limited, the New York Mercury, and the Empire State Express. Those famous trains were known for grandeur, comfort, speed, and were mainly used by the wealthy. Those specific liners were the way people traveled, especially wealthy people.

The whole system of trains in the United States quickly declined during the 1960s. The completion of the Interstate Highways and the growth of trucking companies nearly destroyed the train business. The Saint Lawrence Seaway opening with the ability to bring ocean-size vessels east on the Saint Lawrence through the locks all the way to Green Bay, Wisconsin, was another big competitor for the trains. The advent of the Interstate Commerce Commission, combined with massive overregulation of the train system, was the straw that broke the camel's back. The overregulation literally put the train systems out of business. Around the 1890s and 1900s, with huge numbers of immigrants coming to New York City from Poland, Italy, and Greece, the trains were used by almost everyone to get to upstate New York. The wealthy would take the trains to places like Richfield Springs, Saratoga Springs, and Sharon Springs to escape the heat in New York City during the summer and bathe in the warm baths that bubbled out of the ground as a vehicle to better their health. As people came into upstate New York and spread out into the beautiful vistas at Lake George, Lake Placid, and the Finger Lakes, the demand for trains became even greater. The New York Central train line was right there waiting in New York City to provide the services that people demanded. Immigrant workers living in New York City would take the trains upstate to work at the resorts that catered to the wealthy. Many also came upstate to work in the lumber industry in the Adirondacks. In Forestport, New York, thus the name, was a train station where the immigrants would disembark and get picked up to work in the Adirondacks, cutting trees or milling lumber. Many of those immigrants couldn't speak English. At some point a long time ago, someone put a mounted buffalo head on the outside of the train station in Forestport. Being that most of the immigrants couldn't speak English or understand English, it was hard for them to tell where to get off the train. The people in New York City would give them a picture of a mounted buffalo head to put in their pocket and tell them when they get to the train station with a buffalo head like the one in the picture, that is where they get off. In Forestport, next to the old train station was the Buffalo Head Restaurant, which was in business for many years and that's where the name came from. The immigrants were told to get off the train when they saw the buffalo head and someone would meet them to provide transportation to Saranac Lake, Inlet, Eagle Bay, or wherever to work lumbering to fulfill the demand for lumber, housing, and building materials in New York City, Boston, Philadelphia—literally all over the United States.

When I went to college, I worked at the Herkimer County Historical Society during the summer. One summer that I worked there was in 1976, the year of the United States Bicentennial. We had a lot of fun with that. While looking through some of the artifacts one day, I found a handwritten letter in not very good English from a worker in the Adirondacks, who was cutting lumber, to his mother in New York City. The worker was explaining to his mother that it was very hot, probably close to 100 degrees, and very humid, possibly close to 100 percent humidity. Even in that heat he had to wear a hat, a mask, gloves, long sleeves, heavy jeans, and so on because the black flies were so bad that if you had any skin exposed, you could get bit many, many times in one day. The welts from the bites would bleed and ooze, then crust over. There was no relief from them. The only option available was to keep your skin covered from head to toe in the intense heat and humidity. You couldn't get enough water in your body to keep cool, and all you did was sweat all day long. It was horrible, but you still couldn't take any clothes off.

Those trains even affected my own family well over three generations ago. My great-great-grandparents arrived from the province of Calabria in Italy sometime in the 1890s with their two small children: Leon, who was my grandfather, and his sister, Olympia. As I understand it, my great-grandfather and grandmother, whose names

I do not know, bought a house at 3131 Fourteenth Street in Queens, New York. Again, as I understand it, most likely they were both buried somewhere in Queens. I think my great-aunt Olympia inherited their house and lived in it her entire life. Later living with her were her son Rocky and his family in the upstairs apartment and my aunt in the downstairs apartment. My grandfather Leon either got a job working for New York Central Railroad and was sent to work in Utica, or he worked for New York Central in New York City, and the job got transferred to Utica. He settled in Frankfort where he met my grandmother Mary Dee. They soon married and bought a house on Orchard Street. They have seven children: my mother Rose, her sisters Grace and Flora, along with brothers Vincent, George, John, and Anthony.

My grandmother's brother, my great-uncle Dominic Dee also worked for New York Central Railroad in Canajoharie, New York. For that matter, Dominic's grandson Anthony Stellitano worked for New York Central Railroad his whole life and retired a few years ago. It was generational, one person to the next, to the next, and so on as the years went by. There is a connection between the wealthy traveling from upstate New York City and my uncle Dominic working for New York Central Railroad at the Canajoharie Depot. It seems that while working in Canajoharie, my uncle would come in contact with the family of Edward Clark of Cooperstown and New York City fame. Apparently, Edward Clark was married a number of times and had a number of families. Clark was extremely wealthy in that as a young man he had aligned himself with Isaac Merritt Singer, the inventor of the Singer sewing machine, and made a fortune quickly. Edward built the Kingfisher Tower, The Otesaga Hotel, The Farmers' Museum, and The Fenimore Art Museum. His son Steven C. Clark is the founder of the Baseball Hall of Fame, and his granddaughter Jane Forbes Clark is still the chairperson of the Hall. History shows Edward Clark as a notorious womanizer. He was married two or three times and during each marriage always had at least one mistress. In between marriages he had numerous girlfriends including one who was a French movie star. He is generally considered, as were many men at that time, an industrialist but also a scoundrel. Clark was once arrested for bigamy for being married to two, possibly three, women at the same time. Between his businesses and the women, indeed, he was a very busy guy. How this all connects to my uncle Dominic is when one of his family members, girlfriends, or whoever got off the train in Canajoharie from New York City, my uncle Dominic would be certain that there was an on-time car, wagon, or some type of ground transportation to quickly get the family and their luggage to Cooperstown. Edward or one of his wives took a liking to my uncle for all his efforts to the extent that when my uncle's daughter Rosemary Stellitano got married, the Clarks bought her a unique mahogany corner table for a wedding gift. Rosemary's sister Georgeanne who lives two miles from us, whom Carol speaks to almost every day and comes to our house often, still has the table. I tell Georgeanne and her son Pat that I hope they both outlive me, but if they don't, I'll take the table. It has history. It was a gift from the Clarks made out of expensive wood, and it's a unique-shaped corner table. Quite interesting overall. The next time I go to Georgeanne's house, I'm going to ask her if I can take whatever she has on table off and flip it over so I can see who manufactured it, when it was manufactured, and where it was manufactured. I really like the fact that it was a gift from the Clarks, likely be close to one hundred years old. Maybe it's one of those period pieces that are on *Antiques Roadshow* valued at $14,000 or more that the owner is not aware of.

Who knows? Even if it is worthless, I still like it.

I really am going to have to take a serious look at that table.

Some of Johnny Kipper's circumstances, as in the case of Johnny Caruso who was never a resident of Orchard Street and thus not eligible to be the king, are loosely connected to Johnny Kipper's bid to be crowned the King of Orchard Street. The imperceptible strengthens Johnny Kipper's case. Which candidate has led the most captivating life, gotten away with the most while doing little or no harm to himself or others is possibly the ultimate criteria as to who in the end is resolved to be the king. It appears now, after approximately six months of collaboration and writing, the terminal algorithm is firming up.

Like the biography of the now deceased comic Chris Farley entitled *Anything for a Laugh*, Johnny, myself, and all the contenders for the King of Orchard Street have been consciously or unconsciously doing just that our entire lives.

Johnny Kipper continued, "Orchard Street was a great place to live, but like anywhere else, there were tragedies we all suffered through. The first one I remember was Carmie Garcia drowning in the Barge Canal. Carmie and Debbie Puzzilla were by the canal playing on the ice, obviously where they should not have been, when the ice broke, and Carmie went in that freezing cold water. Can you imagine the terror that went through that poor girl's mind, drowning and being trapped under that ice? It makes me want to cry for her now close to sixty years later. She was probably in third or fourth grade, maybe fifth. She was beautiful. I can still see her in my brain. If my memory serves me right, her body wasn't found right away. By the time a dive team was assembled with equipment, at least twenty-four hours went by. Keep in mind that was sixty years ago. I couldn't imagine what the family was going through during that period when she was missing. Heartbreaking, to say the least. I don't know how anyone could recover from that. The suffering must have been unbearable for Carmie in that water and her family waiting for information.

Another poignant tragedy was my dear cousin Barbie Caruso's death. At least Barbie's family had some options, granted temporary ones, and a little time to process the circumstances. Although in the end, it didn't make much difference. Barbie developed cancer in her leg that was so advanced when it was identified that almost her entire leg had to be immediately amputated. We all thought she was going to survive and was good for a while, then the cancer came back with a vengeance. More developed and metastasized than the first time. Talk about shock and disbelief. It was worse than the first time. Horrible for the whole family, and I mean the whole family. Fourteen aunts, uncles, and about sixty first cousins. I had never felt anything like that in my life. I think in the end, Barbie didn't live another month after the cancer came back the second time. I must have just started at Sullivan County Community College when I got the news.

I couldn't get home fast enough. I was so sad. My poor cousin. What a tragedy. It still hurts to this day."

We had to take a break. We both had a drink. Then noshed on some chips and soppressata. It didn't help.

I asked Johnny, about thirty minutes later when we got started up again, why he wasn't at Jimmy DeRollo's house for New Year's Eve. He explained that Jimmy had invited him, but he had been working all day and didn't want to go out again. He and Emily decided to stay home and watch TV. I continued to fill Johnny in as to how the King of Orchard Street came up with Jimmy and me. It was Jimmy's opinion that first, we should change the name of this book to *The Pope of Orchard Street*. Jimmy felt we were wasting our time writing it also. The King of Orchard Street was determined decades ago. When I asked Jimmy who he felt was this already determined King of Orchard Street, he explained his position. He asked who first came to mind whenever Orchard Street was mentioned. I told him I didn't know. Jimmy was emphatic that it was Johnny Kipper's Uncle Rossi Caruso. He raised a good point. I then proceeded to tell Jimmy how earlier that day I had spoken to my uncle John Iocovozzi who lives in Palm Coast, Florida, about how Carol and I were leaving soon for Georgia, and if he was comfortable with it, we would also visit him in that we had not seen him in a while. Uncle John had just turned ninety years old. Of course, he was happy for us to come. The discussion then turned to if he wanted to be part of the King of Orchard Street project, which of course, he did also. I was very happy that he decided to be involved, having been born in 1932 and clearly having been on Orchard Street in the 1930s through mid-1950s. A living "primary source," if there ever was one, for a period of time prior to my time. The discussion with Uncle John Iocovozzi then turned to almost the same discussion I would have with Jimmy about four hours later. Uncle John felt that the King of Orchard Street was already determined also. As matter of fact, he had two kings.

Uncle John carried on. "In the 1930s my brother Vincent was the king. The entire street loved him. He was big, tall, and about as gregarious as a person as you could get. When he walked or drove down the street, everyone waved to him and called out his name. It was wonderful. After Vincent in the 1930s, my brother George took over in the 1940s. He was the same thing. Always dressed sharp, quieter than Vince but equally as friendly, and the whole street loved him. When he drove or walked by, it was like a parade. People waved to him, called out hellos and his name. It was wonderful just like Vince."

Jimmy and Uncle John raised valid points. That got Johnny Kipper thinking.

"Maybe Jimmy is wrong on one hand but right on the other. I like *The King of Orchard Street* better than *The Pope of Orchard Street*. Jimmy is wrong about the title, but maybe he is right about my uncle Rossi. He was my idol growing up. Uncle Rossi always had a new Cadillac. I think I told you how he bought every niece and nephew a present for Christmas, and I mean probably sixty or seventy of us, every single one, and delivered them to us. He never had a job but always had money, nice clothes, and a fancy car. At one point he had a hot dog stand on Main Street in the front and a craps table in the back, with cards and gambling also taking place twenty-four hours a day. Like a miniature casino, all 100 percent illegal. Everyone, including the police, knew what was going on, but no one ever stopped him. He loved me like I was his son, and I loved him equally as much. He was like Frankfort's version of John Gotti. Naturally, watching my uncle Rossi, Frank "Chico" Sanders, Chico's brother Luke, Earl De Luke, and the rest of the crowd gambling all day, we all picked up on it early. It was illegal to gamble, but so what? Who were they hurting?

"One afternoon my brother Frank and I walked over to a pool hall or something that Ming Bianchi had, and I bought some pull tab tickets. I might have bought two or three dollars' worth, and I won fifteen. I was maybe twelve years old at the time. Ming was a good guy, but you had to watch him all the time. He was always trying to stay one step ahead of everyone else, often not legitimately. When I went to the counter to collect my winnings, Ming told me three kings was not a winner. It had to be four, even when I showed him the back of the tab, which said three was a winner. Again, he insisted it wasn't a winner, but if I went through the trash and found another pull tab with three kings, he would pay me. I knew three was a winner and was determined to collect the fifteen dollars. At probably twelve years old, here I was going through the entire trash can to find another three kings pull tab to collect my illicit winnings. Sure enough, I found one. Most likely Ming knew full well my three kings were a winner and just didn't want to pay. Like I said, you always had to watch him, or maybe he knew there was an already paid three kings winner in the trash and wanted to see if I had the gumption to find it and make him pay. In any case, I stuck to my guns, and he paid me. Reluctantly.

"This possible King of Orchard Street, Johnny Kipper, was on his game way back in the misty past of 1966. How about that?"

Ming did have a good side, though, and at times it came through. The spots may have been few and far between, but they were there.

Johnnie seemed to like the idea of Ming having a good side, so on he went.

"Even though there were times when Ming was way off track, he did some good things too. When I played varsity football in high school, before a game on Saturday, a bunch of us would meet for breakfast. I don't remember exactly where, but Ming got wind of us meeting and would show up. He would have coffee and sit to talk to us. Ming always wished us all good luck and urged us to play hard but don't get hurt. We all looked forward to him being there. It was great fun. When we all were ready to leave, Ming would pay for all our breakfasts. It was a good gesture on his part, and we all really appreciated it."

That made Ming's good side pop into my brain.

I asked Johnny, "Do you remember when there was a very poor family living in the apartment above Viti's Bakery with probably five kids? Ming would at random times go to Melrose Market to buy three of four bags of groceries and give them to these people whom he didn't even know. Or how about when he would go find Charlie Bommarito on Christmas Eve? Charlie had a severe drinking problem, but Ming would find him and bring him to his house for Christmas Eve dinner. Ming could be very difficult, but at times he had bright spots. What a dichotomy. Ming never lived on Orchard Street, so he can't be considered for the king, but he really did tear Frankfort up."

Johnny restarted. "As a little kid, I loved being around my uncle Rossi and his crowd. They were all good guys, just loved to gamble. I don't remember any of them ever having much of a job, but a lot of the things I apply in my business I learned from watching them gamble. When Chico died, my uncle Rossi put a dollar in his pocket, so he didn't die broke.

"Funny that some of those guys never had any money, but when the Addolorata had their festival parade on Orchard Street, they all had money to pin on the saint. They had money for that and to gamble but never had any in their pockets."

I told Johnnie that Donnie said the same thing. That we were in our own little world there. We thought the whole of creation were Italian Americans, and all that mattered was what happened on those five small blocks of Orchard Street. We lived there, and we died there. We laughed and cried there. We found joy and pain in each other. We found comfort and solace in each other. No one went unaided. No one went uncared for.

From there what has happened to this world? If the world went back to emulating Orchard Street from those long past days, would we all be better off? I don't see any plausible argument that could deny the world would be better off if we all just "practiced a little Orchard Street."

I doubt Johnny Kipper, Donnie, John-John Tubia, myself, or any potential King of Orchard Street would disagree with that proposition.

I wanted to talk more. Johnnie wanted to talk more. I defer to him, and he continued to make his case.

"I think we all pushed the envelope a little bit, some more than others, but never to the extent anyone got hurt. We messed around pretty good. We covered up for each other, but it was never anything harmful or dangerous. In reality what happened was the opposite. In the end we helped each other and protected each other. My best memories were being at my grandmother's house with all of my cousins, and I mean a lot of cousins. Just simple stuff, like Christmas dinner and all the holidays being together with a lot of very funny people. It's not like that anymore. Everyone is spread out doing their own thing. The daily connection just doesn't exist anymore. I agree with Donnie 100 percent. Times have changed, and I don't think for the better. We used to do what seemed like everyday stuff for hours and not think anything of it. I feel bad about it too, like Donnie. Who would have thought way back then, when it was so common, it would be so rare now? Who would have thought what seemed to mean so little then would mean so much now? Everything just went along smoothly. Now everything is so disrupted. It really makes me sad. Time is horrible like that. It just keeps moving and, in the end, eats all of us up. Great memories burned on my brain.

"Simple things like waiting for the water to boil to cook pasta for dinner at my grandmother's house meant so much to me. Simple but dominant, easy but beguiling. There never seemed to be many dramatic ups and downs. Mostly an even keel. Probably, the most disturbing incidents of my young life on Orchard Street were the death of my cousin Barbie Caruso and Carmie Tubia drowning. Consistency was the word I think best describes our day-to-day lives, and that consistency bred contentment. Not a bad way to live. How I wish it was like that now. There is just too much turmoil in the world. I think that is what makes people so unhappy. That turmoil causes so many problems in people's own houses and throughout the entire world. The only other big thing I can remember was when Lucy Dade was murdered. I was in that store every day. Somebody killed that innocent woman. Who did it and for what we will never know. That was obviously a huge tragedy for us all because we all knew her and saw her all the time. I used to be in her store sometimes two or three times a day. I would go to buy those airplanes with the rubber band in the middle. Half the time I would break the plane before I even got it home. If I did get it home in one piece, I would fly it a few times and, sure enough, get it stuck in a tree or by mistake step on it, whatever. Almost a guarantee that an hour or so later, I would be back in the store buying another one, only to repeat the same pattern again and again. If I wasn't back in the store, my father went to buy me a new one.

"Do you remember those planes? They were paper thin, like papyrus. If you picked them up wrong, they would snap in half. The manufacturer most likely had made a fortune on those planes because we broke so many of them. In and out of Costanza's store, buying candy. In and out of Sam Talerico's store on the corner of Orchard Street and Railroad Street all day, buying more candy. I'm surprised I even have teeth with all the candy I ate."

I agreed, as in my case too. My memory kicked in with a good, maybe true, legend only potential King of Orchard Street would have heard.

"Johnny, how about those pockmarks on the still standing from 1890 Masonic building, on the corner of Main Street and Litchfield Street? Let's compare two possible kings' recollections of the same legend."

Johnnie picked up immediately.

"You and Donnie and I used to walk to that corner, likely without permission, to look at the pockmarks on the northeast corner of the building. I don't know where one of us got the idea. Maybe it was true, that those marks were gouged out by bullets from a Mafia hit of somebody on that corner. When the assassins sprayed the guy with bullets from machine guns, obviously, some of the bullets missed and knocked pieces of individual bricks out of the wall. The guy being shot staggered across the street to the northwest corner of Main and Litchfield and died there. Did that really happen, or was it the collective imaginations of three six- or seven-year-olds running away with them? I don't know for sure. If my memory from sixty years ago serves me correctly, the Frescos who lived a little south of the Masonic building on Litchfield Street verified that story for us. Could it be true?"

I answered, "I don't know, but a little research on the topic shows interesting info. The Mafia was mostly put out of business in the area in 1990, when a huge federal racketeering case decimated what small existence there still was. At various times beginning in the early half of the century, this area was run by crews backed by the Mafia in Buffalo and New York City's Columbo crime family. The Utica area was often known by the moniker "Sin City." The last breath of mob activity really went out with a bang. Salvatore and Joe Falcone allegedly ran the rackets from Prohibition until the 1970s. When Joe died and Sal retired, a vacuum existed until Columbo family backed Dominic Bretti, fresh out of jail, who took control. Bretti was again later jailed for murder, attempted murder, and racketeering in 1982. I understand he was released in about 2018. From 1970 to about 1990, there was a lot of activity in the area, it seemed, to settle old scores. First, a man named William Conley was blown up by a grenade in South Utica. David Sgroi was shot outside Rome, and five or six years later, Albert Marrone was killed walking home after dinner at Alfredo's. Then the action moved to Syracuse when a produce dealer, Albert Schiano, was found dead near the Onondaga County line. In 1979 Dawn Grillo, allegedly a mob wife, which is a name I do remember, was strangled for skimming money from the Columbo crime family and possibly cooperating with the authorities.

"There was another attempt when an alleged mob associate Richie Clair, a bar owner, had his bar bombed when he was already in police custody for potential involvement in other crimes. Another name I also remember was a lawyer named Joseph Daquino who was killed in what was likely a case of mistaken identity or was a scary message to Daquino's boss, another lawyer, Louis Brindisi. There were a few more situations like a topless dancer named Carla Feliciano was killed in Woodside, New York. Angelo Grillo was gunned down in Cornhill. Tommy Bretti, Dominic's brother, was injured in a bomb attack, and George Sandouk was killed in his apartment for refusing to pay tribute money to run his sports gambling operation in the area. I don't know if any of it is true, and it certainly is none of my business, but I do remember seeing some of the names in the newspaper a long time ago, and minimal research presents those names again. I really didn't know any of the victims either. It seems like that was the end of the whole thing.

"As far as in Frankfort, there is nothing of any record evident, but there were a couple of deaths attributed to some sort of feud among the residents. I don't know if you remember Billy Schuster from

Frankfort who worked at the Union Fork and Hoe, but he wrote a book entitled *Dark Times in Frankfort* that details these alleged feuds and their end results. I read the book a few years ago, and Billy made no mention of anything on the corner of Main Street and Litchfield Street. I showed those pockmarks to my children when they were little and told the same story that we told. In the end I think it was you, Donnie, and me letting our imaginations run wild. Yet who knows? There is an old saying 'Every rumor begins with a grain of truth,' and that may be exactly what happened to us back in about 1962. For lack of a better term, let's call them Legends of Old Orchard Street.

"Speaking of the Frescos, do you know that their old house is the oldest existing building in Frankfort? Look at the keystone at the top. I think it says 1860 or even earlier. King of Orchard Street notwithstanding, that place scared the snot out of me when I used to walk by as a kid. It was originally built as a Methodist church, but I was convinced it was haunted. As I walked on Litchfield Street, when I got to either side of the building, I would sprint across the front of the house because I felt for certain a ghost or something would grab me and pull me in. Even being a young potential King of Orchard Street, it was real fear. Fear is not an emotion a king should entertain, but I sure felt fear there. Is that a strike against my possible enthroning as the King of Orchard Street? A moment of weakness? For a king? It can't happen! Maybe I should leave that part out?"

That statement got a chuckle from both of us. We pressed forward.

Johnnie continued. "Do you know even I as the possible King of Orchard Street also have a similar type of strike against me. At one point I used to shine shoes. A king? Never. It can't happen! I agree with you 110 percent. It cannot happen. Still, it did happen. Only for the right reasons, though. Such as to buy more candy at Sam Talerico's store or more balsa wood airplanes at Lucy Dade's store after I broke my fifth one for the day and my father wouldn't buy me anymore. At least for that day.

"My uncle Sammy from Amsterdam made me a box to store all my shoeshine equipment that I would carry over to the corner of Main and Litchfield Street. We must have spent a lot of time there.

My cousins Ronnie and Eddie Scalise and I would sit on the box and wait for people to get off the bus from Utica to shine their shoes. It all started when we saw this Black kid about our age, probably from Utica, who would get off the bus and set up to shine shoes all day, then take the bus back home at night. Eddie, Ronnie, and I all thought we could do that too. We asked this Black kid if he thought it was a good idea. He told us that he did pretty good shining shoes there, but if we were going to do it, he wouldn't come back, and we could pick up his business. We all agreed. I am not sure how the topic came up, but at some point my uncle Sam heard about it and made us a shoeshine box. Just like that we were in business overnight. We charged $0.25 a shine and did good. I bet there were days we earned three or four, maybe even five dollars, which we split three ways. You could buy a lot of candy and balsa wood airplanes with a dollar or two then. One guy, I can't remember his name, was a clerk in the Frankfort Police Department. We would shine his shoes every day when he went out to lunch. He was our best customer by far.

"Eddie, Ronnie, and I were there when Bennie DiPiazza killed Noreen Jones. I can't remember if we were there shining shoes or just hanging out on the corner, but we knew something bad had happened. We were sitting on the curb when the police brought him out. It was very bad. People were gawking and pushing to get a look. Horrible scene for sure. Bennie has been in jail for about sixty years now. Truly heartbreaking for all the families involved. I can't imagine what their lives have been like since that day. Apparently, with his cousin Richard Talerico's help, Bennie was paroled at one point to live in Albany, but it didn't last very long. Soon after he was released, he got arrested for shoplifting or something minor and was then found to be in possession of some sort of weapon. Clearly, a paroled killer can't do those things, and he was right back in prison in no time. What a cataclysm and still causing devastation six decades later for the families. Horrible lifetimes of hurt caused by a few seconds of quick overreaction in 1964. Like an ancient Greek tragedy with the choir singing in the background, telling the actors and audience to beware. That something bad was about to happen that would have terrifying long-term effects."

"That's intense stuff," I told Johnny.

"How did we get from shining shoes to spending your whole life in jail? Whew. That's enough of that. Let's get back to more lighthearted King of Orchard Street tales. How about Tommy Dovi and Donnie with the diesel fuel in Tommy's car?"

Johnnie jumped right into the narrative.

"Did Donnie include that in his account? He had to. I wasn't there, but to hear Donnie tell it is comical. I could hear Tommy telling Donnie, 'Fill it right up, buddy, all the way" in that monotone voice Tommy had. The car went a hundred yards and died. Tommy was all upset. Donnie couldn't have cared less, left Tommy and started walking home with Tommy cursing him all the way east on Orchard Street until Donnie got home on Litchfield Street. That's an Orchard Street saga if there ever was one. That incident brings to my mind another potential King of Orchard Street's tale that I witnessed but is really not part of my chronicle.

"I must have been about eleven or twelve years old and was in my room on a very nice summer day with my window open. Out of nowhere I heard all this loud screaming and swearing. My first impression was someone was hurt. I looked out the window to see what was happening, and there was Alex Rosemyer running alongside a moving car that was picking up speed, holding the driver by the collar with one hand and punching him in the head and face through the open window with the other hand as the car was accelerating. Finally, after probably one hundred and fifty yards of chasing this car, Alex let the guy go. When he walked back to my house, I asked Alex what had happened. Alex told me they guy gave him the middle finger as he was walking along Main Street, and he wasn't going to let him get away with it. Alex chased him down and gave it to the driver good. That is a King of Orchard Street saga too, not for me but rather for Alex, and I'll leave it at that."

Vinny

I always remember a sweet, dry smell. It was everywhere. It never went away. Goodness, there was nothing wrong with it but was always there. As a matter of fact, it was very nice. In the summer it was stronger, sweeter, and more pungent mostly, I imagine, because of the warmer air. In the winter it may have been weaker because of the cold air, I would think, but it was still there. It was nice. It was actually very nice. I was probably twenty years old before I realized where it was coming from. I might have been on Orchard Street visiting my aunt Josie, who was my grandmother Mary's younger sister and my dear cousin Russell Marchione's grandmother, or I might have been at Puzze's on the weekend, having lunch and a drink. I don't quite remember why I was there or what I was doing, but I do know suddenly I realized where the smell was coming from. It was from Corrado's Feed Mill on the west end of Orchard Street. For the past probably thirty-five or forty years, it has been known as Browns Feed Company. George Corrado was the mayor of Frankfort in the late '40s and early '50s and a prominent businessman. George's house on the corner of Main Street and Cemetery Hill was recently occupied and then sold by a longtime friend Bob Reina after Bobby retired. George's house still remains on the corner with a very colonial stoic appearance. An old office and apartment building on the corner of Main Street and Litchfield Street in Frankfort sat there for many years also. It was a large four-story brick building that housed apartments and businesses such as Brady Thomas's Insurance Agency. George donated a clock, as literally every small village in America must have, to hang off the side of that building until the building I believe burned and was later demolished. The clock was taken off and saved. I hope. I don't know where it is, but hopefully, it was not lost or given away in that it was proudly hung on that building for probably seventy-five years.

George's feed mill had a loading dock. Erected over the loading dock was a large hopper. Farmers would pull their trucks in under the hopper. The hopper would then be loaded with various feeds from the top, be it wheat, corn, rye, barley, or whatever the farmer was interested in purchasing that day. When the hopper was opened to dispense two or three tons of grain into the farmer's truck, a thin dust would also be dispensed. Not dust in the sense of being dirt or something harmful but rather a fine powder of clean, sweet-smelling grain. I only realized where the smell came from all those many years later when I noticed, while doing whatever I was doing on Orchard Street, a thin brown powder on my car, on the rails of my aunt Josie's porch, or wherever I first noticed it. Only then did it become evident to me where the smell came from. It was the grain powder being released into the atmosphere when the hopper was opened at Browns Feed to fill up trucks.

I noticed the other evening while attending the Frankfort Marina Days that George's old hopper had been torn down and replaced in the back of the feed mill with a fully covered bay enclosed by two large overhead doors that now prevents most of that grain powder from escaping. That smell was nice. That smell was everywhere, and it took me about twenty years to realize where it came from. Yet now it is probably gone. It permeated Orchard Street and the vicinity and added a sweet smell to an already very "sweet" environment." I had much the same experience when I went to college in Oswego, New York. In Fulton, New York, a village about ten miles South of Oswego, there was a Nestle chocolate plant. As soon as you drove into the Fulton city limits, especially on warm days, you could smell that chocolate being manufactured in the plant. If the wind was right, there were even days when you could smell chocolate ten miles north of the factory wafting through the air in Oswego. It was a wonderful smell equal to the wonderful, sweet smell of the grain from Corrado's Mill on Orchard Street.

When I think back to those early years on Orchard Street, it becomes evident to me that the whole environment was effortlessly moving along with little or no disruption coming from inside or out. Consider the Milky Way, a small corner of the cosmos gliding effortlessly, serenely through creation guided by the power of existence. Consider the Earth and even smaller corner of the universe gliding effortlessly, serenely through creation again guided by the power of existence. Consider Orchard Street and its environs, it too gliding effortlessly, serenely through an even smaller corner of creation guided by the King of Orchard Street. Maybe that king knew it at that time or not and possibly doesn't even know it now, but he was the guiding force. The inductive/deductive concept reminds me of the famous Russian nesting dolls. The forces at play on Orchard Street worked in a similar manner. Those forces worked in the same perfected manner as creation. As simple as the nesting dolls or as majestic as the universe.

My mother, father, sister, and I lived in a small two-bedroom apartment upstairs in what would have been my grandmother's house. When my grandmother passed away, my aunt Flora bought the house, and my uncle Jim made part of the upstairs into an apartment. My family lived in the apartment, and my aunt, uncle, and her family lived in the remainder of the house. We occupied the upstairs, and my aunt's family occupied the downstairs and a small part of the upstairs. There was a large wraparound porch that, if you walked to the right, was the entrance to my aunt's apartment. If you walked straight, the stairs led to our apartment. When you walked into our apartment to the right, there was a small bedroom that my sister and

I shared at some point. If you went straight ahead across the hall, there was a small living room, something like my cousin Damian Iocovozzi would term "The Museum" years later in my mother's house on Fourth Avenue. Proceeding down the hall, the first door on the left was my mother and father's bedroom. In that bedroom, to the left, there was another small room like a walk-in closet. I believe that's where my mother and father put my bassinet when I was a baby and later, I believe, a small bed for me. If continuing to proceed west in that hall, at the end was a small kitchen. Across the kitchen there was a sink up against the outside wall. A table was placed on the right side of the kitchen. Walking through to the right and taking one step down was a living room on the north side of the house facing the Mohawk River and Barge Canal. A couch occupied the right-side wall of the living room with two chairs on either side of the step-down entrance from the kitchen. Also on the right side of the living was a door that was kept locked, which led into the hall and a bedroom on the second floor of my aunt's apartment. That bedroom was shared by my cousins Verna and Matti. I found out on Thanksgiving this year that the room at some point was also shared with Verna and Matti's younger brother Joseph Favat. The sisters were in no uncertain terms not pleased with the arrangements.

We spent most of our family time together in the living room watching TV that was placed against the back wall with rabbit ears on it to get the best reception. My dad and mom were always busy with my mother running her own business and my father working in John's Market as a butcher. I sat in that living room for countless hours on the floor or on the couch, playing with my toys, watching TV, or looking out the window toward the Mohawk River and the Barge Canal.

I have come to realize as the years passed that our house on Orchard Street was the ideal environment to raise a family. My uncle Jim Favat, aunt Flora, and their three children Verna, Matti, and Joseph lived in the downstairs apartment. While my dad, mother, sister, and I lived in the upstairs apartment, setting up a model habitat for constant interaction between two closely related young families. All of us spent hours sitting in the driveway with my grandfather's grapevine growing thick, green, and healthy above us or by the banks of the Mohawk River, where the Frankfort Marina is now located in my great-grandfather's garden, as we called it, Grandpa's Grove. Grandpa's Grove was a favorite place for me to spend my time. Although I shouldn't have been there because it was on the other side of the railroad tracks that my mother and father warned me practically every day to not cross, I couldn't resist. I was there constantly most times by myself.

    I never remember my great-grandfather George Dee being there, but his garden was always planted, weeded, and watered. I don't think my great-grandfather owned the land, and I'm not sure who did, but whoever it belonged to, he either paid to use it or the owner just allowed him to plant his garden there. My grandmother's property ended at the railroad tracks, and the garden was on the other side of the tracks a short distance east of my grandmother's house, which definitely made it not on her property. Of course, the number one crop to grow was tomatoes, number two crop was peppers, and number three crop was zucchini. Then came the seasonings: the first, naturally, garlic; the next basil; and the third parsley to complete all the flavors of classic Italian cooking. The Grove really did look like a grove. There a small clump of three or four trees in the middle with a rectangular perimeter about twenty feet by thirty feet cleared out for the actual garden. In the shade of the trees, I vividly remember there being two classic lawn chairs that are known as clamshell, shellback, or tulip chairs. The style of the chair was at first called a motel chair because it was commonly seen in front of roadside motels and oftentimes by the pools of those motels alongside probably the most famous road in America, Route 66, America's Main Street. I recently had the pleasure of driving on a section of Route 66 in the Mojave Desert National Park. To state it was a pleasure does not do the drive justice. Water for keeping the garden green in the case of drought was brought in by hand from the close-by Mohawk River. The water was collected by buckets, hand sprinklers, or rain barrels, which dotted the landscape, to not incur any expense in watering the garden. Sitting in the Grove by myself, with my friends, or any of my cousins was a guaranteed fun experience. It was always cool, and we sat there in the shade kibitzing at one hundred miles an hour. Even though I wasn't supposed to be across those railroad tracks and I knew it, I just had to go. The distant memory of the experience of sitting in that grove lights up my brain like a Christmas tree right now on Tuesday, October 4, 2022, at 10:37 a.m. Being in Grandpa's Grove or anywhere on Orchard Street with my three cousins Verna, Joseph, Matti, any of my relatives, friends, and neighbors was constantly restorative. An exhilarating time in my life that I will never forget.

When my aunt Flora and uncle Jim had somewhere to go, they had my mom and dad on-site to keep an eye on their children as they went in and out of the house to school, work, or to socialize with their friends. My uncle Jim was severely wounded in World War II, as I recall by shrapnel, almost the entire length of his left side from his calf up to his left kidney. I don't think he ever fully recovered from those wounds and spent the remainder of his life using leg braces, eventually being confined to wheelchair due to the shrapnel wounds and a stroke he suffered in his late thirties. Uncle Jim also suffered from poor kidney function most likely traceable to the wounds inflicted on his kidneys by shrapnel. Unfortunately, he passed away in 1962 at the age of forty-four. A true American hero who, not immediately but in the long run, gave his life for his country. He was fortunate to live long enough for his children to grow into young adults. The house was originally owned by my grandmother and grandfather. I have no recollection of either my grandfather Leon or grandmother Mary, but I do have a vague recollection of my grandmother's father and my great-grandfather George Dee, whom I and my grandmother lived with. After my grandmother's death, George then lived with his granddaughter, my aunt Flora, in her apartment below ours on Orchard Street. That is the way families took care of each other in those days, wistfully. The world could use much, much more of that care these days.

Funny how I can recollect an ancestor from three generations ago but not any from two generations ago.

Life has some strange twists and turns.

As for our house and Orchard Street, the constant interaction between the two families was extraordinarily close and consistent. I would spend my days wandering in and out of my aunt Flora's apartment, interacting with my cousins, aunts, and uncles still living in the area while soaking up every second of it like a sponge.

Being that my mother ran her own small business in the hallway and wraparound porch of our house, she would not schedule any customers after about four thirty in the afternoon. My father would get out of work usually by five and be home by about five thirty for dinner. My aunt Flora's house ran on a slightly different schedule in that she was a stay-at-home mom, and my uncle was usually home from work by about four. Considering that small time difference, the Favats would eat dinner promptly at five o'clock. In that window between the Favats having dinner and my family having dinner, I saw my opportunity. At just about five o'clock, I would be sure to make my way to the downstairs apartment where dinner was just about ready to be served. Of course, my aunt would invite me to stay for dinner. I readily took her up on her offer and took a seat at the table. Imagine? As luck would have it, within five minutes of finishing dinner with the Favats, my dad would walk in the front door and proceed up the stairs for dinner with my mother, sister, and I. When I heard him come in the door, I would thank my aunt and uncle for dinner and quickly move up the stairs to have dinner with my own family. An exceptional daily opportunity to spend high quality time interacting with close family members and have two good dinners to seal the deal. It's no wonder that I've never been thin in my life. Not with that beginning. Two dinners every day?

The close family living situation and the constant interaction between our two families led to many endearing settings. At times when my mother and father had places to go at night, perhaps a wedding, a birthday party, or were just out to dinner together for some husband-and-wife time. With my aunt Flora living downstairs, we had a built-in babysitter. My sister and I would go to my aunt's apartment sometime after dinner, most times on a Saturday night, to watch television with my aunt. Television was only the major networks CBS, NBC, and ABC, their signals being picked up by an over-the-air antenna that was placed on the roof to do away with those now passé rabbit ears. Cable and satellite TV would not be invented for many years to come. With any luck we might receive two signals from each network, one being from the local affiliates in the Utica/Rome area and the other being from the Syracuse or Albany affiliates. The ironic part of that was they were all the same networks; even if they were affiliates from outside of the area, the programming was the same. The newscasts were different, and the local commercials were different, but the programming from the networks was the same. We would spend our evenings munching on our popcorn and watching Perry Mason, The Jack Benny Show, The Jackie Gleason Show, Lawrence Welk, and others in that first generation of television programming. It was a major experience to watch entertainment to that degree so readily, right in the comfort of your own home, a phenomenon that changed America right from the second it became available. As the night progressed, my aunt would usually make popcorn and Tang to drink for which we would spend a quiet comfortable night. As the evening wore on and it started to get dark, my aunt would always tell me that by the end of the night, I would be sitting on her lap. My usual response was that I was a big boy now, about six or seven, and I didn't need to sit on anyone's lap anymore. Big boys such as me just didn't do that.

My aunt would always respond, "You'll see. Just give it some time."

As the night progressed and I started to get sleepy, little by little I would move closer to my aunt. First step might be to sit on the chair next to her. Then I would come closer, sitting on the floor by her feet. In about another half hour, as I got sleepier, sure enough, I would climb on to her lap and fall asleep in seconds. To be sure, the perfect lap to sleep on for a potential King of Orchard Street.

How fortunate and comfortable I was.

One night, while my aunt was babysitting us, Aunt Flora and I were sitting at her kitchen table doing some kind of craft project. As we sat there cutting and gluing, we discussed that when the project was finished, perhaps I could hang it in my bedroom. I would have to do two things to hang my project. First, I had to get permission from my father, and second, I would need some thumbtacks to hold up the project. My aunt went looking through one of the drawers in her kitchen and found five or six thumbtacks. Now that we were finished and had everything we needed, we started to clean up the kitchen table. Inadvertently, I dropped one of the thumbtacks.

When I told my aunt that I had dropped one, her only words to me were, "Don't worry, you will find it."

We looked around the kitchen, under the table, and the chairs briefly to try to locate the missing tack.

Again, my aunt Flora warned, "Don't worry, you will find it."

A prophetic statement as to what was about to happen next.

Within about a minute of walking around the kitchen barefoot, I stepped on the tack. Without a doubt, I had found it. I let out a high-pitched yelp that frightened even myself. There was the tack stuck in the bottom of my foot. I immediately sat on the floor and started to cry. My aunt quickly sat me up on a chair and consoled me that I was all right but we had to take the tack out. Now I was even more upset because the tack had to come out immediately. The only option was for my aunt to grab it and pull it out. I was a wreck over the whole idea, sitting there on a kitchen chair with my foot sticking out, crying not like a big boy who did not need to sit on anyone's lap anymore. My aunt went and got a Band-Aid and some rubbing alcohol, leaving me to be consoled by my sister. My aunt assured me that the removal would only take a second, and it would be best if I looked the other way. I sat there crying and shaking like I was severely injured, which plainly I was not. My aunt held my ankle with one hand, grabbed the tack with her other hand, and quickly pulled it out. At the exact second she pulled it out, I looked back to see that deep-red oxygenated blood squirt out to my aunt's dress. It must have squirted out about three inches, but for a seven-year-old boy, it looked like it squirted two feet. My aunt then took a white washcloth, cleaned up the puncture hole, put some alcohol on it and a Band-Aid over it. When I saw that deep-red blood on that clean white washcloth, it frightened me even more than seeing the blood squirt out on my aunt's dress. Again, I began to scream. I was certain it was never going to stop bleeding, and that was going to be the end of me.

THE KING OF ORCHARD STREET

Thank the heavens some sixty years later that wasn't the end of me due to my aunt Flora's quick first aid work, which gave me my chance to someday possibly win the "beauty contest" known as the King of Orchard Street.

How blessed I am to have lived through what I thought at that moment was a life-threatening circumstance to still have an opportunity to make my case as the King of Orchard Street. All due to the house and family life I was fortunate enough to be born into.

The biggest cultural phenomenon that occurred in my early years was the advent and distribution to the general public of televisions due to their drop in price, allowing the average American to purchase TV or, as they were called in those days, a "television set." My children asked me many years ago if I ever remember a time when there wasn't television, and I told them that I did not. Television had always existed from the day I could first remember such things. I asked my father the same question when I was very young, and he replied that, of course, there was a time when he could remember hardly having radio, let alone a TV. As the saying goes, he sat there "watching the radio." Television wasn't even on the radar yet until my dad was probably twenty-five or thirty years old. It was some scientists' concept prior to that. The first models were too expensive for the average person, thus only the wealthy could afford one. As is always the case when manufacturing became more systematic with any product, the price drops, and televisions became available to the average person at a cost they could afford. Television in old days wasn't very fancy. The screen itself was probably twenty-four inches by twelve inches. The cabinet that housed the screen was the biggest part of the television, probably three feet wide and four feet high. When I was a child, people would say that one of these days you were going to hang your television on the wall like a painting. I thought to myself then that would never happen. How are you going to be able to do that, especially when I was sitting there looking at that huge cabinet housing that little screen? Sure enough, probably twenty years ago, televisions were flattened out to the point you do now hang them on the wall like a painting. Clearly, they are much more sophisticated and much more functional, but they do hang on a wall. Will wonders ever cease?

Television in those days was very grainy and basic. Saturday morning was the day when literally every child in America who had one watched TV. The Saturday morning programming with Howdy Doody and Buffalo Bob was probably the most successful children's show of all. *Howdy Doody* along with another show *The Lone Ranger* taught values and lessons that need to be retaught again today for certain. The ranger stood for honor, dignity protecting the marginalized, and helping people who need your help no matter who they are. The other equally important lesson the ranger and his sidekick Tonto imparted was to always hold the people who did harm to others responsible. Those values are timeless, and they need to be stressed every day to all people in perpetuity.

Sky King was another radio program that quickly evolved into a Sunday afternoon television programming. *Sky King* was based on the true-life personality of Jack Cones known as the "Flying Constable" of Twentynine Palms in San Bernardino County, California. Coincidently, Carol and I have been to Twentynine Palms. From his Flying Crown Ranch, Schuyler "Sky" King flew his Cessna 310 twin-engine airplane high above the blue cloudless California desert, resolving issues of trespass, water rights, larceny, and mistreatment of others, to name a few. Sky's program convinced every young male Sunday afternoon TV watcher that to be brave, successful, and happy, you had to fly a twin-engine Cessna 310 like Sky's that he aptly named Songbird. The make/model of Sky's plane was prominently displayed on the plane during the opening and closing credits way ahead of its time in respect to the modern concept of branding. Sky and his nephew Clipper and niece Penny always seemed to have a solution to the problem in twenty-five minutes no matter how big or small the concern. The television version starred Kirby Grant as Sky King, Gloria Winters as his niece Penny, and Ron Haggerty as Sky's nephew Clipper. Mitch was the local sheriff portrayed by Irwin Mitchell who was always fair, intelligent, and quick on his feet. Mitch was the officer whom Sky relied on to resolve the more difficult issues and close out each case.

Eventually, the western theme–based shows were replaced by cartoons. In the long run that movement went from Saturday or Sunday morning programming to evening programming, where westerns proved even more popular, providing a huge windfall in the more lucrative evening time slots. Those early daytime westerns developed into *Bonanza, The High Chaparral, Rawhide,* and others of the same nature. Evening broadcasts tended to draw more viewers, more advertising, and more money due to a larger home family-oriented audience rather than children only. The change proved hugely beneficial. A bigger market made for bigger money.

A similar situation evolved from the 1950s Saturday programming of the science fiction genre. The early science fiction, mostly of the outer space format, such as *Space Patrol,* captured a huge audience of children on Saturday morning. Eventually, science fiction lost its place on weekend mornings to cartoons also. That time slot move also generated a big return. Much like the western theme–based shows, those early science fiction–theme shows soon developed into strong evening programming. *Lost in Space, The Time Tunnel,* and *Voyage to the Bottom of the Sea* found big audiences. Although that wave of programming was mostly space-oriented, it still was a niche market in evening family-based programming as opposed to the weekend morning kids programming.

Two situations that at face value looked like an error eventually developed into a long-term, wider, more profitable circumstance. I doubt anybody then scheduling programming at any of the TV networks saw it coming at the time, but it certainly did come and certainly did prove much more beneficial. Television, at that point, had indeed taken control of America.

The Mickey Mouse Club was another prominent television program on weekends and after school during the week. One of the stars of the club, of many, who went on to greater fame was a local woman from East Utica by the name of Annette Funicello. Annette went on to star with Frankie Avalon in the classic beach movie of the 1960s *Beach Blanket Bingo* and numerous other young adult–oriented movies. Annette continually starred in movies such as *Babes in Toyland, Back to the Beach,* and *How to Stuff a Wild Bikini.* She made famous an entire genre of youth-aligned movies, whose format is still popular today.

Felix the Cat and *Top Cat* were big hits and literally on every channel. All of these and more were a huge draw for every child in America who was lucky enough to have a television. My father used to say that my grandmother Mary had the first television on Orchard Street, and practically everyone in the neighborhood was at one time or another invited over to watch this magic contraption called television. On Saturday morning, I would sit on my living room floor watching TV, playing with my toys, eating dry Cheerios from a bowl while looking out the back window of my apartment at the Mohawk River and the Barge Canal whether they were frozen or not. I can still hear train whistles on the other side of the Mohawk River in Schuyler. Very distant-sounding train whistles yet audible in my apartment. I could hear the "boom" of a train disconnecting the engine in Schuyler and then hooking up again to pull only a few cars over the connecting spur to drop off their loads of lumber for milling into handles of shovels and rakes at the Union Fork and Hoe, then proceeding to the west end of the street to pick up or drop off grain at Corrado's Feed Mill. Dynamic sights, sounds, and smells that I don't think have ever been replicated for me in my sixty-eight years of existence here on earth.

The before-school weekday morning programming likely did more harm than good, at least in my case, in that once I got all snuggled up in my apartment living room, I didn't want to leave to go to school, church, or wherever. The only thing that pushed me out the door was the sound of my friends on Orchard Street playing outside. On TV in the morning, it was Gumby and Pokey, the first claymation cartoon to hit the airwaves in America. *Captain Kangaroo* starring Bob Keeshan ran for twenty-nine seasons and did 6,090 episodes. Captain Kangaroo did songs, skits, games, and vaudeville along with his costar Mr. Green Jeans. The original theme song was "Puffin' Billy" but in 1974 was changed to "Good Morning, Captain" for an unknown reason. Through the years the program was awarded The Daytime Emmy Award for children's programming numerous times, the Peabody Award twice, and Bob "Captain Kangaroo" Keeshan was awarded the Daytime Emmy for Outstanding Performer in Children's Programming at least once. *Romper Room* was a huge franchise that ran for almost forty years, originally was produced by Bert Claster with his wife Miss Nancy as the presenter. Miss Nancy had the Magic Mirror with her famous rhyme, "Romper, bomper, stomper, boo. Tell me, tell me, tell me, do," which she sang as she looked through Magic Mirror to see "Tommy and Frank and Scott too." I was amazed with that Magic Mirror. I was surely convinced for many years that Miss Nancy was able to see out from that screen at children all over America. I would bet a lot of money that I wasn't the only child in the United States who felt that way. The ultimate children's classic, at least in my opinion, was *Popeye the Sailor*. Popeye was created By Elzie Crisler Segar. Popeye first appeared as a character in the daily King Features comic strip "Thimble Theatre" in January of 1929 and eventually morphed into his own character in the comics, then later cartoons, and eventually into movies.

Kukla, Fran and Ollie, first airing in 1947 in black and white, employed gentle satire to teach valuable lessons such as self-respect, fairness, and kindness to all by using puppets interacting with the live characters of Burr Tillstrom and Fran Allison. The program was developed by Tillstrom and won numerous programming awards for outstanding children's television in 1950, 1954, and again in 1971. It was a black-and-white series full of Lewis Carroll type of programming and puppets reacting to various types of daily experiences. Although short-lived, only from 1947 to 1957, compared to other children's programming of the era, it was a huge success with massive viewership. Many television historians consider it a precursor to *Sesame Street*. Local afternoon weekday programming was filled with a variety of children's shows also. The local NBC affiliate WKTV ran *Bozo the Clown* starring Ed Whittaker as Bozo. I once appeared on the show with my Cub Scout troop and our den mother, Mrs. Betti, a deceased friend of mine Tom's mother. Bozo did simple tricks and played simple games with the children in the studio and closed by giving everyone in attendance a prize. It was wonderful. I think that was the only time, at about eight years old, I was in WKTV's studio until about two months ago when I did a noontime newscast interview concerning my first book *Ruthie Deeply*.

Where has the time gone?

Those being the days before cable television, we watched TV with the signals picked up by an antenna on our roof. We were able to pick up a CBS affiliate in Schenectady, New York, licensed as WRGB, which was the property of General Electric broadcasting and is still in business today. Up until 2012 we continued to watch WRGB at our camp at Pine Lake by an over-the-air antenna. When I was a child, WRGB broadcast a friendly Count Dracula character who also did tricks, played games with local children, and had cartoons. A very similar program to our local *Bozo the Clown*. We all tried to watch both every day, although I must say the Count Dracula character did frighten me a little.

Kids Say the Darndest Things with Art Linkletter was also an afternoon staple and another program I literally ran home to watch. I YouTube-searched it the other night to refresh my memory. First thing I noticed was Art being rude to one of the kids on the show when the boy, of likely seven, waved to someone in the audience. A child spots perhaps his dad in the audience and waves. What would anyone be expecting him to do? Possibly, no waving from the stage was a policy of the show to keep the content moving in a limited amount of airtime so that programming did not get bogged down in morass of waving. Yet there had to be some "give and take," and I would think programming that dealt with children would have a keen awareness of such an issue. When I watched the program as a child, the backdrop proved interesting to me. It was a tag board that had what looked like handmade drawings of roosters, chickens, kids, and so on. It looked strange to me then, and watching again the other night, it still looked strange. I am not certain of the material the board was constructed from or if they were indeed handmade drawings, but the backdrop was unique. Now that I think of it, some sixty years later, the drawings looked like native cave drawings from five thousand years ago. Those drawings may have been placed on that board to convey primitive ideas. That was what struck me then and now as strange. As did Art Linkletter's rudeness to a child.

The reruns of the 1950s the *Adventures of Superman* starring George Reeves as Superman and Noel Neill as Lois Lane were a definite afternoon hit. In about late spring of 1977, prior to the release of the first modern *Superman* movie in 1978, starring Christopher Reeve and Marlon Brando, the original TV Lois Lane was touring the country to promote the movie in which she had a small cameo appearance. Her scene depicts a woman and her small son riding in a railroad car with the old-fashioned seats facing each other. The boy is looking out of the window at a rural scene of barbed wire fence and fields with a dirt road running along the barbed wire. As he gazes out of the window, he sees a trail of dust and a young man running so fast he is passing the train. When the child alerts his mother, she looks out the window and dismisses the incident as nothing. The mother does a quick double take when she realizes what is happening and is astonished at the scene she is watching unfold. That woman was Noel Neill, the original Lois Lane on TV in the *Adventures of Superman*. Lois made a stop at Oswego State University where I went to college, as did my brother-in-law Bob Pacific, along with father-and mother-in-law Nick and Therese Ciufo and thousands of other New Yorkers since the college's founding by Edward Austin Sheldon as Oswego Normal School in 1861. To promote the upcoming movie release, Noel was hired to visit various venues across the country. She wore the Lois Lane–style dress from the TV show with the white collar and six big white buttons arrayed side by side in twos, her hair in a bob covered by the little pill box hat to generate effect. Lois filled in the audience about filming the TV show, her cameo in the movie, and finally opening the discussion for questions. Naturally, the college-age audience had many questions. After the questions progressed for a while, I raised my hand to ask one.

Surely, Lois/Noel noticed and called on me.

She said, "Next question. Sir."

In true potential King of Orchard Street form, I stood up and posed my question. "Can I kiss you, Lois?" I asked.

She was a little taken off guard but said, "Sure."

I went up on the stage and planted a big kiss on Lois/Noel's cheek. She got a huge kick out of it. So did I. The audience got the biggest kick of all.

I waved to the audience, walked back to my seat, and laughed and giggled about the encounter for the rest of the night, which now recalls another situation that might help my odds of being the King of Orchard Street.

Many years later, in 2005 my wife, children, and I went to Disney World in Orlando, Florida. We stayed at the Polynesian Hotel and did all the typical tourist activities: Magic Kingdom, EPCOT, Universal Studios, and the like. One must do an activity being breakfast with Cinderella at the Disney Castle with my approximately seven-year-old daughter Alaina. I guaranteed to my children that once we got there, I would kiss Cinderella. When we finally get seated and the breakfast was being served, Cinderella eventually made her way over to our table in true Disney style for small talk and pictures.

At long last the opportunity I was waiting for had just fallen in my lap. The discussion ensued in much the same fashion as with Lois/Neil.

I queried, "Cinderella, can I kiss you?"

By then my children and my wife were on about their fifth shade of red.

Cinderella replied, "Of course."

History repeating itself? Out of my chair I went again and planted a big smooch on Cinderella's cheek.

Lois/Noel's was a kiss. Cinderella's was a *smooch*. I had to. It was likely to be my second and probably last chance in a lifetime to kiss a star. That concept has proven out so far. Yet who knows what will happen tomorrow?

Thank God, I can still kiss my wife and kids. I want that opportunity to last a long time.

In the end the King of Orchard must have chutzpah for his entire life. It cannot fade or wither, because if it were to, that could cost the holder of the title, the title itself. Certainly, lifelong chutzpah is one of the main skills required to obtain and keep such an extreme honor as the title of the King of Orchard Street.

THE KING OF ORCHARD STREET

Saturday afternoon reruns of old movies were a big TV draw, especially in the cold winter months after being out in the snow all morning. Slippila and Sachala or Slip and Sach along with their friends starred in numerous movies known at various times by different names such as *The Dead End Kids, Bowery Boys,* or *Little Tough Guys*. The movie franchise started as a Broadway play entitled *Dead End* written by Sidney Kingsley in 1935. The play quickly moved to Hollywood in 1937 and was put into production making movies. The original play opened at the Belasco Theatre in New York only and ran for over two years with almost seven hundred performances. Only recently did I realize how many movies were made by this talented group of young actors with such big stars as James Cagney, Humphrey Bogart, Ronald Reagan, and Pat O'Brien. Huntz Hall, Billy Halop, Leo Gorcy, and others in their roles as the Bowery Kids had long acting careers and still can be found creating mayhem on the screen right up to today in reruns and on YouTube.

The school lunchtime favorite was *Jeopardy* starring Art Fleming. Unlike the modern set, where the answers are on a television screen, the *Jeopardy* of my youth had the answers on cardboard placards covered by another cardboard placard. When the contestant picked a category and an amount, the cover placard would slide up to reveal the answer to which the contestant had to provide the question. The placards were arranged like the modern version, and the format of the game was the same as today but clearly much more low tech.

At night during the week, we all watched *Batman, The Green Hornet,* and *The Monkees*. The Monkees were a television phenomenon in itself. The band was formed to conceptualize around a proposed TV series. The series then launched a forty-year career for the band with the television program ending after only a two-year run. The original theme song, "Hey, Hey We're the Monkees" was written by Bobby Boyce and Tommy Hart of the one-hit wonder "I Wonder What She's Doing Tonight." The Monkees went on to a string of top ten hits such as "Last Train to Clarksville," "Pleasant Valley Sunday," and "Valeri." The remaining Monkees are still popular today in oldies concerts across the United States. Certainly an amazing run stemming from such a simple concept.

As time progressed, the original bodyguard for the Green Hornet on the program *The Green Hornet* was Bruce Lee, the future international star of the '70s and '80s kung fu movies. Bruce was a tragedy in that he portrayed this clean-cut, superfit, athletic kung fu master, and in reality he had a serious drug problem and ultimately died of an overdose. Bruce also had a son named Brandon who was killed on a movie set when a live handgun that he had put up to his head jokingly went off and killed him. Recently, a camera person in a western called *Rust*, currently being filmed in New Mexico, was killed when tragedy struck again. A live handgun being used on the set apparently went off, shooting and killing one of the camera people. Maybe a clue to the movie industry that perhaps live handguns should not be used in movies anymore? A reasonable option to pursue?

Always the next day in school, a main topic was what we watched on TV the night before. The boys in our class often discussed the commercials we saw for new toys from Hasbro or Mattel, while the girls mostly discussed whether Davy Jones was the cutest Monkee or Paul McCartney was the cutest Beatle. Different topics for different people but all relevant for all of us.

There was no cable television yet, but on Sunday, WKTV would usually broadcast the Buffalo Bills/AFL game at 1:00 p.m., and WTVH in Syracuse would broadcast the Giants/NFL game at 4:00 p.m. The American Football League and the National Football League had not merged into one National Football League with two conferences, the American Football Conference and the National Football Conference. They were two independent leagues with different sets of teams playing each other only. There was no Super Bowl in those early days, only an AFL championship and an NFL championship. On June 8, 1966, the two leagues merged into the National Football League comprised of the two conferences, the AFC and the NFC. On January 15, 1967, the Super Bowl was born. The first Super Bowl was played between the Green Bay Packers coached by Vince Lombardi and the Kansas City Chiefs coached by Hank Stram with the game being won by Green Bay 35 to 10.

After football, the rest of the night was all about family programming. A huge audience viewership belonged to Mutual of Omaha's

Wild Kingdom starring the American zoologist Marlin Perkins and his colleague Jim Fowler. As Johnny Carson of *The Tonight Show* fame so frequently and comically pointed out, there was Marlin sitting in his office looking at photographs of alligators while Jim was down the river wrestling with an alligator. Johnny pointed it out again and again. Everyone laughed every time Johnny joked, and it was the truth. With those five words, "Mutual of Omaha's Wild Kingdom" that show instantly became the most popular nature program in America and probably one of the first. The show was very educational to the extent that it explored the relationships between animals and other animals, animals and their environment, and, to some small degree, animals and humans. It was very educational and very entertaining.

The Ed Sullivan Show brought the Beatles and the Rolling Stones to America along with native-born American entertainers like Elvis Presley plus hundreds of later famous comedians and singers. Of course, *Bonanza* and *Dennis the Menace* were Sunday night staples too. A blue haze filled every living room in America. Television was the medium that everyone wanted to see and everyone paid the most attention to.

With the advent of cable television, suddenly, local channels were not only available but also programming from New York City on a network called Metromedia, which consisted of WPIX, WNEW, and WOR. All these stations still exist and are available on many cable TV networks. The new programming from these networks exploded all over upstate New York. You could watch the Yankees on WPIX and the Mets on WOR. *The Joe Franklin Show* was broadcast nightly from New York City for probably fifty years beginning at 1:00 a.m. and always maintained a large late-night television viewership. Many of Joe's guests were Broadway stars who had just gotten off work from the evening performance and walked over to the WOR studio to appear on Joe's show. Joe's show never went national but was a huge hit in the metropolitan area for many years. WNEW broadcast a ten o'clock news, which was unheard of in upstate New York. The news began with an announcer intoning, "It's 10:00 p.m. Do you know where your children are?" Unprecedented in this rural area.

Local news programming was at 6:00 p.m. and 11:00 p.m. National news was at 6:30 p.m., which defined the news day. Thus, years later CNN was obviously a shock. News channels now broadcast twenty-four hours a day from Hong Kong, Australia, China, and Europe. Nonstop news is now the norm, and I am not sure that is necessarily good.

The funny part of the entire situation, at least locally, was that broadcasting was from 6:00 a.m. until 1:00 a.m. The local NBC affiliate broadcast *The Tonight Show* with Johnny Carson, which was live at that time from 11:30 p.m. to 1:00 a.m. The station then went off the air with a playing of "The Star-Spangled Banner," an announcement that "this concludes the broadcasting day," and then the infamous test pattern from approximately 1:00 a.m. to 6:00 a.m. Sometimes now I will turn on the television at about 3:00 a.m. to check out the news on Bloomberg, BBC, or International CNBC. All over the world the various stock markets are open, cities are busy, and people are working. I'm still amazed by that compared to what I saw when I was seven or eight years old, which I thought that was quite amazing enough back then. Times have changed, and again I'm not sure if it's for the better. Television may not have been as powerful then, but it may have been, in the long run, better. Only time will tell.

Although television was a new and fascinating phenomenon to us, we found after a while it got tedious. Being very young, the natural inclination was to spend as much time outside as possible. We found many ways in any season to keep ourselves outside and busy. The North Side School, which my mother, her brothers, and sisters attended as children, was on the south side of Orchard Street. Across Railroad Street, on the north side of Orchard Street, were a parking lot that also served as a playground/basketball court and a large field on the east end of the property for baseball, kickball, or just running around. In the winter the Village of Frankfort DPW would remove the snow from the playground/basketball court and then, with snow, create a perimeter of snowbanks, leaving an uncovered space about forty feet by fifty feet. Being that the snowbanks were high enough to hold water inside, the Frankfort Fire Department would flood the cleared area with water and create an outdoor ice-skating rink. In those days there was nowhere for children to ice-skate except on a rink built like the one on Orchard Street, frozen ponds, or lakes. The only local indoor ice-skating rink was at the Utica Memorial Auditorium, when ice was down, and that was only used minimally for shows such as the Ice Capades. There were no indoor skating rinks like the Town of Whitestown Recreation Center or the New Hartford Recreation Center that could be used by the public or local school's hockey teams. The Village of Frankfort also constructed a small building on the side of the rink that was open in the front with some benches installed inside to sit on to change from boots to ice skates. When the winter was over, the building was removed and stored at the DPW's garage until the next winter. It was a very popular winter activity for children and adults to meet at the ice rink and skate for an hour or two. When it snowed again, an informal group of children would voluntarily show up with shovels to push the snow off the rink, usually while on ice skates, back to the already existing snowbanks to expose the ice that had previously been put down. If the children in the village didn't do it, at some point the Village DPW would. After the fresh snow was cleared off the already existing ice surface, the fire department would then return and flood the rink with water again, thus creating a fresh coat of smooth ice. When it snowed again, the process would be repeated so that one way or another that rink was always available to the residents in the Village of Frankfort. A perfect example of how simple cooperation can create an enjoyable environment free and open to the public, a concept that somehow we have lost sight of.

In the winter the village would also close up the Hilltop Park, the real name being Lehman Park, and block off the road that led from the park down past the swimming pool to Litchfield Street. As soon as that road was closed and some fresh snow came down, the snow-covered road became a perfect place to ride a sled. Kids would gather at the top of the hill with toboggans, sleds, flying saucers, lunch trays stolen from school, and at times just a piece of cardboard. After a little running start, we would jump on our sleds and ride down the hill to the bottom, hoping that we stopped by the time we got to Litchfield Street where the traffic was zooming by. A much more dangerous environment than skating at the ice rink on Orchard Street but free and fun too. After a few days of kids sliding up and down the hill, if no more snow fell, the paths we made with our sleds would harden up and become very fast. It was an accident waiting to happen for days on end, but as luck would have it, I never remember anyone getting seriously hurt there.

    The summer also provided another enjoyable environment free and open to the public. The Frankfort swimming pool and playground was a huge public area built by the Works Projects Administration during the Great Depression. The main pool ran from north to south with the south end being about forty feet wide and about one foot deep for the kiddie pool area. That end provided the intake for fresh water to move in. The pool then ran north for about seventy feet to the other end, being about fifteen feet wide and the deeper end of the pool to a depth of about ten feet. On the north end was a diving board and the outtake for the water to flow out. The water was pumped directly into the south end from Moyer Creek about twenty feet below the elevation of the pool and flowed out back into Moyer Creek on the north end of the pool. On the south end was also a lifeguard house and a chlorine well to hopefully keep the water safe to swim in since it was coming directly out of a creek. Also, on the south end was a red-and-white trimmed lifeguard house with bathrooms and changing rooms on either side. Behind the guardhouse were swings, teeter-totters, and another about thirty-foot-by-thirty-foot wading pool about two feet deep with water bubbling directly out of the ground from the many freshwater springs in the area. In the center of the wading pool was a metal grate that you could stand on and feel the force of the water coming out of the ground pushing the bottom of your feet. On the back side of the kiddie pool was an outflow so that the height of the pool never rose to above one to two feet. With water flowing from a natural underground spring or being pumped directly out of the creek, it was always cold and not uncommon for fish to be sucked right in with the fresh water. Most times if any fish did get sucked into the pool, they were killed by the chlorine and floated to the top for the lifeguard to skim out of the pool. At times some fish did survive and swam happily in the pool right along with us.

The pool usually opened up to the public around July 1. Prior to the opening on warm days, we would swim in Moyer Creek. After the pool closed around Labor Day, there would still be warm days, and we would swim again in Moyer Creek usually until the end of September. Yet while the pool was open, that was the place for swimming. When I was a college student, I worked as a lifeguard at the Frankfort Pool for two summers. I always felt that it was the best job I ever had in my life. I asked the pool director if he would station me in the kiddie end of the pool where the water was only one to three feet deep so that if any child were to have a problem in the water, I could just jump in and grab the child out without the risk of a rescue in deep water. With the water being so low, there was really no swimming involved, only pulling the child out to the side of the pool. It was the perfect job. I was paid $1.85 an hour, had little responsibility since the water was so low, and could spend the whole day working on my suntan and flirting with the women. If I could have done that job for the rest of my life and earned $250,000 a year, I would be a lifeguard at the Frankfort Pool right up to today. It's the consummate way to make money and have fun.

The pool schedule was to be closed on Monday, a day we would swim in the creek, if need be, and open Tuesday through Sunday from 9:00 a.m. until 11:00 a.m. for swimming lessons, closed for lunch from 11:00 a.m. to noon, then reopen for public swimming from noon to 5:00 p.m., closed again from 5:00 p.m. to 6:00 p.m. for dinner, and then open from 6:00 p.m. to 8:00 p.m. for public swimming. When the pool opened in July, my friends and I developed a plan to get in the pool at 9:00 a.m. rather than wait till noon for public swimming to open. Even though we all knew how to swim, we would sign up for the swimming lessons from 9:00 a.m. to 11:00 a.m. so that we could get in the pool earlier. A group of about seven or eight of us would show up for the lessons and hurriedly get in the pool feigning that we didn't know how to swim. None of us were the best swimmers in the world, but we had the basic idea and could swim well enough to protect ourselves. The lifeguards who had worked there the previous summers already knew it was a swindle but went along with it anyway. The lifeguards who had never worked at the pool before took a little while to figure out what we were doing but then went along with it also. I think the lifeguards like Donna Rae DeLuke and Maryann Walawender all knew what we were doing but went along with it because, if for no other reason, we made them look busy, and they were able to keep what was an enjoyable summer job.

A symbiotic relationship if there ever was one.

A railroad spur ran in my grandmother's backyard probably fifteen to twenty feet north of her house. My mother and father must have told me a thousand times not to go on the other side of those train tracks because on the other side, down a hill, was the Mohawk River. Obviously, a dangerous situation for a five-year-old. Did I listen? Not for one second. As soon as my parents or my aunt Flora went in the house, I was on the other side of those train tracks. At one point, I don't remember exactly how it happened, I was playing in my backyard when I fell and hit my head pretty hard in those steel tracks. I don't remember if my mother or my aunt saw it happen, but I had a pretty good-sized lump on my head. I remember we iced it, and there may have even been a small gash. My mother wrapped a bandage around it to keep it from bleeding. I thought that bandage was the coolest thing. I looked like the toughest guy on Orchard Street. It made me feel very macho, made me feel tough and dignified. I wanted to keep it on. My father told me once the swelling went down and healed, I could take it off. I didn't want it off. I liked it there. I was tough. I was macho. It made me feel like the King of Orchard Street. Little did I know, someday I just might be the king. In any case, right there, right then, at least in my opinion, I was the King of Orchard Street.

Only time and you, the reader, will prove me right or wrong.

An ironic situation I used to hear my mother repeat time and time again concerned all the families that lived on Orchard Street, big and small, through her youth and even into mine. There was one family that had probably fourteen children. My mother's family was big enough with seven, but this particular one was huge. My grandmother Mary Iocovozzi went out of her way every day to make sure her kids were all fed, their hair was combed, in the winter they had boots, gloves, and jackets on when they to North Side School, were out playing, visiting, or whatever they were doing. The other much larger family was not as fortunate as my mother's. With all those kids, obviously, it was difficult to dress and feed them all properly. They would be out in the rain and the cold or the wind with no jacket, snow boots, gloves, or hats on. Pretty much nothing. Rarely was one of them ever sick with a cold, fever, or the flu. They were rarely at the doctor's office; all of them were generally in good health. My mother used to continue that no matter how hard my grandmother tried to keep her kids healthy, they were always sick. One would catch a cold, and it would spread to everyone. My grandmother would nurse everyone back to health then, and someone would catch the flu, and it would spread to everyone again. It was this constant cycle of my mother, her brothers, and sisters all constantly infecting each other with something. Nothing that was ever deadly but certainly made them all sick. Meanwhile, the other kids never had anyone sick. My grandmother Mary just couldn't understand it. No matter how hard she tried, her kids caught everything, and the other kids caught nothing. I think every infection doctor in the world asks the same question to this day, especially in the age of COVID. How does one person catch COVID, become very sick, and at times die, and another person who may not be vaccinated never catches it? If they do, it's minimal with some discomfort, then they're well and off on their way. How does that happen? Mary Iocovozzi wondered about that question in 1935 as, I bet, did her sister, my aunt Josie DiCamillo, just one hundred feet east of my grandmother living on the corner of Orchard and Litchfield Streets. Just as I would venture, Dr. Anthony Fauci asks that same question in 2021. Is there an answer? I don't know, nor does anyone else. We all collectively should keep our fingers crossed and hope that someday that simple question can get definitively answered.

Maybe the King of Orchard Street, whoever that ultimately is, has the answer.

A more connected to the King of Orchard Street debate comes to mind.

When I was probably six years old, a woman who lived across the street from my grandmother's house by the name of Josephine Vaccaro was looking out her front door. Josephine lived by herself, and I never remember a husband or any children being in the picture. A bunch of us were playing when Josephine called us all over. There must have been two or three of us, perhaps Santo Falcone, John Kipper, and I. I'm not sure who was there, but there were two or three of us at least. I remember Josephine handed me a paper bag that was heavy. She told me and the others to take it down by the Barge Canal and just throw it in the brush. She handed me the bag, and off we went. As we were walking down the hill to the canal, I opened the bag up to see what was in it because it was heavy. When I looked in the bag, I was amazed in that it was full of silverware—knives, forks, spoons, and so on. I don't know. It may have been just costume silverware, or it may have been the real thing perhaps worth quite a bit of money. I wasn't exactly sure what to do with it. I thought maybe I should bring it home, give it to my mom. Maybe I should just throw it in the brush like Josephine asked me to do, or maybe I could find someone who wanted to buy it. I wasn't sure how to proceed when I was told specifically, to cross the tracks, walk to the canal, and toss the whole bag in the brush. For all I know, it could still be sitting there some fifty-five or sixty years later. I have no idea why Josephine would have wanted to dispose of the dinnerware, but she did. Then I did. I intend to go to a Christmas at the Marina tomorrow night, November 27, 2021—the Marina being near the spot where I dumped Josephine's silverware some sixty years ago for a tree-lighting ceremony. I think I'll take a walk over by where I dumped that bag of silverware in probably 1962—I bet I can pretty much pick out the location—to see if all of it is still sitting there. It may very well be. Maybe Josephine chose to give that bag to me only for disposal because she felt I may have a chance sometime in the distant future to be chosen as the King of Orchard Street.

Donnie likely doesn't feel that way, nor does Johnny Kipper, yet the jury is still out. I urge you, no matter who the final choice is, to make that choice only after deep consideration. It being a long pursued, hard to earn, equally hard to maintain position to be crowned the prestigious King of Orchard Street.

    When I was at Johnny Kipper's house two weeks ago, he brought up the name of the Hotalings, a family that lived on the corner of Orchard Street and Tisdale Avenue. The house has long been demolished, but there is an incident that I recall on that corner vividly as if it happened yesterday. Most likely I was wandering around by Corrado's Mill when Mr. Hotaling, I believe his name was Chuck, came walking around from the back of his house. In his yard he had a chicken coop as many people did in those days including my father when he was growing up in Herkimer. The reason so many people had a coop was so that there were fresh eggs every morning for breakfast, baking, or so many things that eggs can be used for in cooking. My dad always loved eggs until the day he died, and that may have been a result of having a constant supply of fresh eggs. After the hen got older and probably didn't produce eggs any longer, she would be slaughtered, plucked, cleaned, and eaten. When Mr. Hotaling came walking around from behind his house with a chicken, carrying it by the legs upside down, I knew what was coming, especially when I saw he had the chicken in one hand and a hatchet in the other. He put the chicken down on the ground and stretched the poor thing's neck out over the curb while the chicken squirmed. With one quick whack, off came the chicken's head. The longtime euphemism for being busy, "I'm running around like a chicken with his head cut off" is 100 percent true. Once Mr. Hotaling lopped off that chicken's head, it stood up with no head and ran around in about five or six circles, good-sized circles, then just dropped on the ground. It had blood literally squirting out through the top of its neck while running in circles. I was horrified, but at the same time, I couldn't keep myself from watching this insane scenario. When it dropped to the ground, Mr. Hotaling picked it up, cut its feet off, plucked the feathers, and gutted/cleaned it. He left sitting there a big pile of feathers, guts, feet, blood, and of course, a chicken head quietly searching for its chicken body. Mr. Hotaling pushed all the remainder in the storm drain, turned, and went in the house to cook the chicken. For the next six to eight hours, maybe it was psychological, I could smell that chicken cooking in the oven whether it was or not. It's something I will never forget seeing, and even today when I hear the phrase, "Running around like a chicken with its head cut off," I can't help but think of Mr. Hotaling and, of course, that poor chicken.

Similar to the story about Mr. Hotaling, Johnny Kipper told a story about his grandmother and pillowcases that she stored in her bedroom. Johnny's story, along with mine, concerning Mr. Hotaling validate each other. There must have been a lot of chickens running around on Orchard Street both with and without their heads.

Two separate potential King of Orchard Street candidates both telling a similar story concerning chickens, of all the living entities on this Earth that has been swinging its way through the cosmos for billions of years. What are the chances? Cross-referencing at its finest.

As most of the candidates for king have mentioned, we all spent hours running around in Corrado's Feed Mill. In the parking lot, behind the building, on the loading docks, in the Drops of Moyer's Creek, literally all over that property in places we should not have been, first because it was private property and second because it was dangerous.

As all this continues to get pulled together, it seems the developing criteria for all potential King of Orchard Street candidates is to have been in numerous places we should have not been, doing many things we should not have been doing.

I have to wonder if in the end those criteria are indeed the "litmus test" for inauguration as the King of Orchard Street. Only time will tell.

As you walked in Corrado's parking lot, on the left side there were always two or three huge sandpiles and a smaller rock pile. I'm not sure what they were used for, but I think they were mostly used to fill in the parking lot when low spots developed from large grain trucks and even tractor trailers pulling in and out all day long. I think the workers would load the sand and stone onto trucks and drive around the parking lot, filling in those low spots that would occur all the from the weight of the delivery and customer's trucks. We all being from age of four to about thirteen, those sandpiles were like a magnet to us. A huge sandbox as it were. We would play in the sandpiles all day long. We would climb up, and the sand would slip down and bring us with it. Climb back up again, roll down again. Many of us would spend the whole day there climbing up and down those piles, much like you see children today on blow-up waterslides. Sand being as granular as it is and dusty, naturally, by the end of a few hours, the sand was in your hair, in your ears, and stuck to your skin. The sweatier you got, the more dust stuck. By the end of the day, I can still remember looking down at my ankles and seeing them literally brown from the dust stuck to me. I could take my fingernails and scrape the dust off my scalp. The dust would collect under my fingernails indicating how thick it was stuck to my scalp. When I got back to our apartment, my mother would take one look at me and order me in the bathtub immediately. Being like any other kid, naturally, I didn't want to follow directions and would argue with her that I didn't need to take a bath. She would run that water to get it warm to fill up the tub, and in I would go, resisting all the way. I would still resist even when in the tub until I got splashing around, and it became fun. The sandpiles were off the books and now suddenly became a distant memory. My mother would wash my hair, scrub my feet, under my arm, and so on until I was nice and clean. She would constantly warn me that if I didn't get that sand and dirt off of me, I would catch leprosy. I didn't even understand what leprosy was or where it came from, but I knew it must have been something bad if my mother warned me as much as she did about it. Years later when I realized what leprosy was and how it spread, mostly through lack of personal hygiene and wearing dirty clothes, I got the idea.

There is local connection to that horrible illness. In approximately 1840, a child named Marianne Cope immigrated from Germany with her parents and settled in West Utica. Marianne grew up to become a member of the Sisters of Saint Joseph in Syracuse. Marianne was one of the sisters instrumental in establishing Saint Joseph's Hospital in Syracuse and Saint Elizabeth's Hospital in Utica. Marianne and many other sisters worked as the first staff in both locations. Marianne also worked to establish Saint Joseph's College of Nursing, which my daughter Alaina, I am proud to say, is a 2021 graduate of and holds a bachelor of science in nursing. In 1883, now being a superior mother, Marianne answered a desperate plea from the Hawaiian government for religious nursing sisters to relocate to Hawaii to care for thousands of leprosy patients living in there. Marianne and six other sisters arrived in Hawaii on November 8, 1883. In 1884 Mother Marianne opened Malulani Hospital, Maui's first general hospital. At the government's request, she then went to Oahu and was responsible for opening the Kakaako Branch Hospital for leprosy patients. Still healthy and certain her work in Hawaii was not completed in 1885, she established the Kapiolani Home for female children of leprosy patients. Her life ended while at work with leprosy patients in Kalaupapa, a remote settlement on the island of Molokai. Marianne was canonized as a saint in 2012 who, along with Father Damien of Molokai, worked tirelessly to end the spread of leprosy. Father Damien was also made a saint by the Catholic Church in 2009. Blessed Marianne Cope and Father Damien were the face of Jesus to those they served.

Indirectly, Mother Marianne and Father Damien, along with my mother, unknown to me at the time, may have saved this potential King of Orchard Street from the scourge of leprosy as I carried a quarter pound of sand on my body into our apartment probably four days a week.

In another lifesaving situation, Mother Marianne was still helping me.

I was at Saint Elizabeth Hospital yesterday for a cardiac stress test, required every other year as protocol due to a heart attack I suffered a number of years ago, which I'm happy to say turned out to be completely normal.

Corrado's sandpiles and my heart getting me into trouble. Mother Marianne getting me out. Twice.

Another potential for the title of the King of Orchard Street is John Tubia also known as John-John Tubia. Together we made plenty of issues while living on Orchard Street. I still feel pain from the day that pedal chain came off John-John's bike in 1961. We decided, being five and seven years old, to flip the bike over in my grandmother's backyard and put the chain on. While, I held the chain,

John-John turned the pedal to thread the chain back on the sprocket. I had my thumb placed on the bottom of the chain close to the sprocket. When John-John turned the pedal, my thumb moved into the gap between the teeth of the sprocket. My thumb was now stuck in the gap on the sprocket with the chain on top of my thumb. John-John and I were looking at each other, trying to figure out what to do next with my stuck thumb in the sprocket. I don't remember if it was John-John's idea or mine, but the only way out was to turn the sprocket the rest of the way around until my thumb came out on the bottom. There being no other adults around, that is exactly what we did. With my thumb stuck in the sprocket, John-John turned the pedal, and my hand went all the way around from the top of the sprocket to the bottom and then out from the teeth. Pretty good-sized hurt and quite a bit of blood as the sprocket spun around. I remember thinking to myself, *This is going to come out eventually, but in the meantime, there is hell to pay*. Needless to say, my thumbnail got chewed up good. As I look at my thumbnail right now at 11:03 a.m. on December 8, 2021, it is still disfigured as it has been since that day in probably 1960. It never grew back normally like the base of a normal thumbnail. In the left, what is now a corner of the bottom of my right thumb, there has always been a weak spot where the skin peels back, and my thumb looks funny for probably sixty-two years. I don't think that's ever going to change.

At another point John-John somehow, probably as a gift, got a BB gun. One afternoon, which I vividly remember being warm and sticky, John-John pointed the BB gun at me and pulled the trigger. Luckily, he missed my eyes and hit me in the forehead. The BB made a little hole, and blood squirted out. I ran inside to show my mother the injury. Instantly, the clock was turned back to when I hit my head on the train tracks in my backyard. My mother got the bleeding to stop and wrapped a bandage around my head to keep pressure on the bleeding. With that bandage on my head, I was tough again. I was macho again. Yet this time I was even tougher because to stop me from crying, my father put a feather in the back of the bandage, like an Indian, which made even more machismo than the first bandage from hitting my head on the railroad tracks. I really thought I was the King of Orchard Street again. No one was going to mess with me with that bandage and feather on my head, and I mean nobody. Everyone knew that I was rough-and-tumble just from looking at me. When my mom decided it was time for it to come off, I didn't want it to come off. I wanted to be tough. I wanted to be the King of Orchard Street. Maybe I still have a chance.

After those early incidents with John-John, we continue to be friends and still are to this day. At one point another Frankfort resident by the name of Joe Tocco opened a small variety store on Frankfort Street in which he sold cigarettes, soda, ice cream, magazines—the usual type of sundry items. The storefront had a door on the right side and a door on the left side. The door to the right was where Joe had a counter and a cash register to pay for purchases. When entering through the door on the left, the room opened up into a wider grocery store–type arrangement of shelves with products. Along the left side wall, Joe placed a large double magazine rack. On the bottom of the left side rack, stacked behind the mainstream magazines, Joe stocked a series of soft-core pornographic magazines. Those magazines were of the nature of *Playboy*, not pornographic, mostly just female nudity. John-John got the idea that we just had to have one of those magazines. Being only seven or eight at the time, clearly, Joe would never sell us one, but together we hatched a plan to steal one. John-John would be the lookout. When Joe walked to our right behind the counter, a large overhead cigarette rack would obscure his view of the other side of the store near the magazine rack. The crime was on. When John-John signaled that Joe had moved into position behind the counter, I would slide the magazine under my shirt, and the two of us would then nonchalantly walk out of the left side door into the street. I must say the plan worked flawlessly. Perfect execution. We then walked about a block away, constantly looking over our shoulders to see if Joe or anyone was following us, to the park by the Frankfort Free Library and opened up the magazine in about two seconds while sitting in a small clump of trees that separated the backyards of people who lived on First Avenue from the Village of Frankfort Park. Want to get the attention of a seven- and-eight-year-old boys quickly? We had never seen anything like the naked women posed all over these magazine pages. John-John and I couldn't believe it. We had a complete anatomy lesson right there.

After we looked through the magazine probably three or four times, next we had to figure out what to do with it. I didn't have anywhere to keep it, and I didn't want to get caught with it. Neither did John-John. How are we going to dispose of it? Who are we going to give it to? Suddenly, for both of us, the guilt kicked in. What had we done? We had stolen something from a guy we liked and treated us well. We went to school with Joe's daughter Franny. Now we were really confounded. John-John and I considered our next move of which there weren't many options. We bilaterally decided that our only option was to bring the magazine back. It had to go back. How are we going to get it back on the shelf without Joe seeing us, realizing that we have stolen it and are now bringing it back? We opened this Pandora's box. Now how are we going to get it closed? The only viable option we had was to bring the magazine back. We decided to use the same plan that had worked so well when we had stolen it, only in reverse. I would look at the magazines, John-John would watch for Joe to walk behind that cigarette rack again, John-John would give me the sign, and I would put the magazine back. If we got it out of there, we sure should be able to get it back in. If Joe saw us, we could tell him we were only looking at it. Joe would not like it and would kick us out of the store, but that would be it. Our minds were made up. Back to the store we headed. We walked in the door the same way we had done an hour earlier. John-John milled around, waiting for Joe to walk behind the cigarette rack. As soon as Joe moved into position, John-John gave me the look again, and I slipped the magazine back on the rack behind the mainstream magazines. The look of relief on both of our faces told the story. The fact that we had gotten the magazine out of the store, looked at it, and put it back on the shelf without getting caught was amazing. We both said goodbye to Joe and walked out the door together as if the weight of the world had been lifted off our shoulders. I decided I would never steal anything again; it just wasn't worth it. I had learned my lesson, I thought, but in the end I really didn't.

I did, now at least, learn what was possible when two potential Kings of Orchard Street put their brains together to construct "the perfect crime," then do the "perfect crime" in reverse, which in the end wasn't a crime at all. Or at best a minor one at least for a seven- and an eight-year-old.

Still, it does bring to mind another inappropriate but true story concerning at least another attempted stealing incident. When I was much younger, my father worked as the Meat Department manager at a grocery store in Herkimer, New York, named John's Market. My Dad had started working there in 1932 at the age of seven before and after school. My father's workweek was from Tuesday through Saturday being that the busiest days in a grocery business are usually Thursday, Friday, and early on Saturday. Grocery stores in those days, especially the independent ones, were nothing like modern ones. Most of the independent grocery stores were probably 40 percent of the size of a modern grocery store. They usually opened somewhere between eight and nine in the morning and were closed by eight in the evening. Unlike the huge grocery store chains such as Kroger, Price Chopper, Walmart, and so on that are open, most of them, until midnight from seven in the morning. Many of them open twenty-four hours a day.

My mother, being a self-employed beautician for over fifty years, pretty much set her own hours. She generally worked perhaps a little bit on Tuesday morning, usually Wednesday, Thursday, and Friday, and until noon on Saturday. She had a pretty good-sized customer base but was able to schedule them around the way she wanted and the customer agreed to. In those days, like most families, we had only one car, and many families had no car. On Tuesday morning my mother would bring my father to work at the grocery store so she could drive his car home and go shopping. She headed right for downtown Utica, first, to the Boston Store, which was one of the biggest retailers in the area. Then she would go to other department stores like Stars in Yorkville or State Street Mill in West Utica. My mom was a real bargain hunter, and she knew all the places to find the bargains. In any case, when she got done shopping, she would come home, and sometime around 5:00 p.m., she and I would drive to the grocery store in Herkimer to pick my father up after work. She would usually send me into the store to tell my father that we were outside waiting. I would talk to my father, the other employees, and customers, then walk back to the car to wait for him.

On one trip, I decided, while walking through the candy aisle, that I would help myself to a few miniature Tootsie Rolls. I picked up three or four miniatures, put them in my jacket pocket, walked over to the car, and got in. I would often sit in the front seat with my father and my mother would sit in the back. After we got a halfway back to Frankfort, I reached in my pocket and pulled out the Tootsie Rolls. Before I could even open one up, my dad looked over and wanted to know where I got them. I informed him that I got them in John's Market. His automatic next question was, "Did you pay for them?" I told him I didn't, but I thought it would be okay seeing that he worked there, and they were only a penny each. I didn't see a real problem with it. In a split second, my father said, "Oh no, you stole those from the store. You didn't pay for them. You have to bring them back and apologize to Johnny, and you have to pay Johnny if you want to keep the candy." I didn't have any money, so I agreed to bring them back to the store, apologize, put them back on the shelf, and that would be the end of it. My dad turned the car around and back to the grocery store we went. I told Johnny Cassella, the owner of the store, what I had done, told him that I was sorry and that I wouldn't do it again. I didn't have money to pay for them, so I had to put them back in the bin. I didn't open them. All I did was put them in my pocket and put them right back on the shelf. My dad then sweetened the offer and told me if I wanted the Tootsie Rolls, he would pay for them, and then I could pay him back. I think he felt sorry for me more than anything else. I had to weigh my options quickly. I had to make an executive decision immediately. Pretty tough situation for a six-year-old to be in. As I ran it through my mind, I realized that we had candy back in the apartment, and I had no money to pay Johnny for the Tootsie Rolls. I told my father I think my best bet was just to put them back on the shelf, which I did, and apologize to Johnny again. Johnny accepted my apologies and told me to never do anything like that again anywhere. What a lesson. Considering how it all played out well over sixty years ago, I think I made a pretty good decision. Granted, I should have never taken the candy without paying, yet be that as it may, I knew I didn't have any money, and I knew I had candy back in the apartment. What was the sense of committing myself to paying my father back for the candy when I could go home and have access to plenty of candy. As with everything else, you must weigh your options fully. The choice that I made was my best option. A very young boy making a very quick, very good decision that ultimately worked out to his advantage. I learned my lesson about stealing. I didn't have to pay for the candy, and when I went home, I had candy in our apartment. Not a bad deal at all. A veritable win-win. Looking back, I am not proud of stealing; still, the whole scenario ultimately played out to my advantage on numerous levels.

While on the topic of executive decisions, my godfather Joseph P. Cristiano of Pleasanton, California, automatically comes to mind. Joe started out as a stock boy at the local Sherwin-Williams paint store in Whitesboro and moved through the ranks of Sherwin-Williams to become a division president. After a long successful career at Sherwin-Williams, Joe moved on to be president and CEO of Kelly Moore Paint in San Francisco, California. He then retired from Kelly Moore and started an exciting after-retirement journey. Joe is currently the founder and CEO of the Northern California Entrepreneur Group, where he mentors entrepreneurs on a pro bono basis. Joe also has founded Napa Community Bank along with the Bank of San Francisco. At the Bank of San Francisco, he has served as the chairman of the board for over eighteen years. Plainly, Joe has been a successful businessman his entire life. As much as he is a successful businessman, what's even more important to me is, he has always been a very big part of my life and continues to be right up to this day. Had Joe ever lived on Orchard Street, he would certainly be a daunting contender for the title of the King of Orchard Street. Each of the contenders for the title are very fortunate that Joe never lived on Orchard Street, or the premise of this book might have had a predetermined outcome.

My contact with Joe is from birth when he dated his high school girlfriend, my dear cousin Verna Favat, who he eventually married. Sadly, Verna died in 1983 at the age of forty-three, yet Joe has always remained a part of all of our lives. As a matter of fact, in February 2022, Carol and I are vacationing in San Francisco, then to Pleasanton, California, to visit Joe and his wife Janet along with their six children and nine grandchildren all of whom are all still a big part of our lives. After Pleasanton, Carol and I will proceed to Palm Springs, then Las Vegas after that. Growing up on Orchard Street, I was in contact with Joe almost every day. He was always ahead of his time in that he had the nicest car—I believe it was a baby blue Cadillac convertible—he wore nice clothes, he was always very glib, and people automatically took a liking to him. He is one of the lucky guys on earth that you just have to like. Wherever Joe went, I wanted to go too. Many times Joe thought he was going to get away with not taking me along when he and Verna went places, but I was having none of it. Joe still feels that my aunt Flora, Verna's mother, always sent me along to keep the two of them on their toes, so to speak because they had a four- or five-year-old with them. I never realized it then and still did not until Joe mentioned it to me a few years ago. I guess my role was really to chaperone, but I didn't know it. I think the point is made.

Joe would often ask me on any given night in the fall if I wanted to go to the cider mill in Ilion to buy a gallon of apple cider. Of course, I jumped at the opportunity. There were two ways to get to the mill. You could travel south on Barringer Road, left on Old Forge Road to Otsego Street, then left on Spinnerville Gulf Road, as Parker's Cider Mill was about a mile up Spinnerville Gulf Road on the right side. The other option was to stay on Route 5S East until Otsego Street/Route 51, turn right to Otsego Street, then left on Spinnerville Gulf Road to Parker's. Joe and I would get in the car, and we'd start driving to whatever route he wanted to take, usually the one on Barringer Road to Old Forge Road. He was notorious for telling me when we got to Old Forge Road that he was lost and wanted me to tell him which way we had to go. Being all of five or six years old, I had no idea, so I would guess. My guess would be a left on Old Forge Road, which was correct, then down the hill to a right on Otsego Street/Route 51, then a short distance over to Spinnerville Gulf Road to take a left. We were both happy with my choice because it proved to be correct. Joe knew all along exactly where to go but got a big kick out of sitting there, watching me wonder and waiting to hear what I was going to say. Having made the correct choices when we eventually arrived at Parkers's Mill, I was thrilled to pull into the parking lot. When I see him now, we still talk about that hysterical true story.

Joe's father, Joe Cristiano Sr., ran a small restaurant named Dibbles Inn in Middleville, New York. On Friday night Joe would often pick up Verna, and they would go to his dad's restaurant for a fish fry. I waited for him to ask me if I wanted to go. As soon as he did, I jumped into that car in a flash. We would drive on Route 5 East to Route 28 North in Herkimer and drive out of Herkimer to Middleville. About a mile outside of the Village of Middleville, the New York State DOT had built a three-foot retainer wall to hold back a hill that was notorious for mudslides, which would cover the road, putting a quick stop to the flow of traffic. The wall still stands today. When I saw that retaining wall, I knew we were close to Dibbles Inn, but I also thought we were one thousand miles from home. I don't know if we'd ever find our way back, especially considering the trips to Parker's Cider Mill when Joe floated the infamous "being lost" scheme. When my kids were young and we would go to our camp at Pine Lake, at times we would drive the same route through Middleville to Pine Lake. I must have told my children and wife one hundred times the story about the retainer wall with Joe Cristiano and my impression of being so far from home. Even now when my wife and I drive by the wall, I tell her the same story literally every time to which she replies, "I know, I know." Her tone of voice and the look on her face tell me she certainly does know. As for me, I will never forget Joe Cristiano, Verna, myself, and the retainer-wall story from the 1960s. Nor will I let anyone else.

A&W Root Beer Drive-In was located in East Utica. Joe, Verna, and I would often go to A&W on a weeknight in his convertible Cadillac for dinner. We would drive in the lot with that big Cadillac and wait for the carhop. The carhop was usually a young woman. She would snap a tray onto the driver's-side door window. The window had to be left up just a little to hold the tray. The woman would take our order, then proceed, I believe while on roller skates, back to the building to place our order. After about five or ten minutes, the carhop would come back to place the burgers, fries, and root beers on the tray attached to the car. The root beer was served in big chilled mugs and had a rich, creamy flavor that overloaded my taste buds instantly. There the three of us would sit with the top down in his convertible and a sky full of stars, while talking, eating our burgers, along with drinking our root beer in those frosted mugs. True American lifestyle at its finest.

Might I someday be the King of Orchard Street?

In that situation, to the mind of a seven-year-old boy, I was already the King of New York State, the King of the United States, and the King of the World. Sitting right on top of this big playground of mine called creation with Joe and Verna Cristiano by my side.

Sunday was also a big day in this sphere that Joe and I inhabited. He would usually come to my aunt Flora's house to see Verna at some point in the early afternoon. When I saw his car come in the driveway, I would run down the stairs to my aunt's apartment to make sure he was aware that I was home. We would all visit for maybe an hour, and then invariably he would ask me if I wanted to go hunting or fishing depending on which season was open. I jumped at the chance. We would then proceed to his mother's house to find his mom, Doris, cooking or baking and Doc watching TV. Doris was a quiet, calm woman with very blonde hair, and Doc was equally quiet and calm. I found out recently that Doc's real name was Francis, which I never knew, and that Doris was very patriotic. Doris would often have Joe and his sister, Donna, sing "The Star-Spangled Banner" together to consistently reinforce their love for this beautiful, free county we inhabit. Joe's sister, Donna, was equally as blonde as her mom and had a comical sense of humor. She passed away many years ago, yet I still think about her.

Joe had bought me a little popgun with a cork on a string at the end of the barrel. The cork could be pushed into the end of the barrel to load the gun. When the trigger was pulled, the cork would pop, thus "firing" the gun at the intended target. Joe would grab his shotgun, and I my popgun. As we walked out to the Flats along the Mohawk River to hunt, we would discuss gun safety, staying away from the river, the scenery, the dangerous "Swinging Bridge," and just about anything else that came to mind. Where we were hunting in Schuyler was probably a mile west of my aunt Flora's house on the other side of the Mohawk River in Frankfort. Joe would take a few shots at some rabbits he saw or maybe a squirrel, and I would shoot at them with my popgun as well. I really don't think we ever killed anything. We just walked through the Flats and had a wonderful time. When we were finished, the best was yet to come. We would go back to his mother's house, two big-game hunters coming in from the cold, and Doris would offer to make us Heidi Milk. I waited for those words to come out of her mouth. I never really knew what she was serving me, but it was warm, sweet, and very good. Doris would heat milk on the stove and gently mix in some sugar with a spoon. She would then pour her wonderful potion in a coffee mug and serve it to us. I was fascinated. The Heidi Milk was delicious. I looked forward to the Heidi Milk more than I looked forward to the hunting. Doris claimed the Heidi Milk was a cure-all for everything, especially the common cold.

On a few occasions, I stayed overnight with Doris, Doc, Joe, and Donna. Stories such as this cannot be made up. They're too vivid, lush, and invigorating to ever not be true. In life you make a few big decisions and millions of small ones. Spending many youthful hours with Joe, Doris, Doc, and Donna while hunting, fishing, and drinking Heidi Milk were probably some of the smallest decisions I ever made in my life. Yet they are the biggest, the most dynamic, and certainly the best. Those experiences will live in my memory forever.

As I got older, Joe and I also went on numerous "real" fishing expeditions. We would drive to his father, Joe Cristiano Sr.'s restaurant in Middleville. When we got there, we would talk with his father for a bit and then walk behind Dibbles to a path that led down to the bank of the West Canada Creek. We would get our fishing equipment ready and stay probably an hour fishing in that spot. I don't think we caught much there, but we were fishing. Next, we would get back in the car and drive on Route 28 North toward Poland and Newport. The right-hand side of the road was pretty close to houses and farms. There was not much room between the road and homes with a good-sized mountain behind the houses rising up to the foothills of the Adirondack Park toward Pine Lake. The homes and farms on the left-hand side of Route 28 toward the bank of the West Canada Creek at spots came within twenty-five or thirty feet of the road. In other places the bank could be two or three hundred yards from the road. Most of that acreage was cornfields, cow pastures, or land lying fallow for future use. In certain spots we could fish fifteen or twenty feet off the road on the banks of the West Canada Creek. In other places we would have to the walk across those cow pastures for maybe two or three hundred yards to access the banks of the West Canada Creek. Often Joe knew people who lived on the right side of the road, and they would allow us to park on their property. From there we would walk across the road and then walk across the fields over to the bank of the West Canada Creek. On the walk over we would again talk about safety near the water, the scenery, and any topic that came to mind. We would usually catch one or two fish in West Canada Creek, but the best fishing was yet to come and much easier to access.

On our way back to Frankfort on Route 28S, on the left side of the road, Joe's uncle also owned a restaurant named Cristiano's. Next door to his restaurant, he had his house and a probably two-acre pond next to the house. It seems that his friends would catch fish in the West Canada Creek, then release them into his pond, especially the small ones, which eventually grew very large. I think at other times he also bought fish from the New York State Department of Conservation to stock his pond. Now we were in a good position. We knew there were fish to be caught. Joe and I would bait our hooks while standing on the side of that pond and put on our bobbers and bait to give our lines weight to ensure long casts into the deep section of the pond. Usually within a few minutes, maybe five or six, we would be catching fish. At times we would catch eight to ten fish in an hour. A great spot to fish, practically guaranteed to catch a number of decent-sized fish. When we were finished, we would throw them all back in the pond so that we could come back another time to catch them again. Over the course of a summer, we would probably catch the same fish three or four different times.

I always told my wife and kids that I taught Joe how to fish and where the fish were but that may be a small stretch of the truth.

The last time I drove by, the pond was filled in, and the house and restaurant looked to be abandoned, although in my mind, the entire property is still there exactly as it was sixty years ago. Indelible.

Joe Cristiano grew up in Schuyler, and his mother's house was about a mile west of my grandmother's house, only on the other side of the river. There was a spot to cross without traveling all the way around to the North Frankfort Bridge. It was in reality a pipeline to transport natural gas from Frankfort to Schuyler that was commonly known as the "Swinging Bridge." It wasn't very big or secure and did swing in the wind. It was definitely not safe to walk on. In the summer, when the river was low, the bridge would be about three feet above the surface of the water. In the spring, when the river was full of melting snow, the bridge was generally about a foot under the water. In effect, you were walking on a twelve-inch pipe suspended three feet below two metal cables on each side of the pipe that could be held on to like handrails with the running water at best four feet below your feet.

One afternoon Joe's younger sister, Donna, decided that she wanted to go with him to visit Verna. Being younger and his sister, Joe naturally didn't want to take her anywhere but reluctantly agreed. They proceeded to walk through the woods to the bank of the Mohawk River and the site of the "Swinging Bridge." Once Donna got sight of the supposed bridge, she quickly came to her senses, turned around, and went home. That made Donna happy and her brother equally so in that now he didn't have his little sister tagging along when he went to meet his love. An example of a reverse Mexican standoff.

Once on the other side of the river, there was another farm bridge that was used to move tractors and farm equipment into the fields that lay in the Flats. It was a short walk from the farm bridge to Route 5S East and then a mile walk into the Village of Frankfort.

One summer night, at about 1:00 a.m., Joe didn't have access to a car, but he had a plan to see Verna. He decided to walk across the "Swinging Bridge" in the dark, next, over the farm bridge, then east to my grandmother's house. Once at my grandmother's house, he was equally determined to get Verna's attention without anyone else knowing he was there. Phase two of his plan now sprang into action. Joe proceeded to toss tiny pebbles at what he thought was Verna's bedroom window to get her attention yet not break the window. What he didn't realize was the window he was throwing the pebbles at was not Verna's. Indeed, it was my father and mother's bedroom window. My dad usually then picked up the story from the inside. He had been in a deep sleep from about 10:30 p.m. when suddenly he was awakened by the taps of pebbles hitting his bedroom window. It being well after dark, when he looked out his window, he could see a figure in the yard tossing the pebbles but could not make out who it was. The story has it that my father then picked up a baseball bat, which he kept in his room for such an occasion, and went out in the dimly lit yard to investigate in his own subtle manner. He ran out of the back door and started chasing whoever was throwing the pebbles through the backyards of other people's houses. At some point they both got running east on Orchard Street, then turning south on Litchfield Street to Main Street, and went east again toward Herkimer on Main Street. Then a south turn on the corner of Main Street and Skiff Avenue. Joe, with my father in hot pursuit, then turned east on Canal Street, the site of the original Erie Canal, and kept running. By that time, a total of about five blocks, they were both likely out of breath. My father stopped chasing, but Joe kept running until my dad was well out of sight. I found out recently the exact route of the chase while I was at Joe's house in Pleasanton. No matter which way they went, that's a story I have heard my whole life from two sources, and it's undoubtedly 110 percent true. Joe never got Verna's attention that night. Yet he certainly got my dad's and scared the daylights out of him too.

As I considered and documented the incidents connected to Joe's attempts to visit Verna, I could see and hear in my mind's eye Marvin Gaye and Tammy Terrell harmonizing:

Because baby there ain't no mountain high enough,
Ain't no valley low enough,
Ain't no river wide enough,
To keep me from getting to you babe.

I was also struck by what so intensely motivated Joe to be with Verna. Was it fate? Kismet? Karma? Providence? Destiny? Or something else?

There is one motivation I am certain of. Pure, unfettered love drove Joe to take such a risk to see Verna. Nothing was going to prevent him from being with her, including but not limited to the Mohawk River, the treacherous "Swinging Bridge," or my dad.

*****

Carol and I drove on Route 5 East in Schuyler the other day to stop at a consignment store that she does business with, owned by a longtime friend Robbi Hughes Breit of Frankfort. While driving through Schuyler, I noticed that the original Schuyler Fire Department, a small stone building likely built during the Great Depression by the Works Project Administration that Donnie and I had discussed earlier, was torn down and was replaced with a more modern building to house firefighting equipment. I was aghast. I told Carol I had to call Joe Cristiano and tell him. He was a member of the fire department back when I was five or six years old. The firehouse was on the other side of Route 5, about 150 yards west of Joe's mother's house. On those wonderful Sunday afternoons and even on some weekday nights, Joe and I would walk across Route 5 to the fire department for me to sit in the driver's seat of the trucks, climb on them, and get instruction from Joe how to safely put up a ladder, get on or off the truck, and so on. Needless to say, activities that any seven-year-old boy would find exciting. Once in a while he even allowed me to give a small blast on the siren. Talk about swelling a young boy's head. Again, I thought I was in control of every fire department in the world. Joe would watch me smiling from ear to ear. He could tell by the look on my face how thrilled I was. I think he was just as thrilled as I was, to watch a young boy having so much fun. I bet right to this day, he is still equally as thrilled when he sees his own children, grandchildren, or any child for that matter, enjoying themselves to the extent I was.

Unfortunately, Joe's career as a firefighter ended abruptly at the age of nineteen when he piloted one of the department's trucks to a barn fire. He was so excited to actually put out a fire that he parked the truck far too close to the burning barn. As the fire grew, igniting more and more bales of hay stored inside, the flames pitched over the truck to the extent that the fire helmets, mounted on the outside of the truck for quick pick up by the responding volunteers and rated to withstand interior fire suppression temperatures, melted into an unrecognizable form.

Through it all, the fire chief remained philosophical and commented, "At least we know our helmets aren't safe."

That was the last word on Joe Cristiano's career as a firefighter.

Many times when I sat in the living room of our apartment on the backside of my house facing Schuyler, I could hear the sirens and the fire whistles from the Schuyler Fire Department. I was certain that those whistles and sirens were Joe Cristiano signaling to me that he was there in Schuyler waiting for me and our next hunting or fishing expedition but ironically no more firefighting experiences. Fascination, beyond description, is the only way I can express the sentiments that swelled in me when I heard those alarms and whistles coming toward me from Schuyler in my apartment on Orchard Street.

Once Joe and Verna were married, they rented a small one-bedroom apartment on Erie Street in Frankfort, in a house belonging to Sam Giambrone. The apartment was probably a total of six blocks from my mom and dad's recently purchased house on Fourth Avenue. There were times when my mother and father wanted to go out to dinner with their friends or just had somewhere to go. On a number of occasions, I would go stay with Verna and Joe overnight. While my mother was getting my bag ready, I would inform her that I was not really certain that I wanted go, that Verna's apartment seemed too far away, and so on. I was a little leery of being out of my own home to sleep and all the things that go through a nine- or ten-year-old's mind when confronted with not being home as he normally is. My mother would convince me that it was fine; they were only going out to dinner, and by eight or nine o'clock they would be home. If there was any problem, Joe would call, and she would come and get me, again being only five blocks away from my house. Eventually, I would buy the idea, and off I would go to Cristiano's to spend the night. Verna, Joe, and I would watch TV while we munched on our popcorn and drank our soft drinks. One movie I specifically remember watching was *The Song of Bernadette*, a 1943 black-and-white movie about the appearance of the Virgin Mary to a group of children watching their flock sheep in a field near Lourdes, France. The movie's premise was the Virgin Mary appeared to these children numerous times and told them to pray the rosary for peace in the world. By eight thirty or nine o'clock, usually I would be asleep. Verna would get me pillows and blankets, and I would get a good night's sleep right there on the couch. The next day, Sunday, Joe would make us breakfast. Soon after that, my mom or dad would call and want to know if I was ready to come home. Now the tables had turned completely. I didn't want to go home. I wanted to stay with Joe and Verna in the apartment. My mom would now have to convince me to come home, which I did reluctantly. My independence from my own family was being helped along by Joe and Verna, but I didn't want to become independent too fast either.

When everything falls away, it all belongs to Joe, Verna, and me. No one can ever take one second of it from us.

I purposely walk by their apartment at times even now, and the emotional response I get is equally as strong as the sounds from the Schuyler Fire Department evoked in 1964. God bless you, Joe and Verna Cristiano, for those cherished memories—past, present, and future.

As Frankie Valli aptly put it, "Chasing the music. Trying to find our way home."

While living on Orchard Street, my mom and dad did not have a lot of money, because my mother was just starting her business and my father was working very hard in the butcher shop, neither one of them was earning a great deal of money. Yet one way or another, they always were able to put together enough money to go on vacation at least once a year as a family. As my sister and I got older and my parents were able to earn more money, they would go on cruises in the Caribbean or winter vacations in Florida when very few people had discretionary money to spend on such activities. While my sister and I were young, our family vacations mostly consisted of trips to places like Lake George, New York, and New York City to visit my mother's aunt and my great-aunt Olympia DeCrescenzo along with her sons and their families, or to Philadelphia to visit my mother's Uncle Frank Dee, again my great-uncle, and his family. When my father and sister came along, we would drive to New York City or Philadelphia, but if my mother and I went alone, we would get there using other modes of transportation.

One occasion my mother and I took a bus from Utica to New York City, then transferred to another bus from New York City to Philadelphia. Uncle Frank met us at the bus station, and we took a train to his house in Upper Darby, Pennsylvania, about two blocks off the Baltimore Turnpike. We stayed with my uncle and his wife aunt Belle for four or five days and visited all the sights in Philadelphia. Uncle Frank was a graduate of the University of Pennsylvania, class of 1929, and lived in Philadelphia for over sixty years, which made him very well-versed in the important sites to visit. On one visit in the summer, we took the train to the historic district of Philadelphia probably two or three days in a row. We made visits to the Liberty Bell and Independence Hall, which was the Pennsylvania State House prior to being the location where the Declaration of Independence was signed and then renamed as Independence Hall. The Liberty Bell was the bell hanging in the tower of the state house, which was rung to summon the citizens of Philadelphia to hear the first reading of the Declaration of Independence. Legend has it that the bell was rung so hard and for so long that it cracked. We visited the site where the Liberty Bell is now housed, Betsy Ross's house, Philadelphia City Hall with the statue of William Penn on the top spire, the Philadelphia waterfront and phenomenon known in those days as an Automat. As we meandered through the narrow streets of historic Philadelphia over a stretch two or three days, my uncle Frank, who always had a very funny, sharp mind, had stories to tell on literally every corner. As I was about seven or eight at the time, my uncle would tell me every now and then to look up quickly at William Penn so I could see him wave. I would look up as quick as I could, and my uncle would tell me just as quickly, "You missed it." I bought it every time, and every time it was worth its weight in gold. I don't think I caught on to the joke till probably five or six years later, and when I did, it was worth more than its weight in gold. As for now, at age sixty-eight, there is no process to put value on those small but marvelous interactions, and they will inhabit my consciousness for the rest of my life as distinctly as the day they happened.

Shortly after that trip to Philadelphia, on a second trip to Philadelphia, I had a first-time experience of flying in an airplane. My mother and I boarded a Mohawk Airlines plane at Oneida County Airport in Oriskany for about a forty-minute flight to Philadelphia, seated in seats that faced each other, which I don't think I've ever seen in an airplane again. My uncle picked us up at the airport, and we went to stay at his house. When we made another trip to the historic district, my uncle promised me lunch at the Automat. On the train downtown, Uncle Frank informed me about the correct way to order lunch. Automats were a 1960s version of a fast-food restaurant where simple food and drinks were served quickly. Automats consisted of a large wall, about twenty feet by five feet, of small doors, the doors being likely ten inches long and eight inches high. Much like a wall of mailboxes in the post office. After you picked out the lunch you wanted and put coins in the slot of the door, it would unlock. Then the customer reached in and grabbed their sandwich. The buyer would then repeat the process for chips, a drink, or whatever else was purchased from another box. By looking through the glass of each door, you could see workers in a kitchen preparing food to replenish the empty boxes and slide in more food from behind for purchase. While I was standing in front of the doors, deciding which sandwich I wanted for lunch, my uncle again informed me to make sure I picked the right one the first time in that if I wanted mayonnaise on my sandwich but picked out the one without mayonnaise, a large boxing glove would come out through the door to punch me in the nose, and someone behind the wall would yell, "Why didn't you tell me you wanted mayonnaise?" Verifiable Philadelphia-style communication in its truest form.

I was very careful to be sure that I had ordered the exact lunch I wanted. The first time.

After lunch, as we walked back through the historic district from the Automat to get a train back to Upper Darby, it started raining. Luckily, my uncle had brought some umbrellas. As we walked along, chatting, a homeless man caught up to us and wanted money. Uncle Frank reached in his pocket and gave the man a few coins as we proceeded to walk away. The guy decided it wasn't enough and continued to follow us, asking my uncle for more money. My uncle, being the smart, friendly man that he was, politely informed the homeless man that we had already given him money and to please leave us alone. We continued to walk, and the guy continued to follow us, insisting that my uncle had to give him more money. Finally, 100 percent out of character for my uncle, he quickly turned around and told the guy to leave us alone right now, or he was going to put his umbrella down the homeless man's throat. I was shocked. I had never heard kind, intelligent Frank Dee talk like that. The homeless man got the message fast and disappeared around a building. Surely an unfortunate incident, but something had to be done. I just never expected my uncle Frank to be the one to do it.

On two other occasions we would travel to Philadelphia as a family, and having made numerous trips to the Philadelphia historic sites, my uncle would take us to Atlantic City. In those days there were no casinos in Atlantic City, but it was still a tourist mecca mainly for the world class hotels, the beach, and the numerous businesses along the Boardwalk. We would spread out our blankets and chairs, swim in the ocean, eat our lunch from the basket Aunt Belle had packed, play penny games in the arcades along the Boardwalk, and really enjoy ourselves all day. On the short ride back to Upper Darby, we were all very much worn out, but it was worth every second. Having been to Atlantic City twice in 2022 for the first time since the early 1990s, it has certainly changed but not really necessarily for the better. When we used to go with my uncle in the early 1960s, it was a family destination. The tourist areas were gaudy and loud, but it was safe. Everything was built around the atmosphere of the beach. In its current state, the casinos have done much good, but the underbelly of a large homeless population, dilapidated housing, little if any decent public housing, and parks littered with trash is nightmarish. To venture one or two blocks off the Boardwalk is dangerous. The casinos were intended to be a boon to the city, and in some cases they are. Yet after nearly fifty years of doing business in Atlantic City, the casinos have probably done as much harm as they have good. It's not the Atlantic City I remember where I, with my dad, mom, sister, Uncle Frank, and Aunt Belle, built sandcastles on the beach. It breaks my heart to see the tragedy of what has happened to a once fine American city.

Those marvelous trips to Philadelphia stemmed from the maternal side of my mother's family. There were equally as marvelous trips to New York City that stemmed from the paternal side of my mother's family. At some point in approximately the 1880s, my great-grandmother and grandfather on my mother's paternal side immigrated from Italy to New York City. I have never been able to determine either of their names, other than my great-grandfather's surname of Iocovozzi, nor have I ever heard any older family members specify their names. It has also never been determined whether they married in Italy and then moved together to the United States or if they immigrated independent of each other and then met in New York City. In either case, one thing is for certain, they married and had two children they named Olympia and Leon. To the best of my knowledge, both children were born in New York City. My mother's aunt and my great-aunt Olympia lived in Queens County, New York, her entire life, specifically at 3131 Fourteenth Street in Astoria, about two blocks east of Broadway. At some point my grandfather Leon, most likely around 1910, left Queens and move to Frankfort. Chances are he made the move due to finding a new job with one of the ever-expanding railroad lines in the United States, or the move was made because of a job relocation while already working for one of the railroad companies. Trains being the most popular means of mass transportation beginning prior to the Civil War and continuing to be so up until the 1960s, the rail networks were in a constant state of growth, especially east of the Mississippi River. That huge expansion had an insatiable appetite for new employees and unlimited job possibilities. It appears that Leon moved to Frankfort alone with no relatives living in the area. That occurrence leads me to believe the move was a result of a job. Shortly after his move to Frankfort, Leon was fortunate to meet and marry my grandmother Mary Dee Iocovozzi. I never knew my grandfather in that he passed away prior to my birth, but he and my grandmother did have seven children. My mother Rose, daughters Flora and Grace, sons George, John, Anthony, and Vincent. Some of those siblings stayed lifelong residents of Frankfort or Herkimer, while others moved to Savannah, Georgia, and resided there for most their adult lives. Uncle John Iocovozzi eventually ended up living in Florida where I will soon visit him to document his opportunity to be ordained the King of Orchard Street.

That paternal side of my mother's family inspired numerous trips to New York City. As a very young boy, most times the trips were for my entire family. As the years went by, they often became trips that only my mother and I would make and even later as adult trips that I would make with one or two of my adult cousins. Interstate 90 and 87 went in both directions, and just as we would travel to New York City, my aunt Olympia DeCrescenzo would travel during the summer to Frankfort, especially in her later years. Aunt Olympia has two sons, Joseph and Rocky. As a young man, Joe along with his wife, Teresa, and their children moved to Savannah, Georgia, and have children and grandchildren still residing there. Rocky spent his entire life living in the family home on Fourteenth Street in Queens, working as a New York City police officer and eventually an officer in long-ago New York City Mayor John Lindsay's office. Being an ambitious man, he also worked for years as a mason and later in life as installer of soundproof rooms while on his off days from the NYPD. In the capacity of working in the mayor's office, he was often in the company of dignitaries and famous people from around the world as they came to New York City in that his job was to provide security for Lindsay no matter what the occasion was. Such a position obviously provided perks. Along with having a New York City police officer's identification, he also had access to many otherwise off-limits events even for a New York City police officer due to his job in the mayor's office.

One afternoon he asked me if I would like to take a ride with him to Manhattan for one reason or another. I certainly jumped at the chance, and off we went. We drove around maybe one block, looking for a place to park, but as usual they were nonavailable. Uncle Rocky told me that if there wasn't a place to park, we would make one. He stopped his car alongside another one, placed the mayor's office badge in the window, and told me to come with him. I asked him if he would get in trouble for having double-parked, and he assured me that he would not because he had "the proper identification in the window." We both got out of the car and walked into the street level of a skyscraper where he conducted his business for probably twenty minutes. As we walked out of the building, I could see his car still there double-parked with no parking ticket or tow truck insight. That situation taught me, at a very young age, how important it is to be with the right people at the right time.

While visiting the DeCrescenzos as a youth, we would often go out to dinner. Uncle Rocky's favorite restaurant was Lum's Chinese in Queens. The way my uncle became associated with the restaurant and the owners was that when he was single, on Friday, Saturday, or whatever night when he got done working with the NYPD, he along with some of his young police officer friends would go to Lum' s for dinner. As the years went by, he became one of Lum's best customers and his friend. With Uncle Rocky and his friends all being police officers, there were certain to be occasions when they could be of help to Lum. For that reason and the fact that Uncle Rocky was such a likable person, he and Lum were friends for many years.

About thirty years after dining on many occasions at Lum's as a child, Carol and I went to New York City when she worked as a tour escort for Utica/Rome Bus Company. The trip was for the weekend to see *Cats* on Broadway. The bus departed on Friday morning with Friday being an unscheduled day for sightseeing and shopping for the travelers, then Saturday being the night to attend the production. We were in Manhattan by two in the afternoon. Carol got everybody checked into the hotel with the rest of the evening free time. I phoned Uncle Rocky and Dolores to find out if they were busy Friday night, which luckily, they were not. We arranged for my uncle to meet us at the Novotel Times Square on Fifty-Second Street. That same hotel, unknown to Carol and me at the time, would play into our future again many years later. After the usual handshakes and hugs, Uncle Rocky told Carol and me that we would take a quick tour of Manhattan, and later that evening we could pick a restaurant to have dinner. Needless to say, a good proposition. We visited Greenwich Village and Washington Square where we were lucky enough to find a parking spot, which my uncle characterized as nearly impossible in Manhattan on a warm Friday night. We walked through the square and the surrounding neighborhoods for an hour, viewed a sidewalk art show, and listened to the street musicians. We were not as lucky to find parking in Time Square and Herald Square but were able to drive at least through. Around nine o'clock, it was time for dinner with Carol and I having the option of picking the restaurant. I asked my uncle if Lum's was still open, which it was. Inasmuch as I hadn't been there since I was a child, if he approved, it was a perfect place. He quickly agreed that it was fine for him, and we proceeded to the restaurant. The original owner, Mr. Lum, was still alive and, of course, was thrilled to see Uncle Rocky. As we sat at our table with Lum making suggestions as to what was the best dinner choices that night, I reminisced with him about how I remember us sitting at a long table with Uncle Rocky, Dolores, my mother, father, sister, myself, Aunt Olympia, and Lum a long time ago, doing exactly the same thing—deciding, with Lum's advice, what were the best dinner options for that evening. I don't think I was six or seven years old at the time, and it was likely the first time I had ever eaten Chinese, but I do clearly remember the food being excellent. Essentially, more than a quarter century later, on the advice of Lum, we placed our orders, and we were not disappointed. Not then and not now. The food was still excellent and only outdone by the memories.

A difficult act to follow.

Particularly more than a quarter century later.

Uncle Rocky and Dolores had three children: Marie, Karen, and Anthony. On a given Friday night, Uncle Rocky along with his wife, kids, and mother would leave after work to come to Frankfort. The family would arrive at my dad's house sometime between 10:30 p.m. and 11:00 p.m. My father would always prepare for them a delicious array of cold cuts, various types of cheese, salads, condiments, and bread. After working all day, the food, and the long drive from New York City, by the time we ate and visited, everyone was ready for bed. We would all spend the weekend visiting and being certain to catch up fully on all the family business. Uncle Rocky, Dolores, and their children would stay for the weekend usually leaving after dinner on Sunday afternoon. Aunt Olympia would stay at my mother's house for the next two weeks, visiting with her nieces, nephews, great-nieces, and great-nephews. While she was in Frankfort, she spent most of her time cooking and baking, but the majority of the time was spent making homemade pasta to share with her local families. The pasta she produced was the best I ever had. During the course of two weeks, she would make many pounds of pasta for lasagna, along with pounds of gnocchi and spaghetti. Aunt Olympia made certain each family in Frankfort got a substantial amount of pasta, of course, distributed equally. The two weeks she was in Frankfort would pass quickly. In what seemed like a very short time, Uncle Rocky would return with his wife and children again on a Friday night, to stay the weekend, pick up his mother, and return to New York City on Sunday after dinner. The time spent with Aunt Olympia was invaluable and fortunately went on for over twenty years. Today, approximately forty years after her death, that time together has proven more precious than I could have ever imagined. I can make a 100 percent unequivocal guarantee that my mom, Aunt Grace, Uncle Vince, and all her nieces and nephews would agree.

As a young boy and possibly someday the King of Orchard Street, even then I knew that I had to expand my activities beyond the limits of Frankfort. In that light, along with the trips to Philadelphia, our trips to New York City provided just the expansion I was looking for. Aunt Olympia's home was located in a section of Astoria that was inhabited by mostly people of Greek ancestry, but there were also plenty of Italian Americans living there too. Across the street from my aunt's house was a playground. A six-foot chain-link fence surrounded the playground, but the gate was always open for the families in the neighborhood to use the playground. On the playground were two sets of swings, two sets of teeter-totters, and open grassy area for baseball, kickball, or just sitting on the grass. A typical New York City playground like something you would see in an old television program.

The response Uncle Rocky's presence got from the other families in the neighborhood always captivated me. Whether he walked out of the front door of his house or out onto the street from the alleyway that led to his backyard, the reaction from his neighbors was the same. There was always three or four people on either side of the street calling out, "Hey, Rocky" or "Rocco." He would quickly call back to them, knowing everyone by name. He was a big, strong man with a heart just as big and just as strong. They were as happy to see him as he was to see them.

I miss him a lot to this day.

Honestly.

On one visit to Queens in the early 1960s, my family along with my aunt Grace's and my uncle Vince's were all at Uncle Rocky's at the same time. I have no recollection of why we were all there together, but we were. While all of my cousins and I were playing on the playground, a potentially serious accident occurred. Mary Lynn Petrilli and Damian Iocovozzi were on one of the teeter-totters, enjoying the ride. At some point Damian decided to jump off. Naturally, Mary Lynn's end of the teeter-totter dropped and hit the ground hard. The impact knocked her completely off the teeter-totter, causing her to strike her head very hard on the blacktop. I don't recall there being any bleeding, but she was clearly incoherent and quickly vomited, the first signs of a concussion. After some rest in the shade and something dry to eat, Mary felt better. I don't think she was ever taken to the hospital and later that day was back to good health. Luckily, she got out of that tight squeeze without an injury, but the occurrence certainly put a scare in all of us.

The playground was always in use and rarely empty until late in the evening. Next to the playground, in a small brick storefront was Parisi's Bakery. Every morning, while we were staying in Aunt Olympia's apartment, usually sometime between 5:00 and 6:00 a.m., the smell of bread being baked fresh that day would escape from the building. That smell coupled with the sounds of the residents moving in and out of their homes created a perfect alarm clock for the entire neighborhood. From the sidewalk in front of the house, looking to the east, the Queensboro Bridge to Manhattan loomed massive in the distance over the Long Island Sound, moving almost 120,000 cars daily between Manhattan and Queens. The official name was the Queensboro Bridge, but for the inhabitants of the neighborhood, it was always referred to as the Fifty-Ninth Street Bridge. Proceeding west along Fourteenth Street to the corner was a small meat market, named Parrelli's, occupying the ground floor of a three-story building. The story was owned by Tony Parrelli and his brother Nick with one of them having ten children to support. The entire neighborhood shopped in that store to the extent the business supported two families, one of them very large. A consummate example of the American dream right on a corner in the microcosm of Fourteenth Street, Queens, New York. The door to the deli was set on the corner of the building with a rounded three-step riser into the store, the classic New York City design. Parisi's Bakery, Parelli's deli, and the playground were the hub of the neighborhood. Not one them was ever empty, and the constant hustle and bustle they generated still enraptures me.

A few blocks back from Aunt Olympia's house was an equally as busy Twenty-First Street. Looking out the kitchen window on the back side of her house, P.S. 126 was visible a short distance away. The school was massive, about eight stories high and left to right filled the entire block. Both Uncle Rocky and his brother Joe were graduates of P.S. 126, a fact they were both very proud of. Uncle Rocky's two girls, Marie and Karen, did not attend P.S. 126 but rather walked every day on Broadway to Thirty-First Street to board the L for a quick train ride to Manhattan to pick up another train that brought them to a private Catholic school that they both attended and graduated from.

I am not sure if Anthony attended the same school, because I think it was a girls-only school but most likely did attend a Catholic school. I am betting the atmosphere at P.S. 126 had changed dramatically by the time Uncle Rocky's kids were school-age so that it was no longer the best choice of a school to attend. Consequently, the best bet was to make the change to private schools.

On one or two, maybe three, separate occasions, at the age of about ten or eleven, I decided it would be a good idea to walk alone to P.S. 126 for some reconnaissance. In that if I walked on Fourteenth Street to the opposite corner from Parelli's Deli, I could turn right, walk to the school, then turn around and walk back to Fourteenth Street. When I got to the corner back on Fourteenth, I could turn left and be right back on Uncle Rocky's block. Needless to say, a very risky endeavor for an eleven-year-old, wandering about the streets of New York City by himself.

Still…a King of Orchard Street adventure, if there ever was one.

Vincit qui se vincit. "He conquers who conquers himself."

Aunt Olympia's house consisted of an upstairs and downstairs apartment that both had the same layout. Her house was the first place I ever encountered a secure buzzer-style front door. The neighborhood was generally a very safe place, but no resident wanted to take easily preventable risks. If an individual wanted to enter the house, they would press the buzzer for either the upstairs or downstairs apartment, and someone in the respective apartment would push a button to activate an outdoor speaker to find out who was at the door. If you were allowed in, someone in the apartment would push a second button to release the lock on the door. Security systems such as that are everywhere now, but in 1962, to a seven-year-old boy from a rural area, the need for a security system was unheard of. Most people in Frankfort didn't even lock their doors at night.

Once in the door, straight ahead were stairs to Uncle Rocky's apartment, and a hallway went along the left side of the stairs to Aunt Olympia's apartment. Upon entering the downstairs apartment, one would see a small kitchen. On the right side of the kitchen was another door to a bedroom, and on the left side was another door to the bathroom. Bearing left upon entering the kitchen was a living room and two other small bedrooms to the right of the living room. The apartment upstairs was the exact same floor plan. There was another door under the stairs to the second-floor apartment that led to a basement. Uncle Rocky used the square feet in the basement to create another small living area. The basement door in the back opened to a concrete patio about twenty feet wide and ten feet across. A brick retainer wall with a gate opened into a grassy area about the same size as the concrete patio where sat an unheard-of situation for a backyard. At least for me. I had the layout of Orchard Street clearly outlined in my brain, but in Uncle Rocky's backyard in Queens, there was something I had never seen. An above-ground pool. I felt like I had been hit by lightning. Uncle Rocky had a pool in his backyard? Not a plastic or blow-up kiddie pool but rather a four-foot-deep fully functioning swimming pool. It even left a little bit of space for Aunt Olympia to plant a garden. Beyond belief.

Another summer when we visited, planting a garden became a big problem. That summer there was severe drought in the metropolitan area, and water usage was very limited. In the summer New York City can get very hot and humid to the extent that air-conditioning is a must. At that time central air-conditioning for residential use was not yet a workable option so that people, if they were lucky enough to be able to afford air conditioners, had small, inefficient window models. The drought was so severe that my aunt placed buckets underneath the air conditioners jutting out of the apartment windows to collect the water that condensed out of them. She then used the water that collected to keep her garden maintained. The entire neighborhood was being resourceful with almost every yard having rain barrels or buckets of some type to collect water from the sky, or if they were lucky enough, to have them from the air conditioners. It seemed like no matter what the weather did, all the gardens got watered, all the cars got washed, and much like Orchard Street, Fourteenth Street off Broadway in Queens County, New York, just vibrated along.

The intense humidity of summers in New York City drives millions of people every day to the beaches of Long Island and New Jersey. The weather forecast being such that the next day was predicted to be the hottest day of the year, Joey DeCrescenzo promised to take me to Coney Island to swim in the largest saltwater pool in the world. The pool was located in a wonderful place called Ravenhall and occupied the entire block at West Nineteenth Street. It was by far the largest pool on Coney Island with the business also containing a gym, handball courts, a steam room, and a small private beach. Ravenhall opened as a hotel in 1867 and grew into a large resort that was destroyed by a fire in 1963. The site was never rebuilt and today is the site of the Abe Stark Ice Rink, some upscale apartments and a parking lot. The original pool was surrounded my lifeguard chairs and bleachers for sunbathers. Just as the weather predicted, not only was it one of the hottest days of the year, but regrettably, the entire day was a washout. Joe and I still drove to Coney Island hoping that we might get lucky and the weather clears long enough to swim in the pool at least for a few minutes. Unfortunately, that did not happen. As we drove back to Queens, Joe could tell that I was very disappointed. He assured me that I was going to swim in a saltwater pool that day no matter how the weather played out. As we parked in the front of Aunt Olympia's house, I could not imagine where we would find a saltwater pool. The pool was in the backyard, but it was not saltwater, and it was still raining. When we walked into Aunt Olympia's apartment, Joe immediately went into the bathroom, filled up the bathtub, leaving just enough space to keep it from overflowing. He then opened a five-pound bag of salt, poured it into the tub, stirred up the water with his hand, and told me to get in because there was saltwater pool to swim in. The entire process provided a perfect opportunity for me to swim in a saltwater pool. I jumped right in with my bathing suit, swimming and splashing away for probably an hour. Joe lined the floor with towels to soak up the water that was coming out of the tub from all directions. In the end, he was right. I may not have swam that day in one of the largest saltwater pools in the world, but I certainly did swim, and it certainly was in saltwater. Thanks to Joey DeCrescenzo. I will never forget that day. and I will never forget DeCrescenzo's Saltwater Pool. Not on West Nineteenth Street in Coney Island, New York but rather on Fourteenth Street in Astoria, New York.

While we were visiting, my family and I stayed in Aunt Olympia's apartment with her and, after she had passed away, by ourselves in her apartment. Uncle Rocky and his family lived in the upstairs apartment, which was close quarters for five people. Aunt Olympia would sleep in her room on the right side of the kitchen in her apartment, while my mother and father would use one of the small bedrooms off the living room, and my sister would use the other one. My accommodations would be sleeping on the couch in the living room. In those days Fourteenth Street was safe to the extent that even in a first-floor apartment, you could sleep at night with the windows open. The living room where I slept had two windows, which would be left open at night. The noise from traffic, people walking along the street, going in and out of their houses and the playground across the street was constant. At night the street got quieter, but there was always a permeation of noise. As I would lay there on a couch getting sleepy, I could hear sirens in the distance, be they police or fire, and wonder why so many people were still not yet at home being it was late at night. The entire environment never got completely quiet. Orchard Street, my daily environment, at night quieted down to practically no sound. I had never experienced anything like the environment surrounding 3131 Fourteenth Street in Astoria, New York, with such constant busyness, and I would bet it is exactly the same today, if not more so.

My fascination with the neighborhood grew each time we visited Aunt Olympia, but another object fascinated me even more. I have no idea where she got it, but my aunt had in her apartment, on a shelf, about a three-foot long stuffed baby alligator. I found it engrossing. There were times when I found it repulsive and wouldn't touch it. There were other occasions when I couldn't put it down. I would turn it over, look at the underside to feel the smoothness of its belly, then flip it back over and feel the roughness of its back. It had legs about six inches long with half-inch nails growing out of the ends of its feet. I would look in its eyes and think for sure it was alive just waiting to bite me as soon as I turned my back. It was stuffed with its mouth somewhat opened. I was always looking inside the mouth at its teeth, thinking at any second, the mouth would snap closed, like a mousetrap, and take one of my fingers off. I was terrorized by the way it looked but at the same time allured by it. That bizarre stuffed alligator kept my attention glued to it for hours. Strange, peculiar, outlandish, and magnetic all at the same time.

In Aunt Olympia's kitchen, in the right corner by her bedroom door, she had two parakeets, which she named Romeo and Juliet. Every day she would feed them, clean out the bottom of their cage, talk to them, then pause briefly, listening to their melodic call and response chirping. At times she would close the bedroom doors and, even more important, the windows of her apartment while leaving the birdcage door open so if they chose to, one or both could fly around the kitchen unhindered. On one occasion Aunt Olympia inadvertently left the kitchen window by the birdcage and the door of the birdcage open at the same time. Romeo was quick to comprehend his route to full emancipation. In the blink of an eye, he was out of the cage door and out of the kitchen window. Aunt Olympia soon came to the realization of what had occurred and was heartbroken. It took a little longer for Juliet to understand the gravity of the dreadful situation, but when she did, her entire world was decimated. Juliet stopped chirping, would not fly out of the cage when the door was left open, and would not eat or drink. On the third night after Romeo's disappearance, Aunt Olympia covered the birdcage like she did every night and went to bed. When she awoke the next morning and uncovered the cage, she was aghast to find Juliet dead on the birdcage floor. The forlorn, lonely life Juliet envisioned for herself without her Romeo was too much for her to bear.

According to the Bard of Avon, "For never was a story of more woe than this of Juliet and her Romeo."

All the trips to New York City were memorable, but the Thanksgiving trips of which we made at least three were the most memorable of all. On Wednesday before Thanksgiving, if my mother would get done working at three in the afternoon and my father be home by six, at five o'clock my mother, sister, and I would eat dinner, and my mother then pack our clothes for a trip to New York City. My mother would want us to sleep for an hour or two because our train would leave at about midnight to arrive in New York City by seven in the morning. Her point being that riding in a train all night was not conducive to sleep. When we arrived at Penn Station, we had to be rested enough to quickly check into to the Americana Hotel, then walk to the Thanksgiving Day Parade a few blocks away. I would go to my room and get my clothes packed, although my mother really already had them packed, and as she suggested try to sleep, which unfortunately didn't work. Ironically, one of the TV stations in New York City that we would receive by way of cable television, I believe it was WOR, would, as a practice the night before Thanksgiving, broadcast the original *King Kong* with the Canadian actress Fay Wray as the female lead with Robert Armstrong and Bruce Cabot as the costar male leads. I never thought about it then, but really it is, in effect, a horror movie about a giant gorilla terrorizing New York City that could only be controlled by the beautiful Fay Wray despite the best efforts of Armstrong and Cabot. Kong's only goal was to possess this beautiful young woman. Fay was certainly worthy of Kong's attempt with her beauty radiating from every camera angle.

When my father would come home from work, he had dinner while we finished getting the rest of our clothes, ready to leave our house around eleven to board the train at Union Station in Utica. The actual journey was probably only about four hours, but the train literally made a stop in almost every city and village between Utica and New York City. The first stop would be in Herkimer, then Little Falls, Amsterdam, Albany, next Poughkeepsie, then Kingston, literally ten or more stops along the entire route before arriving at Penn Station in Manhattan.

One year, while disembarking from the train, a situation occurred that is burned in my consciousness. While getting off the train, I didn't step fully over the gap between the train car and the platform. On that trip, at about ten years old, I slipped between the train and the platform. Having never spent a skinny second in my life, my father quickly grabbed my arm to pull me up, but the real savior of the incident was my somewhat protruding tummy. As I got up on the platform a conductor rushed over to check if I was okay. My dad lifted up my shirt to see, but all that happened was a few minor scratches.

Rescued by the tummy. Who says being thin can save your life?

Upon arriving in Manhattan, the conductors would quickly unload our luggage off the train, which we just as quickly gathered together, and then walked directly across the street to our accommodations at the Americana. By the time all of this transpired, it was about eight in the morning, just in time to walk to the parade route for the parade to start at nine. It was imperative to be standing on the route when the first attraction went by and, more important, to still be on the route when the last float went by, with the rider of the last float being the star we all came to see. It was family tradition to view the parade on Fifth Avenue as close as possible to Thirty-Second Street so that we could proceed to walk three blocks or less to Herald Square and Macy's Department Store where all the attractions were guaranteed to perform. Usually we were lucky enough to get there right as the parade started. I clearly remember the bands being robust and numerous. The segments from the various Broadway shows got the crowd cheering from the minute they stopped in front of a specific section of the block. As a seven-year-old boy looking up at those massive balloons, I couldn't help but to be very impressed. The music of the bands and the singing and dancing of the actors mixed in with that cool November air made me awe inspired.

It seems now when I watch the parade on TV, it is still impressive, but the bands and actors don't stop to perform for the crowd lining the street as frequently. The best locale for entertainment and television spots was always and still is the reviewing stand directly in front of Macy's Department Store. I'm not sure if the entertainment stops at other points along the parade route at all anymore. On one occasion, probably the first time I had ever seen in my fully intoxicated person in my life, a woman stepped out from the crowd and proceeded to stagger along Fifth Avenue. I was in full amazement as to how incoherent this woman was. I had never seen an individual in such a condition as that woman in my life. Thank goodness the police quickly moved in and in a very subtle manner escorted the woman off the parade route and hopefully to the hospital. Being about eight years old at the time, I interpreted the entire scene as tragedy and still do.

As the parade began to wind down, we were all tired from being on the train all night and would return to our room at the Americana Hotel. As I lay there on the bed, slowly falling into a deep slumber, I had the wonderful opportunity to look out through the hotel room window and see the parade still winding itself along Fifth Avenue. A cheery sight to behold while drifting off to a deep sleep.

After we had all slept for about two hours, my father had previously made a reservation at the famous Mama Leone's Italian restaurant where we would go for a Thanksgiving dinner with all the trimmings. Mama Leone's would be loud and full of people. We would order the family-style Thanksgiving meal complete with the whole turkey, which the waiter would carve, stuffing, sweet potatoes, cranberries, and a pumpkin pie for dessert. After dinner we would walk back to our hotel, all of us in a bit of a food coma and still very tired from the overnight train ride. We had to get into bed early because Friday was a big day too.

Early on Friday morning we would be out for a good breakfast and walking tour through Manhattan. We would be always certain to make our way through the Diamond District and peruse the fabulous jewelry displays in the windows. We would continue walking through the Garment District to check out the latest fashions and, of course, Herald Square, one of the major commercial intersections of Midtown Manhattan. Naturally, we made a stop at Macy's after a pretty extensive walking tour of the midtown neighborhoods. We would have our lunch on the street from a food cart, then return to the Americana for an afternoon nap because we had a big night ahead. At about five o'clock we would find the nearest restaurant for dinner because our next stop was Radio City Music Hall. Radio City was as impressive then as it is now. The first activity of the evening was a movie. The movie that made the biggest impression on me was *Bullit* starring Steve McQueen as a San Francisco detective assigned the task of protecting the brother of a hot-headed mob boss so that he could testify and bring down his brother Pete Ross. When two mob hit men enter the scene, Bullitt finds himself completely enveloped in a maze of double crosses and complications. The highlight of the movie is the famous automobile chase scene through the streets of

THE KING OF ORCHARD STREET

San Francisco. The forest-green Mustang that Steve McQueen drove became an instant icon due to that chase scene. The car was eventually located in a junkyard in California and restored. It now resides in a collection of famous automobiles in Southern California. A remake of Bullitt is currently in the works directed by Steven Spielberg and starring Bradley Cooper. After the movie was the Rockettes. What can be said about that more famous than ever American icon, the Rockettes? All those young, lithe dancers, accompanied by stunning props, wardrobe, and faultless live music are entertainment at its finest. All those legs, legs, and more legs really get and hold the audience's attention. The last slice of a superb evening was the live nativity scene with camels, cows, sheep, and of course, the manger. World-class live entertainment still going strong to this day. When I asked my father about forty-five years later what the admission price was per person, the best he could recall it was less than $5.

There is nowhere in the world anymore where such an enormous degree of enjoyment can be purchased for $5 per person.

To top off, one such Friday on our way back to our room, walking through the lobby of the Americana Hotel, we had to pass by the in-house restaurant and bar. As we walked along, my father stopped quickly and noticed in the bar the legendary NBC anchorman Chet Huntley of the original NBC Nightly News broadcast. What an ending to a long, extraordinary day to see an internationally famous newsman relaxing with a drink in a bar after a long day's work just like any hardworking individual.

By then, after another long, entertaining day, it seemed anything was possible.

Friday required another good night's sleep because on Saturday we were off again. Uncle Rocky would, at some point on Saturday, come to pick us up to spend the day and overnight at his house in Queens. Once again we were ready early before my uncle came to make certain of another trip to Times Square along with Rockefeller Center and the ice rink sitting below the most photographed monumental sculpture in all of New York City, that of *Prometheus* created by famed American sculptor Paul Manship due to his fascination for anything mythological and, of course, the towering Christmas tree.

In the early 1960s Times Square was relatively safe and clean. All the streets merging in Times Square had buildings with every storefront occupied by a business. The entire area was filled with camera shops, record stores, arcades, sporting equipment stores, restaurants, and almost any kind of business imaginable. We would walk a few blocks away from Times Square to see the Chinese parades go by in Chinatown, even a few blocks north to sit in the tip of Central Park or south to sit in Bryant Park. In one such store my dad bought me a gyroscope, which fascinated me for years. The gyro was set spinning at a high rate by pulling off a string that was wrapped around a center stock. Once the gyroscope started spinning, it would balance on anything. It came with a stand that allowed it to tip left and right, but I soon realized then I could balance it on any type of point. Within a few hours I had it balancing on the tip of a pen, the point of a Phillips screwdriver, a pin, anything with a point. That toy kept me busy for hours, watching it spin and looking for new perches for it to spin on. I think it made my mind spin just as fast as it did while looking for other ways to make it function.

We managed to fit all those experiences in before Uncle Rocky came to pick us up.

Once he got there, we were off to his house for lunch and to spend the rest of the afternoon relaxing prior to our night out for dinner, traditionally at Lum's. Once back from dinner, we would spend the evening relaxing and watching TV while making our final preparations to go home on Sunday. When Sunday morning came, we would be up early and ready to go to Penn Station. Aunt Olympia would make us breakfast while we finalized our preparations to leave, and she would be certain to make pepper and egg sandwiches that we could eat on the train when we got hungry later on. She would wrap the sandwiches in wax paper and put them in a paper bag. They were perfect for the four- to five-hour trip home in that they needed no refrigeration, The sandwiches contained so much grease that it would escape the wax paper to the degree that the paper bag would be covered with two- to three-inch grease spots almost covering the outside surface of the entire bag. The paper bags and Aunt Olympia, whether by chance or design, essentially made the sandwiches much healthier for us.

Healthy or not, those were great sandwiches and now even greater memories.

As my children were growing up, I told them stories about these Thanksgiving trips to New York City and what a wonderful experience they were. Once they got to be middle school–age, I asked them if they would like to take a vacation to perhaps Las Vegas or take a Thanksgiving weekend trip to New York City to see the sights. Fortunately for all of us, they chose the trip to New York City for Thanksgiving.

We tried to lay out the trip to mirror the trips I used to take with my father and mother for Thanksgiving. A Darjeeling Limited experience, so to speak. The main difference being that the trips I took with my parents did not include a Broadway show, yet this trip with my own children would. I prepurchased tickets to see Jersey Boys at the August Wilson Theatre on West Fifty-Second Street directly across the street from our accommodations at the Novotel Times Square. I also prepurchased tickets for the Christmas Spectacular at Radio City featuring the Rockettes and, of course, the live nativity scene just as we did with my mom and dad for Friday night the day after Thanksgiving. Much to my chagrin, a movie was no longer included with the Christmas Spectacular, which startled me in the sense of how times had changed. We left on Wednesday, the day before Thanksgiving, at about nine o'clock in the morning and arrived at the Novotel at about two in the afternoon for check-in. Once in our hotel room, we took the short two-block walk south to Times Square for a very early dinner, I believe at McDonald's. After dinner, we quickly walked back to West Fifty-Second Street and got in line at the theater. The show started at promptly eight o'clock with the doors opening at seven fifteen. As we were ushered into the theater, I couldn't help but think what strong ambiance the small old-fashioned Broadway theater had. When the lights dimmed and the show began, the first song was in French for about two minutes. I was confused and thought we had entered the wrong venue. After that first song, one of the actors appeared on the stage and began to tell in English the history of Frankie Valli and the Four Seasons. From there the play soared like an ICBM. The crowd went completely hush. The songs and dialogue started to flow while the entire theater was lost in the atmosphere for over two hours. The entire evening was a lesson in the dogma of early rock 'n' roll. All the Jersey Boys classic hits were there: "Can't Take My Eyes Off of You," "Big Girls Don't Cry," "Beggin'," "Sherry," and on and on. The tragedies and successes of the band members' personal lives were also vividly portrayed. Jail sentences, gambling problems, issues with organized crime, divorces, and untimely deaths were laid out on the stage like the threads of a tapestry. The pain and joy of everyday human existence wonderfully painted for all to see. When the show was over at about ten thirty, I think my wife, children, and I were never so enraptured before as we were after those two and one-half hours inside the August Wilson Theatre. After that performance, it was impossible not to purchase a copy of the soundtrack in CD form.

Oddly, for Thanksgiving the entire weekend was warm and dry. After the show, we walked back to Times Square to spend some late nighttime taking in the warm air. We all sang the Jersey Boys soundtrack out loud fearlessly over and over as we walked to Time Square, in our hotel room, in our van, on the way home, and for two weeks after we were home. I never had that Broadway show experience on the Thanksgiving trips to New York City with my own mother and father, but this trip ranked right up there with any that I did have.

After that fun filled evening, all of us drifted off to sleep in our hotel room in less than five minutes. I don't think anyone even brushed their teeth.

We all were up early on Thanksgiving with a full day scheduled. From our hotel room, as when I was a child, we could see the Thanksgiving Day Parade route on Fifth Avenue. We were washed, dressed, teeth brushed since we probably didn't brush the night before, and ready to go for the two-block walk to find a good spot on the parade route. The morning was a beautiful, crisp start to a cool cloudless day. As we walked over to get a viewing position, the sun was about twenty degrees above the horizon with the skyscrapers casting shorter and shorter shadows as the sun rose. The shadows of the buildings on the sidewalk shrunk as we walked from perhaps fifteen feet from the front of the building onto the sidewalk to when we arrived at our vantage point to about five feet. The parade was as stirring as it had ever been. There were large marching bands from colleges and high schools all over the United States, numerous song-and-dance segments from a variety of currently running Broadway shows, the massive floats, and the traditional balloons. One of the featured artists of that year's parade was CeeLo Green. Green was perched twenty-five feet up on the top of a float that stopped directly in front of us while he performed two songs. As the sun rose higher that morning and the temperature got warmer, the entire event multiplied in significance for my wife, children, and me. We were very hungry, but we couldn't leave. The most important event of the parade hadn't occurred yet. I have told my wife and children for years that earlier and earlier each year merchants begin selling Christmas products as a ploy to get the consumer to spend more and more money earlier in the Christmas season. The Christmas season started after one person made his way south on Fifth Avenue in New York City on the last float of the Macy's Thanksgiving Day Parade. Clearly, we couldn't go anywhere until that event occurred no matter how hungry we were. About five minutes after having the same discussion for the hundredth time, there he was towering over the majesty of entire parade. The man we had all come to see.

Santa Claus.

Now it was the season of Christmas.

As we walked back to our hotel, all of us were equally as enamored as when we walked out of the August Wilson Theatre the night before, only on this walk it was because of the Macy's Thanksgiving Day Parade.

The re-creation of those trips to New York City when I was a child, at that point, could not have been more precise. Just as I used to watch the remainder of the parade from my hotel room in the Americana when I was five or six, from the Novotel on Broadway and West Fifty-Second we could look south toward Times Square and again see the parade winding through the streets of Manhattan.

We luckily got a table at the restaurant in the Novotel and indulged in a sumptuous breakfast of eggs in a variety of styles, sausage, bacon, juices, coffee, hash browns, bagels, lox, and cream cheese, all for a very reasonable price. While we sat at our table watching the tail end of the parade meander through Times Square, I was struck by the inaccuracy of the old adage, "You can never go home."

I found at breakfast that Thanksgiving morning that you certainly could because I just did.

After being out so early and a delectable breakfast, we're all ready for a nap in the afternoon. Once we started getting hungry again, I called Ellen's Stardust Diner, a 1950s-style restaurant with singing waiters and waitresses whose other, hopefully, long-term career goal was to sing, dance, and maybe someday star in a Broadway show. I was lucky enough to get a reservation for about an hour later. As we all emerged from our sleepiness, we got dressed and made it over to the diner on time in that it was literally across the street on the Broadway side of the Novotel. As the waiters and waitresses moved from table to table, performing little song-and-dance skits, we placed our orders. The food was good, but the show was even more entertaining to the extent that most people, when they're finished their meals, don't want to leave their tables. Most of the customers wanted to stay and linger over their coffee with free entertainment exhibited everywhere in the multilevel restaurant. Finally, as it was getting late, we left Ellen's, and in an almost balmy night in late November, we again walked to Times Square to unwind before bed because the next day, Friday, was an equally busy day.

When I awoke on Friday morning, I called Dolores DeCrescenzo to find out if she was busy that night, and if not, perhaps we could meet her somewhere. When Dolores answered the phone after the usual chitchat, I informed her that we were in New York City at the Novotel on Broadway and had tickets for the Radio City Christmas Spectacular at seven o'clock, but up until then, our day was pretty open. Prior to going to Radio City, we were, as we did when I was child, going to Herald Square and, of course, to Macy's to view the displays in the department stores and the jewelry store windows in the Diamond District. Our intention was to do our walking tour until about 5:00 p.m., then have dinner and be at Radio City for the show promptly at seven. Dolores informed me that she had some errands during the day, but she could have them finished by five, and then she would pick us up at the Novotel. She had a nice restaurant in Queens that she frequented not far from her original house on Fourteenth Street, whose specialty was numerous varieties of gluten-free pastas and raviolis. She decided on that restaurant because she knew my son has celiac disease, and the available dinners would be a perfect fit for him. Dolores was certain that if she picked us up at five o' clock, we could have a leisurely dinner, and she could get us to Radio City by seven. When five o'clock came, as we were waiting on the Broadway side of the Novotel, Dolores pulled up to the curb exactly on time. As soon as Carol spotted her, we all climbed in the car for a trip back over the bridge to Queens. As always it was great to see Dolores again, and she looked her usual cheerful, content Dolores DeCrescenzo. She filled us in on the busy day she had, driving all over Queens and Manhattan, completing errands although she had gotten in not one but two car accidents that day, and she smiled through it all. Dolores had our reservation set for five thirty, and we walked in the door at exactly that time. The menu was all gluten-free pastas including raviolis stuffed with rabbit, goose, lobster, and just about any filling that existed. The pasta was all made in a kitchen in the basement of the building, fresh each day and strictly gluten-free. The restaurant had an Italian décor, and I'm still not quite sure how the waiters remembered all the available pastas for the day, but they did. There was likely twenty available for the day plus the full regular menu. Our orders ranged from lobster to goose or rabbit raviolis, each one being as delicious as the next, and we were certain to share them all. While absorbing the atmosphere around the room, I leaned over to my son and suggested that he keep his eyes open because there was a distinct possibility that at any second, Don Vito Corleone could walk in the entrance with his "family" for Friday night dinner. That observation really focused his attention on our surroundings, and who knows, maybe we did just miss the Don on our way in or out. Assuredly, a very interesting dinner only surpassed by the very interesting company. Immediate family and otherwise.

Time moved quickly, and at about six thirty we had to depart for Radio City. I got in the passenger seat with Dolores driving, my son, daughter, and, I assumed, Carol in the back seat. As Dolores started to drive away from the curb, my son asked me where his mom was. I told him that she was supposed to be in the back seat with him and Alaina. When I turned to look, much to my surprise, Carol was not in the car. Then I looked out of the rear window as we drove away, and there was Carol standing in front of the restaurant. Dolores, being hyperfocused on driving the car after two car accidents that day, had no idea what we were talking about until I told her that we left Carol standing on the street with a homeless man asleep on the sidewalk beside her. When I informed Dolores of Carol's whereabouts, she quickly U-turned and went back to get her. Three car accidents in one day? Thankfully not. As it played out, Carol was holding the door to the restaurant open for an elderly man with a walker while we all loaded in the car and drove away. A potentially big problem for all of us, thank goodness, averted. The issue was now the precious minutes we had wasted to arrive at Radio City by seven. As luck would have it, traffic was minimal, which quickly got us back over the bridge to Manhattan. Double lucky, there was an open spot directly in front of Radio City where Dolores could pull to the curb. We hustled out of the car, thanked Dolores for the excellent dinner, and got in line to enter the famed 1932 Art Deco jewel, Radio City Music Hall. We were ushered to our seats with about five minutes to spare before the lights dimmed, and again I knew we were in for a treat.

There was a marvelous message in that bottle.

As the lights dimmed, the audience quickly settled into their seats. My children were sitting on either side of me as the curtains rose to a scene of a busy New York City street corner; both their eyes widened, and the look on their face was perfect. On the right side of the stage was a twenty-five-foot-long replica of a New York City bus with fifteen windows along the side of the vehicle. With perfectly timed music, in each window, one at a time, a single Rockette in a red female elf outfit snapped into view. From the left side of the stage, a replica of a taxi moved into place with the driver and a passenger both being Rockettes in the same red female elf outfits as those on the bus. When the taxi came to a halt, the two Rockettes inside opened their doors and proceeded to the middle of the stage. At the same time the Rockettes on the bus moved in a single file around the front end of the bus to join the two who left the taxi while about twelve more gracefully moved into position from either side of the stage to altogether to form one of those world-famous Rockette chorus lines of twenty dancers, just as the orchestra rose into full accompaniment. The Rockettes on the stage began a kick line while moving uniformly to the front of the stage. Once more, as in 1963 when I was eight and, prior to that, their first show in 1925, even before their 1933 relocation to the recently opened Radio City Music Hall, there were legs, legs, and more legs across almost the whole width of the stage from left to right. To put it mildly, a beguiling sight to behold. A variety of song-and-dance skits connected to Christmas then continued for well over an hour. During that time my children did not say a word or take their eyes off that stage for one second, nor did anyone else in the audience except me to check the reactions of my children and the entire audience as the show progressed. The Rockettes ended just as they had started with a kick line that overwhelmed the entire audience literally with each euphoric kick. Enchanting and overpowering at the same time do not do the performance justice. Accordingly, the highlight of the Rockettes had not even commenced yet. On cue, moving in a circular pattern, the largest group of Rockettes to appear on the stage yet formed a chorus line now that filled the entire stage from left to right. As the music rose, the line did circular patterns around the stage and slowly broke into smaller chorus lines, then quickly reformed the long chorus line. The largest number of dancers that had yet appeared on stage. After about fifteen minutes and at a hardly noticeable pace, the Rockettes in groups of two filtered off the stage until it was empty. Enchanting.

In the now lowered lights from stage left, a manger scene quietly formed on the stage complete with a stable, straw, fences, goats, camels, and other live farm animals. All the previous scenes had now led up to the perpetual Radio City Christmas Spectacular live-animal manger display. From stage right a woman dressed in white entered.

She was riding a donkey while sitting sidesaddle on a powder-blue blanket, holding a baby, with a very humble man leading the donkey on a rope. As the woman dismounted the donkey, with the man's help, she took her place inside the manger and ever so gently she laid the baby in the crib while the man and the farm animals moved closer, gazing at the child with a stark white light shining on the baby. The backdrop of the sky full of stars with a white light projecting from the largest star in that sky was a jolting recognition of mankind's infinitesimal relationship with creation.

After about three minutes of that perfectly still scene, from the right side of the stage, three men dressed in colorful robes and crowns entered, leading camels on ropes and carrying small treasure chests. The men moved over to the baby, then slowly knelt on one knee and opened their treasure chests as bright lights shone from inside each chest and from above, all as the orchestra played a flawless rendition of "O Holy Night."

From left, right, front, and behind me I could hear people quietly being moved to tears.

The message didn't need a bottle now. It was crystal clear.

Here on earth was a Savior who would rescue mankind for eternity.

I have never seen my children or so many people around me as moved by an experience as that night in Radio City Music Hall. There is no place in the world like New York City for the Christmas season. Everyone should be as fortunate as we were to experience it at least once.

I was fortunate to experience it five or six times with an unfeigned gratitude to my father and mother. How fortunate I was to again experience it with my wife and children. I only hope that my children can experience it with their children. Then on and on for generations to come.

After those numerous experiences as a child in New York City with my parents, the next three or four years passed quickly. As my sister and I became young adults, as often happens, we were no longer interested in family vacations with our parents but more interested in the comings and goings of our friends. In about 1969, at the age of fourteen, I made my last trip to New York City or Philadelphia with my parents. The lack of interest by my sister and I in any more of those family trips freed my parents up to continue to make similar trips by themselves. For about ten years after our last family trip, my parents continued to make weekend ventures to visit Uncle Rocky, attend various popular Broadway productions, and board ships for weeklong cruises to the Caribbean. Specifically two shows that they attended starred in the leading roles two actors who eventually became world-famous performers. Along with Uncle Rocky and Dolores, on one weekend, they attended *Mame* starring Lucille Ball as Auntie Mame and, about two years later, went on a second trip to see *Camelot* with Richard Burton in the lead role as King Arthur. At that time to attend a live performance with those two young actors in their respective starring roles was an enormous opportunity. As was the case with my wife, children, me, and the *Jersey Boys* many years later, my mom and dad bought both soundtracks to the plays in twelve-inch vinyl album forms. At home we listened to those soundtracks on a full-size, six-foot cabinet-style stereo for months.

Often it seems the more things are different, the more they are the same.

On two other occasions, as the winters dragged on, my mom, dad, Uncle Vince, and Aunt Rose Iocovozzi booked February cruises on the Homeric Cruise Lines to places like Saint Croix, Saint Vincent, and other US Virgin Islands. Again, they would drive to Queens on Saturday to stay at Uncle Rocky's house, and the next morning he would bring them to the boarding pier. On each occasion they had a wonderful time on these beautiful islands, at captain's dinners, in the casinos, dancing, and attending the onboard shows. Just like with *Mame*, *Camelot*, and the *Jersey Boys* they always came home with albums produced by the various bands playing on the ships to continue listening to the songs they had spent the night dancing away to. A warm, bountiful experience for them that they continued to relive once at home. The ship line they traveled on was Matson Lines, and the specific ship was the Homeric, which was docked at a New York City pier until late 1970s. The Homeric was originally named the Mariposa and was one of four sister ships in the Matson

Lines "White Fleet." During World War II the Homeric served as a troop carrier bringing supplies and support forces to distant shores in Europe. For six years the ship was mothballed at the Bethlehem Alameda Shipyard in Alameda, California, while her engines were overhauled. Matson Lines bought the ship and renamed her the SS *Homeric*. Matson then sailed her to Trieste, Italy, for reconstruction as a passenger ship. Once the reconstruction was complete, the Homeric could house 1,243 passengers,147 in first class and 1,096 in the tourist class. Both my father and mother on their return home marveled at the first-class luxury and accommodations on the ship. They really enjoyed themselves on those cruises, and they both earned every second of it.

My father used to love to tell the story that at one point they had made reservations for dinner and to hear a specific band for dancing after dinner. When they went to the restaurant along with my uncle Vince and aunt Rose, there was a mix-up as to whether their reservations were confirmed. After some discussion, the maître d' of the restaurant attempted to close the door of the restaurant literally in my uncle's face. My uncle was having none of it. Vincent was a tall, stocky man who could be quite intimidating if he chose to be. When the maître d' started to close the door to the restaurant, my uncle literally stuck his foot in the door and forcefully reopened it, demanding a table. In what I would bet were very colorful terms, he vehemently expressed to the maître d' that he wasn't leaving until he had a table.

The discussion quickly ended right there, and within a minute the two couples were comfortably at their table, placing cocktail orders.

Put an old sailor back on a ship, and there is no telling what might happen.

No further discussion ensued.

In September of 1960, I entered kindergarten at Reese Road School. Having been a middle school special education teacher for over thirty-four years at a local urban school district, I still find myself inspired by the fact that no matter who I talk to, there is always one or two teachers in a person's life who really helped them to grow into successful, happy adults. Many times it seems that that teacher was their kindergarten teacher, which makes sense because that's the first person, outside of their parents, whom they were exposed to. My kindergarten teacher was a wonderful woman named Mrs. Marrs. She was young, probably only in her fifth or sixth year of working in education when I entered her class. She was very tall and thin, well-dressed, and truly was interested in every one of her students. Education in those days, specially at such a beginning level, was a lot different than it was even when I retired over nine years ago. Kindergarten then and even first grade when I started school was mostly based on socialization and acclimation to an educational environment. In Mrs. Marrs' class, academics revolved around some basic skills. We were taught to read basic sight words, write the letters of the alphabet, at least be able to say our names and addresses. As the school year progressed, Mrs. Marrs taught us to eventually write our names and addresses, count at least to twenty-five or thirty, and write the numbers to twenty-five or thirty. We learned colors, shapes, and simple spatial relationships such as first, last, in the middle, left side, right side, up, down, and so on. I understand that kindergarten instruction now goes much beyond those simple exercises we did because a number of children have attended preschool programs where those concepts that once belonged in kindergarten are now taught in preschool. It sounds like a great idea to me, but what happens to the child who has no access to preschool whether due to money, family circumstances, or location? It seems to me we may be making a big assumption that certain learning readiness skills should already be in place by time a child enters kindergarten. Yet there is a real possibility that the readiness may not have taken place to the level we assume and maybe not at all. That is strictly my opinion, but I think it has some validity. At some point after lunch, Mrs. Marrs would direct us all to pull our cots out onto the center of the classroom for twenty to twenty-five minutes for nap or rest time. Each classroom had a small elevated stage area perhaps six inches off the floor for us to store our cots and to be used for Show and Tell, skits, or for playtime. I doubt if you would find any such circumstances occurring in kindergarten classes across the United States anymore.

I think Mrs. Marrs is responsible for the fact that I always enjoyed school. Fortunately, school was never really a problem for me, and I think Mrs. Marrs had a lot to do with that.

When I went to first grade, my teacher was Mrs. Welch who for many years was a customer of my mother's in her beauty shop. I can still remember exactly where Mrs. Welch lived on Erie Street, near Sam Giambrone's house in which Joe and Verna Cristiano rented an apartment when they were first married. Mrs. Welch was probably ten years older than my mother, about forty-five to fifty years old when I was in her class. She was another good teacher whom I remember very well. A situation arose several times, which really wasn't a problem; it may have been indicative of future situations. After doing about fifteen or twenty minutes of instruction, Mrs. Welch would assign the entire class seatwork for us to practice what she had just instructed. As we completed the assignment, Mrs. Welch would walk around the classroom and help individual students. I was lucky in that I usually caught on quickly to whatever Mrs. Welch was teaching. While the other kids were completing the assignment, I was usually done and then would take it upon myself to walk around the classroom helping the other kids. I don't think it was really a problem for Mrs. Welch, but she'd rather that I didn't do it. To alleviate the situation, she would have me stand out in the hall, not so much as a punishment for misbehavior but more to keep me from distracting the other students so that she could help them. The janitor at Reese Road School was a man named Pat Amendolare whose family had been friends with my mother's family for three generations. When Pat would be working in the school, sweeping the halls, emptying the trash, mopping the cafeteria after lunch, or whatever he was working on at that time, he would see me standing in the hall and ask Mrs. Welch if it was okay if I went with him to sweep, empty the trash, and so forth. Again, I think not being in the hall as a punishment, Mrs. Welch would agree. Pat and I would then move through the school completing his daily work. I can remember, as if it were yesterday, Pat emptying the garbage in the cafeteria and me standing there handing him the clean garbage bags to put in the pails. I can remember, as if it were yesterday, pushing a big, probably four-foot-wide broom up one side of the corridor and down the other as vividly as the day I did it. One incident comes to mind, this time for misbehavior, and looking back after all those years of teaching, I think Mrs. Welch may have gone too far when she had me stand in the classroom closet with the door closed. When the school day ended and my classmates were all dismissed, I was left still standing in the closet. When the school bus went by my house, and I didn't get off, obviously my mother was concerned. She called the school in somewhat of a panic, which is understandable, and the principal, a man named Rudy Egnazyck, went to Mrs. Welch's class to find out where I was. Mrs. Welch was horrified. She had forgotten about me and left me standing there in the closet. Needless to say, that was an issue. Being that my mother knew her for a long time as one of her customers, she did not make a huge problem of it and was pretty understanding, but she certainly was not thrilled about it. My mother thought then and, I think, even now that Mrs. Welch had stepped over the line.

My willingness as a first grader to help my classmates may have been an early harbinger of the possibility that I would someday make a career of teaching. Pat Amendolare picking me to be the one to help him in his daily work at Reese Road School may also have been another early indication of my potential to someday be the King of Orchard Street. The king title being a huge honor that can only be bestowed on me by you, the reader, and my competition is formidable.

John-John

I first mentioned the concept behind and the possibilities for *The King of Orchard Street* when I ran into John-John Tubia and his wife, Brenda, at Sangertown Mall. After we talked a few minutes, I mentioned to John-John the King of Orchard Street project. That really got his attention as if throwing a hungry tiger a steak. He listened intently for about thirty seconds, then made a flash decision that he was ready to jump right in. He mentioned that it was something he had thought about for a long time, and he had stories that he could tell for hours on end. We discussed my time line, which would likely start in about a year from that date and would probably take two to three years to write, edit, publish, and so forth. John-John was interested. I think if I had my laptop with me, he would have started right there. I further explained that there were other people ahead of him to tell their stories like Donnie Ruffalo, Johnny Kipper, and myself, but eventually he would get his chance.

After that discussion, John-John's attention quickly turned to his number one issue in this world other than his wife, children, and grandchildren, that being high school and college basketball. If there ever was a basketball enthusiast in this world, it is John-John Tubia. We then discussed a group of individuals in Herkimer called the Herkimer 9 that has recently begun to raise funds to field and enter a team named the Herkimer Originals in a minor league called the American Basketball Association. Sports history generally accepts the inventor of basketball as a professor and instructor at Springfield College in Massachusetts Dr. James Naismith in about 1891. The purpose of Naismith, legend has it, inventing the game was to keep young athletes in shape during the winter months between football, baseball, and soccer. The original basketball was a soccer ball with laces on it, and games were run strictly as a conditioning program. The Herkimer 9 dispute that fact. Their contention is that basketball was invented in spring of 1891, but before Naismith in the fall of 1891, by William Lambert, the director of the Herkimer YMCA. Perhaps not long before Naismith in Massachusetts but, the Original 9 contend, still definitely before Naismith. All of prior invention theory is based on a book written by Frank Basloe entitled *I Grew Up with Basketball*. Lore has it that Lambert invented the rim, was the first person to put the rim on a backboard, and his mother knitted the first net.

As with basketball, the origin of baseball is equally cloudy. For well over one hundred years, baseball has generally been known to have originated in Cooperstown, New York, by a prominent West Point graduate, and later Civil War general Abner Doubleday. Although Doubleday never laid any claim to be the inventor of baseball, a letter from mining engineer named Abner Graves around 1860 gave Abner Doubleday credit as being the inventor of baseball. Others claim it was not even invented in the United States but was played as an American version of the English game rounders. A third theory is that the first game ever played was in Elysian Fields in about 1815, at the corner of Washington and 11th Streets in Hoboken, New Jersey. A bank clerk in New York City named Edwin Kytril is said to have written the rules. Edward Widmar, a Harvard student, credits Alexander Cartwright with writing the original rules for baseball based on an October 21, 1845, letter in a New York City newspaper reporting about a game between the New York Ball Club and a team from Brooklyn. Clearly many theories about where major sports originated but nothing to assign the origin of each to who, when, and where exactly.

Since the beginning of March, the date today being April 8, I had been waiting for the opportunity to contact John-John Tubia to determine if he was still interested in the King of Orchard Street project. I waited until mid-April because I knew that the 2022 NCAA basketball tournament was in full force until then. I would love to be a fly on the wall over the past five or six weeks for a few hours a day to find out with John-John was doing. Yet I really don't need to be that fly, because I know what he was doing. From the first game at about noon, with teams from whatever conference, to the last game that ended at about midnight on about four different channels, John Tubia was watching the NCAA tournament. I bet while watching two or three games on the Quick View, he was DVRing another one. I bet when the men's tournament wasn't on, he was watching the women's tournament. I bet on the NCAA's off nights, he was watching the games he had on DVR and the NIT tournament. I bet that now that all three tournaments were over and the high school girls tournaments were in full swing, he was watching that. He'd still be watching DVRs, replays, and videos of those games probably until June or July. To rise to the top of any business, sport, career, and the like, you must have full devotion to what you're doing. You don't rise to the level of John Wooden, Dean Smith, or Mike Krzyzewski without full dedication to your career. Given the right opportunity at the right time, John-John Tubia might have been able to rise to that level of success. From a CYO basketball player with Sam Reina as the coach and his now Frankfort legendary phrase, "Judas Priest," to a Frankfort High School varsity and JV player, to pick up games as children in the North Side School playground, and later as teenagers and young adults at the Frankfort Hilltop playground, John-John Tubia has been consumed by basketball.

Still, I know there is a lot more to his life than just basketball. Now with the process of determining the King of Orchard Street, John-John Tubia is about to get the chance to tell his story.

I know it'll be rich and lush. I'll bet my last dollar that it will be hysterical too. As only John-John could do it.

*****

I spoke to John-John on about April 20 concerning a date for us to begin working on *The King of Orchard Street*. He was happy to hear from me as we exchanged the usual pleasantries.

We then began to discuss a time line. John-John told me he and his wife, Brenda, were planning on a vacation to Myrtle Beach, South Carolina, about April 24 and returning on about May 1. John told me that he would call me when he got home from Myrtle Beach or, as they call it in Whitesboro, Myrtle Debbie. I have no idea why it is called that, and I have only ever heard it in Whitesboro, but that is the slang name I hear all the time. John-John suggested we could probably start working on about May 5. I told him I would wait to hear from him when he got home, and we could set up a start date. He called me on May 3, and we agreed to meet on May 5 for our first session, then see how it went from there to set up other dates. He informed me that he and Brenda had decided not to go to Myrtle Beach after all because he checked the weather for that week in the area and the forecast was rainy and the temperature was only in fifties for four out of seven days that they intended to be there. He thought it would be a waste of money to go if the weather was not going to cooperate, so he called the hotel and rescheduled for the beginning of June when the weather was likely to be better. The hotel agreed to make the change without a problem, and the reservation for June was confirmed. That worked out good for both of us because John-John didn't get stuck in bad weather while paying hotel bills and we could still arrange a date during the first week of May to begin his take on the King of Orchard Street. We agreed to meet at his house in Herkimer at 10:00 a.m. on May 5. My guesstimate is we will probably work on *The King of Orchard Street* for two or three hours to get started and then arrange other dates as needed. It will be good to see John-John and spend some time with him since I don't get to do that very often anymore like we did when we spent hours together as kids on Orchard Street. These sessions of reminiscing, discussing, and revising always prove to be a lot of fun no matter whose story is being told. I bet all our brains, individually and collectively, really light up as each session progresses, and that is indubitably a good thing. We will start tomorrow at 10:00 a.m.

I got to John-John's house a little later than I had planned, probably around 10:30 as opposed to 10:00. I knew exactly where he lived, the street at least, because I drove by that neighborhood for many years on my way from Frankfort with my mom, dad, and sister to Pine Lake. I always thought it was a quaint little section of Herkimer with two or three picturesque streets running side by side West Lake Avenue and Lake Street that both became dead ends when they ran into a decent-sized lake named Mirror Lake at the end of both streets. Both were very serene neighborhoods that always reminded me of a Swiss Alps village that you might see a picture of in a promotional brochure. A very stable, inviting look for sure. When I got to the front of his house, John-John was waiting for me at the door as I parked my car in the street. When John-John came out of the house, he directed me to put my car in his driveway to prevent it from getting hit because "they drive way too fast up and down the street," but he wanted me to park on the left-hand side of the driveway so Brenda could get out of the garage when she's ready to go. When I walked in the house, Brenda was storing some items in the kitchen cabinets. It is a very nice, neat house that reminded me of my father and mother's house that I grew up in, likely built around the same time, the early 1900s, but obviously built to last as it sure did. If only those walls could talk. John-John and I sat at the kitchen table. We started to reminisce and discuss what we've been doing lately. The usual small talk about children, grandchildren, and health that invariably begins most conversations when you see a longtime friend that you have not seen in a while. After we went back and forth, Brenda got her bearings as to what we were doing as did John-John and the discussion turned to the more mundane aspects of writing a collaborative book. I explained how I didn't think there would be any problems between him and me with an endeavor such as this, yet sticky situations have been known to occur. I discussed with him that there were four options, at least that I was aware of currently, that he could eventually choose from and probably even more, but I would have to consult with an attorney about that at some point. He could choose one at any time, and again there were probably even more than four. Option one was that he could back out right now, and we would not go any further. Option two is that we start this process, but at any time he could back out, and whatever we had done I would sign off as his property. Option three was that we finish his take on the King of Orchard Street, and he then could sign off that I am the author, the sole owner of all the rights to *The King of Orchard Street*, and thus only I would be eligible for any of the benefits or proceeds that might come of it. Option four is I am the author, but he is the sole owner of his end, and he can do whatever he wants with it, and only he would be eligible for any of the proceeds or benefits of his section. Again, we would both have to sign off on whichever option he chooses of the four outlined or, if there are more options, whichever one he chooses based on the entire universe of options available. Still, all the options required more legal information. All of this would have to be ironed out at some point before any publication agreement was signed and paid for to ascertain what belonged to who. I explained to John-John that I would pay the publication fees, but the proceeds after the publication is where the issues usually arise. John-John told me exactly what I hoped he would. That he would want nothing from this project other than to get his story told. He had no long-term plans. It was just a fun thing that he wanted to do, and whatever happens, happens. Exactly the way I felt too, but I wanted to be clear that at some point we had to come to a formal agreement to prevent any misunderstanding.

I am not prepared to lose a lifelong friend over an innocent "beauty contest."

John-John agreed completely. All he wanted was his story told, which was all I wanted too.

He quickly scanned his notes and began.

"I remember playing two-hand touch football in the street all day with Johnny Kipper, Donnie Ruffalo, all the Scalise boys, and Jimmy Congelo. We always had to be on the lookout for cars moving east and west on the street for fear they didn't see us. When one of us would spot a car coming, the person would yell out "car" so we could all get out of the way. At night we changed the game to hide-and-seek. Mostly we hid behind parked cars, in people's backyards, or by the railroad tracks. We spent a lot of time being in places that were unsafe for small and unsupervised kids. We were constantly in the street, by the railroad tracks, near the Mohawk River, Barge Canal, and in other people's backyards, which was all trespassing. All the places we should not have been. All unsupervised, very dangerous places for children. We would hunt by the "Flats," which is what filled up with water when the Mohawk River overflowed, shooting at about anything that moved with Eddie and Mike Scalise as our hunting partners. Johnny Kipper, Jimmy Congelo, and I would fish from Moyer Creek down through the Barge Canal and right into the Mohawk River. We caught all kinds of fish. We would catch trout, huge carp, and sometimes even a bass or pike. Especially in the spring when the water was high, we could pull almost anything out of that water. Johnny Kipper loved to fish. He would stay there all day, happy as he could be. Before the Frankfort Pool opened up, we would swim in Moyer Creek a lot too. We had a rope that hung over the creek from which we used to swing out with over the water and drop in.

"One hot summer afternoon, we were all there swimming, and one of the families that lived on Orchard Street showed up to swim. Not a big deal, we all swam there. There must have been twenty of us in the water swimming, fishing, or whatever. The father was really skinny, and his wife was pretty obese. As I was swimming and splashing around, I looked over and here was the guy and his wife doing whatever they were doing. I really wasn't sure what it was they were doing but it really caught my eye. When I pointed them out to my cousin Alex Rosemyer, he filled me in. Here was the two of them in broad daylight on a rock with probably twenty kids around, three or four of them their own kids, having sex. I have to admit, looking back now, it was funny. He was lost in her charms, shall we say, completely insensible, with about ten kids watching the two of them from the bank of the creek. I have no recollection of her situation, but the entire scene was certainly compelling from my perspective. That sequence of events has been burned on my mind since the day it happened. A few years ago, one of my wife's relatives died, and naturally we went to the wake. As I was sitting there, a guy came in and told my wife's cousin that he was a minister who came to pay his respects to the deceased. He continued that he knew the deceased very well, and if the family didn't mind, he would like to say a few words. I told Brenda right away that I knew the guy from Orchard Street. He was one of the kids of the skinny guy and his wife who were having sex while ten of us eight-to-fifteen-year-olds watched. All a true story right up to a wake about three years ago. I hope for the family's sake, he really was a minister, or it was a great example of rebranding yourself some fifty-five years later. I am not really certain which of the couples' kids he was, because they had four or five, but I got a huge kick out of the whole thing from way back in about 1963 right up until that night in 2019. Sardonic, to say the least.

"One of the things I laugh about is, is it "crik" or is it "creek"? I have always said "crik," and most locals say "crek." Which is it? English is a weird language. We used to walk the railroad tracks up to get to the creek. As the trains went by, there were often many hobos riding them. We used to compete to see who could walk on one rail the farthest without falling off. It got to be a real competition. Sometimes the hobos would see Moyer Creek and jump off the train to wash in the creek, get water, swim, or just sit on the bank. They seemed hopeless but at the same time content. It was not like they wanted anything, mostly to just be left alone. I don't remember them ever saying anything to us. They were harmless. I didn't really feel sorry for them, because it looked like they were doing what they wanted to do, living how they wanted to live. How can you fault them for that? They were content. Looking back, maybe they had the right idea. We spend our lives chasing what? For what? We all end up in the same place. Truly philosophical questions that maybe those hobos had a clearer knowledge of than we do.

"Wow, I really got philosophically offtrack there.

"A clear instance I do recall concerning a hobo was a nice summer day when we were at the creek, and somebody, I don't know who, shot a good-sized snapping turtle. One of the hobos hanging out by the creek wanted it, so whoever shot it gave it to him. The guy cleaned the turtle out of the shell and made turtle soup cooked over a campfire. I recollect thinking that it smelled good but would not eat any because the turtle came out of the canal, which was dirty. The hobo had a few cooking utensils, a spoon, and a bowl. The poor guy must have been hungry as hell because he ate that soup real quick. I think he did offer us some, but we all turned it down. I found out years later that turtle soup is a delicacy, and it could not have been made any fresher in that it was just pulled out of the canal, but even at that, I wasn't eating any of it.

"We would walk farther and farther west on the tracks every day. When we got to Nicastro's farm, we would usually stop at what we called the Swinging Bridge. When we walked across the bridge going north toward the Schuyler side of the river, I would look down at what was in reality a twelve-inch pipe we were walking on and see the whirlpools of water spinning around beneath me. Talk about scaring the snot out of maybe a ten-year-old kid. I would run across to the Schuyler side but eventually realized that I would have to cross back to get on the Frankfort side and then home. It took me a while to figure it out, but eventually I got it. Duh!

"Alex Rosemyer was always the brains of it all. He was the one who figured out where we could get the wood and nails to build forts, boxcars, or whatever we had in mind. At one point Alex got some cut short telephone poles that we dug holes for and placed in the ground to use as pillars to build on. He got a bunch of lumber from somewhere, and we started to build a clubhouse. We must have had some adult help because we built a nice one on property that belonged to the New York Central Railroad. The fort had two floors and was high enough to stand up in. Looking back, it was nice. We didn't have any windows, but it was warm inside. Some adult with knowledge of carpentry, maybe even my father, must have helped us build it. The entire structure must have been there for two years, but eventually, New York Central realized it was on their property and tore it down. We were heartbroken when we saw it demolished, but kids being kids, we just moved on to the next King of Orchard Street adventure without even thinking about it. What a carefree ever-widening environment we lived in. It was about as near perfection as an individual could find in this world anyway.

I am so happy and proud it all happened and would give anything to do again."

Tears fell for the first time from John-John. Tears for about the third time from me since the group of us started writing *The King of Orchard Street*.

We stopped, got a drink of water, went to the bathroom, and started up again.

"At one point," John-John continued, "it was a big thing to put a penny on the railroad track and wait for a train to come by and run it over. Dangerous? A bunch of seven- to twelve-year-old kids waiting by the side of a railroad track for a train to come by only about ten feet from where we were standing? After the train passed, we would all go get our pennies, which would be flattened right out. Then we started putting nickels being that silver looked better. Eventually, we stopped doing it altogether because a rumor spread that the penny could derail a train when the train ran it over. Of course, that was only a rumor, but we all believed it. I mean, could one single pebble flip over a motorcycle traveling sixty miles an hour? I doubt it, but it kept us away from the trains at least somewhat. Yet I bet there are instances of people who got hit by trains while trying to put their penny down or go pick it up. The best bet is to never put anything on a train track or even go near one."

I agreed with that wholeheartedly.

"I don't know how many times my mother told me to stay away from those train tracks and how dangerous it was to go anywhere near a train. She must have told me ten times a day, but I never listened for one second. They were like a magnet for all of us. Thank God no one ever got seriously hurt or killed," I added.

John-John nodded his head in agreement.

"My mother told me the same thing all day long too. I never listened either. Do you remember the illegal dump we had on the side of the hill sloping down to the canal? My mom would give me bags of garbage to throw in the dump. The whole side of the hill was covered with garbage bags from every household on the street. It must have been 100 percent illegal, but no one cared. There was no DEC in those days, and if there was, they didn't pay any attention or got paid to overlook everything. Who knows what was dumped there illegally for years? Now, you go to jail for ten years if you get caught dumping like that. In the end it was weird to do it, but it never seemed to hurt anything except smell in the summer. Even at that, it was hard to tell if it was the dump or the canal that stunk.

"Smell or not, about four o' clock we would all gather on the north side of Orchard Street, by your grandmother's house, and wait for what we called the Gum Truck to come by. A guy, who I think lived on Orchard Street, worked for Beech-Nut at the factory in Canajoharie. Apparently, at the end of the shift, if there was any gum that was defective—maybe the packaging was wrong or the color of the gum was off—the employees could take it home. Whoever this guy was, he would take a bunch of whole packs of gum and come to Orchard Street to pass it out to us. He did these two or three times a week, and we were thrilled by it. What a memory, free gum regularly to a bunch of kids. A piece? No, the whole pack. A slice? No, a piece of heaven right there in the middle of the block on West Orchard Street. Rip-roaring fun that I will never forget. There were other guys who worked on the trains who would do the same kind of thing. When the engine would disconnect from the main train in Schuyler, it would pull cars of cut trees to the yard at the Union Fork and Hoe to make handles for shovels. The cars would unload the lumber, then move west to the other end of Orchard Street to drop off grain at Corrado's Mill. At the end of the train, there would be a caboose for the employees to sleep, eat, or whatever they did in their off-time. I remember the back of the caboose had a small platform with steps and a rail like you would see in the old cowboy movies. The workers would come out on the deck and throw us packs of gum, just like the Beech-Nut guy would do from his truck. The pack everyone wanted was the Fruit Stripe. If you were lucky enough to pick a pack of Fruit Stripe, it was above and beyond the regular luck of getting free gum that day. Again, could it get any better than that? The best spot to wait for the caboose was your grandmother's backyard, like the best spot to wait for the Beech-Nut guy was on the sidewalk in front of your grandmothers' house. Was that a coincidence or an indicator of who lived there eventually being the King of Orchard Street? Hmm, makes you wonder?

"I was eleven or twelve years old when the whole thing ended. We got free gum right up until then. How it eventually ended was pretty sad, but in the long run it was human nature that stopped it. As the years went by, kids from other neighborhoods got wind of what was happening and started to show up on Orchard Street at about the time the Beech-Nut guy or the guys in the caboose would come by with the free gum. Naturally, we didn't like the idea, since it occurred in our neighborhood. If you didn't live in our neighborhood, you had no right to be there or get the free gum. Up until then there was never any problem. We all got the free gum. We all shared what we got including at times, reluctantly, the Fruit Stripe–flavored ones. When other kids from outside Orchard Street got involved, it started problems. It summed up the whole environment of Orchard Street. We all lived together there, helping each other out, keeping an eye on the street, and the general rule was live and let live. It stayed like that every day until usually an outside force made an issue. Then, perhaps unknowingly, we "circled the wagons" and protected ourselves. How the situation played out with the gum was a template for the entire way of life on that street. In the end, once we started arguing and there were problems with other kids from outside the neighborhood, the whole state of affairs ended. Maybe the Beech-Nut guy got another job or Beech-Nut stopped giving its employees the gum with a flaw. Maybe the guys who gave us the candy from the caboose started working on another route. Maybe they got tired of hearing us argue and just gave up because they knew how it was before other kids got involved. The only thing I know for sure is that it ended. That generous, humble, sensible, almost daily experience was finally ended by good old-fashioned human imperfections. Now that makes me sad. That makes me miss the good old days, and they aren't coming back."

Sad?

Nostalgic?

To state it compassionately, John-John sighed, took a deep breath, collected his thoughts, referred to his notes, and continued.

"I have another great Alex Rosemyer story. Again, he was always the brains of the operation, he was the one who always came up with the ideas, the materials, the whatever we needed to make it work. One day he decided we should build a raft to float on the Mohawk River. I don't know, he might have watched *The Adventures of Tom Sawyer* the night before on television. In the morning he had it all thought out, and we had to put the plan into action. Of course, we never considered it might be dangerous, or we might be breaking a law. After Alex laid out the plan for us, we all jumped right in.

"First, I don't know where he would get them but told us he would procure the necessary materials. We would need barrels, boards, nails, rope, and the like. None of has had enough money to buy what we needed, but Alex assured us he would get everything we required for the project.

"Sure enough, within two or three days, we had all the materials that we needed. We had four fifty-gallon drums. We had about fifteen eight-foot lengths of lumber an inch thick and about ten inches wide. We had nails for which I think we pooled our money together, about three dollars, to buy them at Corrado's, and we had rope. Everything we needed to get this project going. We set out to work. Again, I think we must have had adult help. I don't recollect who, if anybody, because after a few days we had this thing finished, and it looked pretty good. It was about six feet wide and about eight feet long, but the big question was, would it float? I'm guessing now, but I think the barrels came from Corrado's Mill, the lumber came off the trains that were constantly running back and forth between the Union Tool Company and Corrado's loaded with lumber or grain, the nails we bought, and the rope…I have no idea. The wood we used for the deck of the raft was some type of hardwood like oak or cherry. Expensive material like would be used on a dining room floor. Imagine using wood like that to float in that muddy Mohawk River. That wood should have been on the deck of a multimillion-dollar yacht, and here we were about to put it on the deck of a homemade raft we cobbled together to float in the Mohawk

River. Goodness, what a waste. Yet lo and behold, miraculously, all the materials appeared, and the raft got assembled. Once we had it assembled, we realized there was another big concern. That being how would we get it to the bank of the Mohawk River? Once we got in the water, it floating or not would be an issue, but for now the project was how to get it to the water? Running east and west behind Corrado's, along the railroad tracks behind your grandmother's and Falcone's house, was a road the railroad company used it to move their employees, equipment, and materials along the tracks. Alex, my cousin Paul Tubia, you remember Paw-Paw, one or two of the Scalise boys, and I were picking this thing up, pushing it, pulling it, dragging it or whatever, trying to get it about two hundred yards to the riverbank. After quite a bit of struggle, we did get it where there was access to the water. Next, we had to get it in the water to test if it would float. We gently slid it down a small hill into the water, and sure enough, it floated. You would think we had just landed on the moon. All our brains, individually and collectively, lit up like a Christmas tree. We were all smiling from ear to ear instantly. We made plans to float down the Mohawk River to Herkimer. We made plans to float down the river to Utica. We made plans to fish day and night, and now we could catch the big fish that we always thought were out in the middle of the river. Our brains really were set ablaze.

"All the time we were doing this all, I don't think any of our parents knew what we were up to, and I think if they had found out, they would have put a stop to it right away. Clearly, it was a dangerous situation right from the start and now even more dangerous with this homemade raft bobbing up and down in the water.

"Even beyond that, talk about cojones. Here's a bunch of us with materials likely stolen from Corrado's and the New York Central Railroad, on the railroad company's property without permission, behind Corrado's, pushing, pulling, and dragging this contraption we had made down to the Mohawk River in broad daylight. Huge cojones there. The kind you can hear clanging as the individual walks along the street, and we thought nothing of it. That's what we had to do, and that's what we were going to do. End of the discussion.

"The next day we set out to board this waterborne 'hooptie' floating in the Mohawk River, but immediately, we came into a big problem. I still think my cousin Alex must have watched *The Adventures of Tom Sawyer* on *The Wonderful World of Disney* the night before he got this raft idea because our problem was now how we were going to make it move. Alex, always with the ideas, went into the woods and found broken tree branches or trees that had fallen, which were about six or eight feet long that we were going to put in the bottom of the river and push ourselves along like Tom Sawyer and Huckleberry Finn did on the Mississippi River. Next problem: the branches kept breaking as soon as we pushed off with them. Plainly, we needed a better idea, and we found it. Someone, I don't remember who, possibly in the makeshift dump we all used, found three or four eight-foot steel poles that people often used to put an over-the-air television antenna on and then attach the pole with antenna to their house. Quickly, another problem solved, and we were ready to go again. I never knew, but the Mohawk and, I imagine, all rivers do indeed have an ebb and flow of the water almost like a tide. We got our raft out in the backwash of the little harbor where the Frankfort Marina is now with three or four of us on it and the "tide" pulling us out toward the actual Mohawk River channel. Needless to say, now we were all scared to death. We pushed with the poles, got ourselves back into the harbor, and dragged the raft up on the bank. Thank God that harbor, which is only one of two natural harbors on the entire Mohawk River, was there. It saved our lives. Over the next few days, we must have gotten out on that thing fifteen or twenty times, but we stayed in that backwash area and out of the Mohawk River channel. Again, I don't think anyone saw us or knew what we were doing.

"After about two weeks on the water, I believe it was my mother who spotted us or figured out what we had been doing all along. Once the word spread, all the adults in each family involved were dead set against the idea that we had activated for about a month. Eventually, someone had to get hurt. The last time I saw the raft, we had done our usual thing during the day and had dragged it up on the bank that night. The next day, when we went back to the river, it was gone. We never found out what happened to it, but I have always had an idea that my uncle Eric was in the end the demise of the whole thing. Do you remember when my cousin Carmie Tubia drowned? Carmie and Debbie Puzzilla were on the ice of the river when Carmie fell through the ice and drowned. It was horrible for all of us. My uncle Eric and aunt Nina were crushed as was everybody else on Orchard Street and in Frankfort as a whole. I don't remember if Carmie drowned before or after our raft. If it was before, it would be terrible to think that the raft was somehow a harbinger of a tragedy that would occur years later. If it was after Carmie's death, I think my uncle got rid of it out of fear that someone else might meet the same terrible fate as his daughter. I suspect the raft was after Carmie's death, and that was the reason my uncle got rid of it. Either way, I have always suspected my uncle had something to do with it. Once my uncle Eric got wind of what we were doing, he pushed it into the channel so that it would float away. I think he was very fearful what might have happened if we continued on that raft. Looking back, all these years later, I think he saved one or all our lives. I think that one of us would have gotten hurt if we continued being on that water. He likely kept our families from a lot of potential suffering. I thank my lucky stars every day that none of us ever got hurt. Not just with that raft but with many very dangerous things we did all the time. Climbing on the trains, climbing on the boxcars, by the river, hunting and fishing. All of it unsupervised and very dangerous. Only by the grace of God are we sitting here talking about it.

"That whole area of Orchard Street and Litchfield Street even toward Railroad Street was in and of itself a small business district. On Orchard Street was Corrado's Mill on the west end of the street. On Litchfield Street was Puzze's Restaurant and the Argonne Grill. In the middle of Orchard Street was Zito's Restaurant, which Rossi Caruso later ran for years as the Grand Prix. On the east end of Orchard Street was Billis's Hotel, the GLF Corporation, and the back entrance to the Union Fork and Hoe Company lumberyard. The bars, restaurants, and hotels that popped up running east to west on Orchard Street were mostly a result of the Erie Canal opening in the 1820s. The canal moved people and commerce east to west for over

150 years and still does to this day but mostly for recreation now. The people on the boats and the employees too obviously need some accommodations, thus all the old hotels sprang up. I think that the house Ruth Morgan lived in with her uncle Wally was at one time a hotel of some sort, but I never remember it being as such. I only remember it as Wally Richardson and his family living there.

"There was one night when I was about ten years old that I will never forget. At about 11:00 p.m. there were five or six of us hanging out on the street. It must have been in the summer because the bars were open with all doors open too. We could hear and see a lot of what was going on inside. A group of us were sitting outside Puzze's, listening to the band, which I think knew about three songs that they played over and over. Above the usual noise coming out of a bar, we could hear yelling, arguing, and people screaming at each other. Naturally, we went over to take a closer look. Puzze had hired a woman, I believe her name was Lillian, to be the bartender at night. Sheppy Caruso and a bunch of his friends were in the bar, and Sheppy was telling some pretty obscene stories about where he had been and what he had done in his life. I imagine the stories were getting graphic and pretty disgusting for that matter. At some point Lillian told Sheppy that was enough. There was a lady in the bar, and enough was enough. Sheppy really took exception to that statement. He looked around the bar and asked Lillian where the lady who was present was. Lillian told Shep that she was a lady, and again enough was enough. That's all Sheppy had to hear. Lillian continued to tell him that he was nothing but a dirty fag, and he needed to keep his mouth shut because he was gross. Sheppy started screaming at her that she was a slut and the last person with any right to say anything like that. Sheppy continued that she had five children all out of wedlock with five different guys, and who was she to talk? Sheppy said that the reason her boyfriend left her was because he was having better sex with him than he was with her. I can assure you it was a lot more graphic than that, and Sheppy made the entire scenario abundantly clear. Another guy sitting at the bar decided to get involved. Shep told him that he needed to shut his mouth. This was between him and Lillian alone. Sheppy threatened to beat the daylights out of the guy. Then he'd have to go home and tell his wife that he got beat up by Sheppy of all people. To add to the embarrassment, the guy's wife knew Sheppy and exactly what he was. After a few minutes, the whole thing spilled out into the driveway between Puzze's bar and his house. Sheppy was beating the hell out of both Lillian and the other guy. Lillian got enough of a beating that she just ran away from the entire scene, and I never saw her again. Sheppy knocked the guy out on the grass in front of Puzze's house. Sheppy could care less about the whole thing, went back in the bar and continued to drink as if nothing had happened. After about ten minutes, another guy came out of the bar, picked up the guy knocked out on the lawn, brushed him off, put him in a car, and they drove away. Clearly not a scene for a bunch of eleven-year-olds to be exposed to, but it happened, and I'll never forget it. I don't think I ever saw Lillian working at the bar after that. That scene was enough to scare anybody away. Permanently.

"Bars weren't the only business on Orchard Street, but there were sure a lot of them. When I was about ten years old, two guys who were Donnie Ruffalo's uncles opened up across the street from my father's house a small, and I mean small, store. I wouldn't even call it a store. It was more like a big living room. I don't think it was thirty feet by thirty feet. It was an early version of what is now called a convenience store. The store was packed with so much merchandise you could hardly move. It was hanging from the ceilings. It was stocked on the shelves that looked like they were going to tip over because they were so front-heavy. There was a counter that had a cash register on it and so much merchandise on the counter you couldn't see the cash register. As with any store, there were deliveries of new merchandise two or three times a week. One delivery guy we all terrorized when he came to make his stop. We would watch for the truck to drive south on Railroad Street, make a right on Orchard Street, and park in front of the store. It was Coca-Cola delivery, and the truck was like the trucks that you see now with rolling four-foot-wide overhead doors on the bed of the trailer that the delivery guy would push up and then unload the cases he needed to bring in the store. We waited for this guy to show up. Once he went around the passenger side of the truck to load his handcart to bring inside, we vaulted into action. When he walked in the store with the handcart, we would run over and grab the bottles of Coke off the truck. They were the small eight- to ten-ounce glass bottles that you would also see in the vending machines in those days. There used to be a saying that if someone wore very thick glasses, the lenses of the glasses were as thick as the bottom of Coke bottles. We used to call them Coke bottle glasses. The guy could never catch us because when three or four of us took the bottles, we would scatter, and he could never catch anyone. He used to swear at us, call us little bastards, Guineas, dagos, wops, whatever he wanted to call us. He would threaten to call the police and we were all going to be in jail, that none of us were any good and we deserved a lot of punishment. The more he tormented us, the more we tormented him right back. We would even go so far as to take bottle openers and open up the soda bottles to fill up our glasses, then run away drinking the soda. We got to the point that this guy made us so angry that we would open up the soda bottles and just let it run on the ground because we couldn't stand this guy. When he went back to the plant, I'm sure he had to pay the bill for any soda he was unable to deliver and couldn't return. We didn't care. That was his problem. We treated him equally as badly as he treated us. At my age, I would never want my kids to do anything like that, but we didn't know, and we didn't care. As far as we were concerned, it was payback for the way he treated us.

"On the other hand, there was another guy, I think he was from Little Falls, who was a Hostess cupcake delivery man. When he would make a delivery to the store, if there was a new product coming onto the market, he would tell us to go into the store and get some of the free samples that Hostess was using to introduce the product. When he came for the delivery one day, I think I was the only kid around, he told me to go in the store and get a free cupcake. I went into the store and walked over to the Hostess display and took three cupcakes. Donnie's uncle, I believe his name was Earl, told me that I had to pay for the cupcakes. I explained to him that the delivery man had told me that the cupcakes were samples to introduce new products and showed Earl the label that was clearly marked free samples, not to be resold. He insisted that they weren't free, but since I came in the store, he would give me one free if I bought one. In other words, buy one get one free. I told him that I wasn't going to pay for anything, that they were free samples, and I showed him the package again. My Dad was across the street and heard this commotion in the store, so he came over to see what the problem was. Earl insisted to my father that they were "buy one, get one free," and I insisted that the package said they were free samples, not to be resold. My father looked at the package and agreed with me because free sample was plainly written on the package. Then Earl still made it a problem in that I could only take one, and I had three. My dad took them from me, looked out the door, and called my sister Debbie to come over. He gave one to my sister, gave me one back, and he kept the third one for himself. At this point Earl was livid. He told my father not to come in the store anymore to keep my sister and me out too. He didn't want my father's business and that it wasn't worth all the problem that I was making for some cupcakes, which he still insisted were "buy one, get one free." My father was having none of it. Free cupcakes were free cupcakes. My father, my sister, and I all turned around almost uniformly and walked out the door, leaving Earl standing there fuming. I don't think Earl spoke to my father for at least a year, and by that time, frankly, the store was going out of business. I think his attitude had a lot to do with that, especially if you would take the time to rip off little kids. Plainly, he wasn't going to go too far as a businessman. As I said, within a year or two of that incident, the store was out of business. It was fair play at its finest.

"When Rossi Caruso was running Zito's Restaurant as the Grand Prix, he made it into a strip bar that really caught all of our attention. You told me that you and Donnie would watch from across the street behind the bushes in front of your aunt Josie's house. We went even farther than that. To the right-hand side of the entrance to the bar was a picture window that showed behind the bar and into what was the dining room years ago. In the area to the left of the bar, Rossi put a stage and go-go cages for the strippers. We would start out kind of nonchalantly, maybe fifteen or twenty feet from the window in front of Internicola's house like we were just talking and milling around. As it started to get darker, we would get closer and closer to the picture window until we were practically standing right in front of it on a little bit of an angle to the right side so we could see strippers in the cages. Rossi who would let us stand there for a while, but then eventually, when the group started to get noticeable, maybe six or seven of us, Rossi would come out and shoo us away. We would move farther down the street to make him happy. Then again little by little we inched our way back to the window. When Rossi would notice us again, he would repeat the process. This would go on to maybe ten or eleven o'clock when we would have to go in because our parents would be looking for us. We were discreet about it in terms of our parents seeing us in that we faked it very well as a bunch of kids just milling around talking. Rossi knew exactly what we were doing. What harm was it for a bunch of ten- to fifteen-year-old boys to watch strippers through a window? At least that is what we thought. At the time it was fine. Yet as I've said so many times, looking back now, I wouldn't want my kids or grandkids doing it. Inappropriate and unsupervised but, on the other hand, live and let live. That's a pretty good spin years later. Don't you think?"

I laughed and agreed 100 percent.

John-John continued. "Behind the Grand Prix, for some reason I don't know, my grandfather had a chicken coop. One coop was for about ten hens, and the other was for a rooster. Every morning one of us would walk across the street to the chicken coop to get most times about a dozen eggs. One morning my grandfather asked me to walk over and get the eggs. Probably being half-asleep, I opened the rooster coop instead of the chicken coop. I don't know how many years my grandfather had that rooster, but it was big, and it was nasty. He had built a little ramp in front of both coops so the chickens and the rooster could get in and out when he wanted them to feed. The second I opened the rooster coop door, that bird came running down the ramp after me. He scared me so much that I just started running west across Falcone's backyard and your grandmother's toward Corrado's Mill. My grandfather, from the other side of the street, saw what was happening and ran across the street. You have to get a mental picture of this. Here I was running as fast as I could with the rooster right behind me, chasing me, and my grandfather right behind the rooster, chasing it. My grandfather was calling the rooster every name that he could think, and little by little he was catching up to it. Finally, when he did catch up to it, he reached down, grabbed this nasty thing by the neck, twisted its neck, then yanked its head off, almost killing it instantly. Then he threw it in the brush over by the railroad tracks. He looked at me, told me to go get the eggs, and said he hated that rooster for as long as he had it. I don't think anyone ever went back to get it so that it could be cooked. My grandfather just left it there. That bird was so old and miserable the meat was probably as hard as concrete anyway.

"The likelihood of there being any more controversy with that rooster didn't exist now. My grandfather had made certain of that.

"My grandfather used to love to eat snails, in French escargot, Italian *lumaca*, or in Sicily *babbalucci*. My grandmother would put them in a pot of cold water and let them soak for a while so that they would swell up. Then slowly she would turn up the heat until the water started to boil and cooked the snails. One afternoon she was making them for my grandfather as an appetizer before dinner. When she turned up the heat, she forgot to put the cover on the pot and left the kitchen for a few minutes. As the water heated up, the snails tried to escape. When she came back, the snails had climbed out of the pot as the temperature of the water went up and were all over the stove, climbing up the walls, on the cabinets. Everywhere you looked there were snails. My grandmother started collecting them off the walls, the cabinets, and everywhere that she could find them, quickly putting them back in the pot to boil. Eventually, she rounded them all up, got them cooked, and served them to my grandfather with his dinner. My grandfather would take a little crab fork to dig them out of the shells and then dip them in some warmed-up butter like you would with lobster. He loved them. That day was even easier because they had all gotten out of the shells when the water started to boil, and he didn't even have to struggle getting them out.

"One thing we always did have was good food. It may not have been the kind of food that you find today in the grocery store, but it was always good. To find the kind of food we used to eat every day,

I bet you would have to look in high-priced specialty shops, and it would all cost a lot of money. We ate it because that's what we had, but today it's like high-priced fancy food. It is what it is.

"We spent way too much time climbing on trains and boxcars. There was one incident when Johnny Kipper and I were running on top of the boxcars and jumping from one to the other as we ran. After about half an hour of doing so, one of the employees for New York Central Railroad spotted us. I quickly climbed down one of the ladders that ran down the side of the boxcar and over to the sidewalk on Orchard Street to wait for Johnny. Johnny couldn't get down the ladder fast enough. He was stuck up there with the employee getting closer and closer to him. I was watching this play out and thinking how he was going to get off that boxcar before the employee got to him. I saw him moving closer to the edge, and I was hoping he was not going to jump off, but that was his only choice. That is exactly what he did. Those boxcars had to be fifteen or sixteen feet high. Johnny jumped off this thing, and as he was coming closer to the ground, I was thinking he was going to break his leg. When he hit the ground, he rolled over into a little ball and somersaulted forward with his legs absorbing all the shock, and got up to ran toward me. For those few seconds I was scared out of my wits thinking he had broken his leg or his ankle or something. It was a long way down. When he got over to me, I was very happy to find out that he didn't get hurt at all. We just nonchalantly walked away on Orchard Street as if nothing had happened. I don't know how he jumped off and didn't get seriously hurt not only by the jump but by the fact that we were playing on those boxcars. We were on those things for hours. It's amazing that no one got hurt after all the time we spent on the boxcars and around those tracks. The activity around those tracks didn't stop day or night. I don't know how any of us didn't get killed or seriously injured."

Sitting with John-John, thinking about those tracks and boxcars, made me consider how right he was that nobody ever got hurt.

Thinking back to my memory of the boxcars, I said to John-John, "Those boxcars that we used to play on have taken on a romantic perspective in American history. The idea of men 'riding the rails' has become very nostalgic. Unfortunately, for many of those men, they were homeless, jobless, searching for some sort of opportunity, and they may not have even known what they were searching for. For most, I understand it was aimless wandering with nowhere else to go and nothing else to do. The most famous man of this nature was Merle Haggard and another, perhaps not as famous but of the same sort, was Arlo Guthrie. Merle was born in Oildale, California, just about the end of the Great Depression. Merle's father died when he was very young, and Merle was deeply troubled by his father's death. Merle was incarcerated several times during his youth mostly for fighting, shoplifting, and small inconsequential crimes. Merle's mother and father moved from Checotah, Oklahoma, during the Great Depression after the barn on their family farm burned and basically bankrupted them. The mother and father then decided that maybe there were better opportunities in California, so they moved their family to Bakersfield. They rented an apartment to live in, but the family couldn't afford the rent. In the meantime, Merle's father, James, got a job working for the Santa Fe Railroad. Merle's mother and father became friends with a woman who owned a boxcar. She asked Merle's dad if he thought it could be converted into a house. Naturally, not being able to afford an apartment, Merle's father jumped at the chance since he had no housing for his family. Merle's father created a makeshift kitchen and bathroom in the boxcar, put up some walls, and separated it into two bedrooms, one for his children and one for him and his wife. Eventually, he added on the boxcar a second bathroom and another bedroom. When Merle's father died, his mother had to find a job to support the family, which left Merle and his brothers alone most of the time. With all the free time on his hands, Merle started to get in trouble. His mother had him placed in a juvenile detention home, hoping that that would correct him. At the age of thirteen, Merle was caught writing and stealing checks, thus placing him permanently in a detention home. While there he met and became friends with Bob Teague. The two of them escaped from the detention home and began to ride freight trains or hitchhike throughout California for over a year. With nowhere else to go, they finally returned to the detention home where they were accused of robbery and sentenced to jail. They were eventually released when the real thieves were arrested. The experience only made Merle more determined to do what he wanted to do with impunity. After being released from jail, he was returned to the detention home, but Merle and Bob escaped again and headed to Modesto, California. Merle held a series of jobs including truck driver, short-order cook, hay pitcher, and oil-well shooter. While in Modesto, he decided he wanted to sing. He got a guitar, and his first performance was at a bar named the Fun Center for which he was paid $5 and given a beer. Things weren't working out for Merle in Modesto, so he returned to Bakersfield and was again arrested for truancy along with petty larceny. That charge got him sent back to the detention home for fifteen months. Upon his release, he was arrested again for beating up a local boy during a robbery attempt. After that release, Merle saw the Lefty Frizzell in concert and was allowed backstage to meet him. As he performed onstage, Lefty could hear Merle singing his songs along with him. After a set Lefty then exited the stage for a break. As the show was about to resume, Lefty refused to go back on unless Merle was given a chance to sing before he returned to the stage. Merle was thrilled to perform, and the incident convinced him that music was the direction he needed to go in his life. During the day Merle would work as a farmhand or on the oil derricks, and at night he would sing in the bars.

"Around 1957 Merle married but was plagued by severe financial issues and proceeded to rob a roadhouse in Bakersfield. He was caught and sentenced to San Quentin Prison in 1958 as prisoner number 45200. While in jail, Merle started a brewing and gambling business that proved very successful. When he was caught drunk in jail, he was sent to a week of solitary confinement where he met a death row inmate named Caryl Chessman who was an author of various essays, letters, and books such as *The Kid Was a Killer* along with *Cell 2455, Death Row*. This encounter gave Merle the inkling that he could change his life this time for good. While in jail, Merle learned that his wife was expecting another man's child, which caused a great deal of stress. He was fired from his prison job and began planning another escape with an inmate named "Rabbit" James Kendrick.

Fortunately for Merle, he was dissuaded by other prisoners from attempting the escape. Rabbit Kendricks could not be dissuaded and did escape but soon after was returned to San Quentin for killing a police officer. Rabbit was sentenced to death and executed. Rabbit's execution again inspired Merle. He earned a high school diploma and kept a steady job in the prison's textile plant. In 1959 Merle saw Johnny Cash perform at the prison on New Year's Day, and he started up his own country band in the jail. Merle was released from jail in 1960 and quickly established himself as a country music star, playing in bars and small arenas throughout the west. Then California governor Ronald Reagan granted Haggard a full and unconditional pardon for his past crimes. Merle was the original 'riding the rails' man for about fifteen years from the late 1940s to about the 1960s. During that period, other than the times Merle was incarcerated, he spent his time aimlessly wandering around in California and Texas by way of illegally boarding trains, hitchhiking, walking, and whatever other way he could transport himself. Sometimes Merle stayed clear of trouble, but at other times he was up to his eyeballs in it. With a lot of luck and a load of chutzpah, Merle played out his life to become one of the biggest country stars ever.

"The other musician that comes to mind in terms of railroad boxcars is a country musician by the name of Lecil Travis Martin, better known by his stage persona, Boxcar Willie. Willie portrayed himself as an old-time hobo complete with the dirty face, the overalls, and the floppy hat. His musical career began at about the same time he enlisted in the United States Air Force as a flight engineer. Lecil was born in Olivia, Texas, and was one of the first country stars to put Branson, Missouri, on the map as a country music destination. In San Jose, California, Lecil entered a talent contest where he used the name Boxcar Willie for the first time. He won the contest with $150 prize, but most importantly, the name Boxcar Willie stuck to him. Willie had to use singing as a part-time vocation because he was still in the Air Force flying daily missions and performing in-flight refuelings. In 1976, after ten years in Europe, Martin retired from the Air Force and became a full-time performer. His first national appearance was on Chuck Barris's *The Gong Show* where he won first prize. Willie became a force in mainstream pop culture when he did a series of television commercials for compilations of other artists' work who were obscure in the United States but had large international followings. His 1980 album *King of the Road* gave him his greatest chart success reaching number five in the United Kingdom albums chart. Willie was inducted into the Country Music Hall of fame in 1981. Boxcar Willie traveled around the United States and the world as a radio host and musician for many years until finally settling in Branson, Missouri, in 1985. Soon after moving to Branson, Willie purchased a theater on Highway 76 or 76 Country Music Boulevard in Branson. He opened a museum and eventually two motels both bearing his name. Willie was one of the first country stars to reside and preform in Branson, paving the way for the city to become nationally known as a country music haven. In modern country music Branson rivals Nashville, Tennessee, as the home of country music. Although Boxcar did not actually 'ride the rails' as Merle Haggard did, his portrayal of such an individual made him perhaps not as famous as Merle but a country star with a huge following. When I was about twenty-three years old, Boxcar did a show at the pavilion at Pine Lake Park where we had a camp for almost fifty years. I didn't attend the concert, but I do remember being in the parking lot listening to the music. I also remember that day Boxcar Willie drew a crowd of well over one thousand people, and everyone seemed to really enjoy his show.

"My point is that those boxcars that Johnny Kipper, you, and I were so dangerously close to so many times have become fabled in American folklore. How will we ever know if Merle didn't jump one of those boxcars in Texas, ride a series of cars up the East Coast, and jump off in my grandmother's backyard on Orchard Street? How do we know that while we were wandering aimlessly up and down Orchard Street, Merle wasn't wandering as aimlessly as we were to Viti's Bakery to get a cup of coffee and a donut? We would never know Merle, nor would Merle know us. Yet with the way these men 'rode the rails' crisscrossing the United States, only God knows if we might have ever crossed paths. I've told my children since the day they were born all roads lead to Frankfort. Possibly in my case, your case, Johnny Kipper's, Donnie's, and Merle's, all of our roads did lead to Frankfort at the same time and specifically Orchard Street. Remotely possible but on some level remotely likely to."

We collectively thought about that possibility for a second.

Then John-John continued.

"What about that small chapel on the corner of Orchard Street and Tisdale Avenue where a parade used to start and proceed to Sheldon Avenue to another chapel at the end of the street there? The Red Band, for which the real name in Italian was the Banda Rossa, would lead the parade followed by the saint to pin the money on the banner. I think the statue was of the Madonna, but I am not sure. That was a big thing for all of us to do."

I added, "Big was not the word for it, and the reason I say that is, all of us remember it—Johnny Kipper, Donnie, you, me, and others—all bring it up. That little parade that had a total of fifty people in it and lasted for probably twenty minutes made a huge impression on all of us, even some sixty years later. It kept alive traditions from Italy, especially for the most recent immigrants and consider the impression it made on us, at the time being third-generation Americans. Those traditions vibrate through the generations and through the decades. It is enigmatic how that happens in just a small scale and through the millenniums for mankind. Clearly mystifying."

We both considered that fact in equally as mystified silence.

Then John-John picked up. "Sundays with everybody making fresh sauce and meatballs were the best. You could smell the food over the entire street. I can smell it now. I would wander from my house to my grandmother's, to Mrs. Caruso's, to wherever the smell led me to get fresh meatballs. Everyone was cooking them. You could walk in any house, and there they were. What I wouldn't give to relive that again. Viti's Bakery, buying cookies for 5¢ each, half-moons, fingers, doughnuts for about 7¢ each. Where in the hell did all that go? We talked about Earl with the 'free' samples of Hostess cupcakes and all the controversy that was created. Even when we paid for them, it all had a life of its own. Where the hell did all that go? The next day you could go back to Viti's and buy the day-old cookies for 2¢, and we sure did buy them. Sam Talerico had the store at the corner of Railroad and Orchard Streets full of candy, gum, soda, and just about everything a kid wanted to eat all day. I think the store had gas pumps, but I doubt if a gallon of gas, which was probably 20¢, was ever sold. The building is still there, but it is dilapidated now. What compelling memories."

That caused another one of those wistful pauses, which you would think we were all getting used to now, but were not.

"There was a mass of kids on the hill behind Sam's store on snowy day," John-John continued, "sitting there on my sled is as vivid to me right now as it was sixty years ago when I was actually doing it. Holy cow, you really have my mind popping with vivid and deep recollections of those blessed days so long ago. The Frankfort Fire Department flooding the parking lot of the playground across from Sam's store to make an ice-skating rink and the volunteer firefighters supervising to make sure no one got hurt or caused trouble. In all the hours we spent there, I don't ever remember there being a problem or anyone ever being thrown out.

"Many people didn't have cars, or if they did, they only had one, which the husband drove to work. In that the women couldn't go anywhere, the vendors came to us to sell goods that couldn't be bought in the stores in Frankfort, or you had to walk to the store to buy. Benny Licari Sr. had a fruit and vegetable truck that he would drive around the village and stop on certain blocks to sell his produce. On the bed of his pickup truck, he built an A frame, probably six-foot-long tiered display to put the produce on. One side was for the fruits, and the other side was for the vegetables. Benny would stop the truck about midblock on the north side of Orchard Street, pull the covers back, and start selling. I bet he sold one-third of the produce he had on the truck right on Orchard Street and during the day had to go back to his house on Third Avenue to restock the truck. He had a great business model. Next to his house he had a garage to store the fruits and vegetables. Next to that he had about an acre of land to grow his produce. No middleman or big expense was involved. A simple form of direct merchandising a long time ago in the fifties.

"Another vendor who showed up weekly was Joe Tehan in his station wagon, whose business eventually became a full-size department store for about fifty years but sadly went out of business about twenty years ago. Joe would show up on Orchard Street at least once a week, if my memory serves me correctly, on Wednesday morning. If business was good, he might even show up twice a week, maybe again on Friday morning. He had the same setup as Ben Licari, only in a station wagon. He too would pull the car on the north side of Orchard Street and park. Joe would fold down the tailgate of the car and open the top half of the tailgate, which was glass. Inside he had concocted two stand-up cabinets that he could pull out on which he had his products hanging from hooks. On the floor of the station wagon, he would have the back seats folded down, and he would have all his wares stacked up. Joe would sell sheets, pillowcases, towels, and small kitchen items that he would have hanging on the racks that he had built in the cabinets. He might even have sneakers, possibly men's shorts, women stockings, and pretty much anything you would find in a department store much like the business he eventually opened as a full-scale department store. As soon as Joe parked and opened that back of the station wagon up, people would start coming out of their houses to go look at what Joe had for sale that day. They were mostly women, but men would also wander over and look. My mother used to buy from Joe regularly. She bought mostly sheets, towels, washcloths, and that sort of items. Being Lebanese or Syrian, Joe was willing to sell just about anything. Lebanon, the Middle East, and Syria have always been the crossroads of the Western World. The route that Marco Polo used in the twelfth century to get from Europe to China, and the Silk Road both passed through the Middle East. With the constant flow of people, goods, and ideas back and forth for centuries, it's in the blood of the people who inhabit the Middle East to be buyers and sellers of just about anything people want to buy. Joe Tehan was no exception to that rule. He would have the price listed of a specific product, say $0.10, but he was always willing to negotiate. If the price of the washcloth was $0.10, people would offer Joe $0.07. Joe would counteroffer with $.09, and they would both agree to $0.08. I remember Joe as very nice and down-to-earth.

He seemed to like the people living on Orchard Street, and they in turn liked him. He was very fair with everyone, and I think he even extended some people's credit that they could pay half and then pay the rest when Joe came back the following week. Most people living on Orchard Street had jobs and some money but by no means was anyone rich. I think Joe understood that perfectly, and being a smart businessman and a good person, he was always willing to help someone in a large or small way. I remember always thinking of him as professional and a good person to be around.

"There was another guy, whose name I have no idea of, who used to come to Orchard Street once or twice a week and sell bleach, only bleach. Like the case with Joe and Benny Licari, as soon as people saw the bleach truck come to a stop, out the door they would come. I don't remember him selling anything but bleach, and I do remember a lot of people buying it. Bleach was cheap and available as a cleaning product for your floors, clothes, or whatever you wanted to clean. People came out and often purchased a lot of bleach. The irony of this situation was the guy who was doing the selling was always a mess. His clothes were disheveled and looked like they hadn't been washed in a month. The truck he drove was beat-up, and his hair was always a mess. When I saw him, the first thing that came into my head was, 'Goodness, this guy could use some of that bleach on himself.' He came to Orchard Street to sell us a cleaning product, and he needed to use some of that same cleaning product on his clothes, truck, and just about everything he had. I really don't have any recollection of his name or where he came from, but he also was a humble guy. In no way was he like that miserable Coco-Cola delivery man. Both Joe Tehan and the bleach seller treated us well. We, in turn, treated them well. The Coke guy treated us bad, and we, in turn, treated him bad. Karma is a bitch.

"What amazes me now looking back is these people obviously saw a market for their products. I would bet they went to many other neighborhoods, but Orchard Street was one of their stops. These vendors pretty much had a captive audience that waited for them to show up each week to make purchases, and the buyers didn't even have to leave Orchard Street. Direct marketing in its most simplistic and profitable form. No middleman, little if any transportation costs, direct sales, and not much accountability because I don't remember ever seeing any receipts. The just knew what they sold, who they sold it to, and how much it cost. It must have been profitable for these guys to keep coming back week after week after week until I was probably fourteen or fifteen years old. Then with malls and shopping centers opening all over the area, over a period of two or three years, it all slowly slipped away like so many things do in life. The process seems so slow and innocuous you don't even realize it is happening until it does. Really eerie stuff.

"Even the stores and the bars on Orchard Street went the same route as the vendors. They were open for many years, then suddenly closed or changed hands, and then they were gone too.

"The bars tended to stay in business longer than the stores did. As I have said, there were four bars on Orchard Street and North Litchfield Street. On North Litchfield Street was the Argonne Grill or Bea's and Puzze's on the opposite end of the street. On the north side of Orchard Street, right in the middle of the block, was Zito's Restaurant, and on the east end of Orchard Street was Billis's Hotel. Again at other times, before my time, there were even more bars and restaurants like where Terry and Larry Stone lived, which at one time I understand was a hotel/restaurant. Most of them went in business in the late eighteenth century to serve workers and travelers on the Erie Canal, which was fifty yards from these various businesses.

"Puzze's served Limburger cheese. All the food was good, but Limburger cheese sandwiches and plates were the specialty of the house. Those bars and restaurants had people in them all day every day. When the door was open to enter Puzze's, especially in the summertime, and people were eating Limburger cheese, you could smell it out in the street. I could never understand how anybody ate that stuff because of the smell, but people loved it. At the other end of the block, moving south on Litchfield Street, was the Argonne Grill. I don't know the original owner's name, but I knew the woman whom we all called Bea. It was her husband's bar originally, but he died young. The bar was named in honor of the Battle of the Argonne Forest in France that was fought and in effect ended World War I. It was the last major battle of the war and was fought along the Western Front of the war between France and Germany. There were over one million soldiers poised on each side of the front, ready to do battle to the end. The goal of the Allies was to reach Sedan, France, to take control of a railroad junction there. The goal was being able to control the flow of military equipment and personnel in and out of Germany, thus putting the German Army under the Allies' control. Ultimately, the Allies won a battle, which put an end to World War I. I understand that the bar was named the Argonne Grill in honor of all the World War I doughboys who were killed, wounded, or returned home safely after a protracted battle.

"When we were about fifteen or sixteen, naturally, we all wanted to go in bars. None of the bars on Orchard Street would serve minors except for the Argonne Grill. At about sixteen, I went in the bar for the first time. Bea was tending the bar and never asked me or any of my friends for an ID until about the fourth or fifth time that I went in. When she did ask me for an ID, I reached into my pocket and pulled out the two or three dollars that I had and a card for a free game of bowling at Thurston's Lanes. Bea looked at the free bowling card, handed it back to me, and walked over to pour me a draft beer. She took a free bowling card as an ID. I don't think she even knew what it was.

"On the weekends at Thurston's Lanes, they used to have what they called Red Pin Bowling whereby if a pin that fell into the number one slot of the rack of pins was red and the bowler rolled a strike, they would be awarded a free game. Red Pin Bowling was a great marketing tool because on the weekends we couldn't wait to go bowling and try to win a free game. We likely paid for three or four games in the hope of winning a free one, which rarely happened. Most people never won, but I was lucky enough at that point to have won a free game. It was nearly impossible to win because the chances of the red pin falling into the first slot were probably one hundred to one, and then the chances of the bowler getting a strike in that frame, depending on the bowler, of course, were probably just as big. Here I was handing Bea a free bowling card for an ID, and she accepted it as proof of age. She didn't care one bit that we were minors. We were all walking money to her, and she was glad to take the dollars all from us, minors or not. In those days nobody thought about serving minors, drinking and driving, ID cards, or anything of that nature. Nowadays, it's a huge issue because of liability. People are often served too much alcohol in bars, then get in their cars and drive often hurting/killing themselves or others. Then the family of the injured party goes back to the place where the alcohol was served and sues for damages. Bar owners and bartenders are too smart now to assume all that liability. These days everything becomes ID, DWI checkpoints, insurance, and many other issues. The government had to do something about the risk of consuming alcohol and driving because a lot of people were getting hurt or killed. In 1971 or 1972 it really wasn't an issue, but it certainly is now."

Certainly, it is a big issue now and rightly so considering all the harm that has been done.

At that point John-John and I took a break for a few minutes, him to answer the phone and me to use the bathroom.

When we started up again, I told him there was a question I had been meaning to ask him since we started, and now would be a perfect time to ask.

So I asked.

"John-John, do you remember the time we stole an adult magazine from Joe Tocco's store on Frankfort Street? I don't remember what the magazine was. I think it was *Playboy*, but you and I concocted an idea that we would steal the magazine off the rack. While you kept an eye on Joe, I took the magazine and slid it out under my shirt, then we nonchalantly walked out of the store. We went up to a little clump of woods that used to be behind the Frankfort Free Library and gave that magazine a good hard look. It really got our attention. After about thirty minutes of perusing it, we had to decide what we were going to do with it permanently. I didn't want it, nor did you, because we both felt that if my dad or your dad caught either of us with it, we would be in big trouble. Then we prepared a Plan B. Bring it back to the store and put it on the rack without getting caught again. Not only was it "the perfect crime" stealing it, but now we needed "the perfect crime in reverse" to bring it back. As luck would have it, we were able to pull it off and get it back on the rack without Joe seeing us either take it or put it back. The perfect crime and then redoing the perfect crime, which we pulled off. To this day I don't know how we did it, but we did."

Immediately, and I mean immediately, John-John's face lit up and he began to chuckle.

"That's what you think happened?" John-John questioned. "I bet you've been thinking that since we did it about fifty-five years ago. I must tell you that you are completely wrong. About ten years after we did it, I was in my twenties. Out of the clear blue sky one day, my father asked me to tell him about the time you and I stole the *Playboy* magazine out of Joe Tocco's store.

"I couldn't believe the words that came out of my dad's mouth. It was ten years or more later, and I had always thought, just as you did up to this minute, that we stole it from the store, then put it back and never got caught.

"Completely wrong.

"Probably two weeks after we did it, Joe saw my father, who was one of his friends, and told him what we had done. Joe explained to my dad that he didn't want to call the police, my father, or yours, because we were shoplifting. Rather he was just going to tell my father or yours—since he knew them both, after all, it is Frankfort—about the incident and see what they wanted to do about it. Joe didn't want to get either of us in trouble. After all, we were kids, but he felt there was a lesson to be learned. Then Joe got the shock of his day. After about thirty minutes, the two of us came back into the store, and he watched us put the magazine back on the shelf. Joe couldn't believe his eyes. He let it go that we took it. Then here we were putting it back, and he was watching us do it both in and out.

"My father couldn't contain his laughter when he told me about it, and neither could I. I thought like you that we had gotten away with it. In the end we didn't. Not for one single second, and I was convinced for ten years we did. You were convinced right up to this discussion we did. How funny is that?"

Now we had to stop. Not for one of those deep awkward pauses we all have experienced many times before, but rather because we were both laughing so hard.

I was bewildered.

I was astonished.

Joe Tocco and John Tubia Sr. both knew the real story but never told John Tubia Jr. until ten years after it happened.

Again, much to my bewilderment, I didn't find out that they all knew the true story until over fifty years after it happened, and only because of our collective efforts to bring *The King of Orchard Street* to life did I find out. I thought we got away with it scot-free for my entire life, and John-John just rewrote over fifty years of history for me in about one minute. The surprise for both of us was astonishing. We sat there for another ten minutes, grinning from ear to ear and laughing about as hard as we could. I never knew up until that moment that we didn't get away with it at all. John-John had known for probably forty-five years, but it didn't strike him how funny it was until he learned that I thought for fifty-five years we had gotten away with it completely.

I urged John-John as we work our way through *The King of Orchard Street* to be sure to read my take on who might be the king to get a clear understanding of the perfect crime and the perfect crime redo. Or, at a minimum, how wrong I was about both.

The Bible says, "You will know the truth and the truth will set you free" (John 8:32 KJV).

I just found out the truth, fifty-five years later, and it set me free like I've never been set free before.

After all that laughter and astonishment, John-John jumped back in with stories of two lifelong friends of ours Terry and Larry Stone who were twins.

He continued, "I think back to all the fun we had with Terry and Larry Stone. Larry was born with, I'm not sure, what possibly was muscular dystrophy, and a bad leg, but he was way ahead of his time. He took a pull-along wagon that kids used to play with back then and adapted it for himself. First, he put bigger wheels on it, which added a few inches to the height so that he could place his bad leg in it, which enabled him to use his good leg to push. He was just as fast using that wagon as we were on our feet. Larry's invention was the precursor of what you see today when people have an injured leg. They use those little three-wheeled carts that they roll along with their bad leg on the cart while pushing with their good leg just as Larry did. Larry was way ahead of his time. He had the idea of one of those scooters in the 1960s.

"The family lived in what was once one of those old restaurant/hotels for travelers and workers on the Erie Canal. In the back of the first floor was a huge living room, which was probably the dining room for the hotel. Terry and Larry were a little older than you and me and were the first ones to turn sixteen and be eligible for a driver's license. Larry convinced his stepfather Wally Richardson to allow him to practice driving a car by backing in and out of the driveway. The car he was practicing in with had a standard shift. At one point, likely Larry thought the car was in reverse when he actually had it in drive. When he let out the clutch and stepped on the gas, the car lurched forward and drove right through the building and ended up in the living room. Larry didn't get hurt, but he wrecked the car pretty good. There was no one in the living room at the time. When word spread as to what happened, we all ran over to see the damage. Larry had made a probably seven-feet-across-and-five-feet-high hole right through the wall of the house into the living room. There were broken boards scattered all over. Wires were hanging down. It was a mess. Wally was standing there with a bewildered look on his face like, 'How am I going to repair this, and it probably will cost me a lot of money.' We all thought it was hilarious, but obviously, Wally didn't. Thank goodness no one was hurt. Then everything got repaired, and we all went about our daily lives.

"Terry and Larry had an older brother by the name of David. Dave, I believe, was an Air Force veteran stationed in Germany for many years. When he was released from the military, he returned to Orchard Street to live with his stepfather Wally and brought with him his wife, a German citizen named Hilda. Hilda was a tall good-looking woman with blonde hair and blue eyes. Being European, she was usually dressed in a very sophisticated fashion. All the boys on the block, being all of ten or eleven years old, would wait for Hilda to come out of the house to go shopping, to hang their clothes on the line, or go in and out doing whatever she had to do that day. A few of us used to wait for her to hang her clothes and lingerie on the clothesline to dry and would sneak over and steal them off the line. A little weird, I must admit now, but for a twelve-year-old boy, very alluring. Hilda must have wondered why every time she hung clothes on the line, some of them disappeared. One day Alex wanted to show me something. We went behind Josephine Vaccaro's house and climbed up on her garage roof by first climbing a tree. When I looked over toward Wally's house, much to my surprise, there was Hilda's bathroom window. I couldn't believe our luck. After sitting up there for about two minutes, Hilda came walking in the bathroom to take her shower or do whatever she was going to do in the bathroom. Talk about real focus. Alex and I were amazed. Apparently, this wasn't the first time it happened to Alex, but it was for me. We did it a few more times and got lucky once or twice more, but the biggest issue was if we got caught up on that roof, what were we going to say we were doing? If Dave Richardson caught us, we would be in real trouble. A potential big issue for sure. We didn't go on for very long because eventually we knew we had to get caught. We made an executive decision to stop. It was a difficult but necessary choice. Soon after that, Dave and Hilda moved away, and I never saw either one of them again.

"Being one of those old hotels from the Erie Canal days, there were a lot of small rooms that Wally would rent out to boarders. One guy who lived there in particular was named Bob. There was no place to park his car at Wally's house, so he would park in the parking lot of Zito's bar and walk west halfway down the block to Wally's house. This guy was terrible to us. We were little children, and he treated us like dirt. He was always calling us names, ethnic names in particular like Guineas, dagos, and so on. Much like the guy who drove the Coca-Cola delivery truck. Eventually, we had had enough and developed a plan to get even. We went to Corrado's Mill and probably bought a dozen four-inch nails. Then we waited for Bob to come home, park his car, and walk to Wally's house for the night. Once it got dark, we snuck over and placed the nails, three for each tire, at about a forty-five-degree angle directly into the tires. We waited a little bit to determine if anybody had seen us, which no one had, and we all went in for the night. We paid attention to Bob's daily ins and outs knowing that he usually left for work about eight in the morning. Knowing what was going to happen, we were all out early the next day standing on the corner by your aunt Josie's house. Like a clock, about seven fifty, Bob walked east on the street to go to work. He got in the car, started it, put it in reverse, backed up about three inches, and in twenty seconds all four tires popped and went flat. Bob got out of the car, looked at the four flat tires and went into a rage. He looked over at us spitting, swearing, calling us all kinds of names, and accusing us for doing it. He told us that he was calling the police and we were all going to get arrested, that he had had enough of us horrible kids. He was out of control. We all just milled around looking at him like he had lost his mind, nonchalantly ignoring him and denying we had anything to do with the situation, like we didn't even know what he was talking about. He stormed back over to Wally's house, and about two minutes later, the police drove north on Litchfield Street. I believe in the patrol car was George Grates, who was the police chief at the time. Bob was telling George that he wanted us arrested because we put the nails in place so that they would flatten all of his tires, that we were terrible kids and should be in jail where juvenile delinquents belong. Bob demanded that our fathers pay for the tires and so on. The guy was completely out of his mind at this point. Looking back, I think George knew the kind of guy he was and knew he likely deserved what had happened to him by whoever had done it. George walked over to talk to us and wanted to know what we knew, what we did, and if we had anything to do with the whole scene. Collectively, we denied everything. None of us knew anything about nails or tires and that we didn't even know Bob. We were just a bunch of kids hanging out there on our street. George walked back over to Bob and told him he couldn't do anything to us because he had no proof that we damaged his property. No one saw us near his car at any time, and unless someone could identify us being near the car, there was nothing he could do. Now Bob was late for work, and he was even more enraged. Finally, someone came to pick him up, and off if he went to work. The police waited around a little while too and then drove away. About a half hour later, George Grates came back to talk to us again, and we were still milling around on the corner. He in effect told us that if we did it, we got lucky because no one saw us. If someone could identify us, then he would have no choice but to notify our parents, and Bob could prosecute us. George had this smirk on his face like he knew exactly what had happened and was giving us a warning, but since there was no proof, he had to let it go. It certainly was not a nice thing that we did, but this guy deserved it. Bob was horrible to us. We were children, and he was calling us all kinds of hateful names on a regular basis. There's some karma in there. What goes around comes around. I can't say that Bob deserved it, and it was a horrible thing to do, but there's a price to be paid for all that unwarranted nastiness. Again, I'll say, what goes around comes around.

"Another pastime that was constantly swirling around Orchard Street and in many places locally was gambling. When Rossi Caruso bought Zito's Restaurant and turned it into a strip bar named the Grand Prix, along with the alcohol and strippers came gambling. On Sunday afternoon Rossi would contact many of his friends for an afternoon of gambling at the bar. About two o'clock or so, slowly the parking lot would fill up with Lincolns, Cadillacs, and other large expensive cars. The crowd would come in for a few hours of heavy gambling. One of the guys would bring in a portable crap table that you could set up on a dining room table. They would have poker and blackjack too. Some intense high-stakes gambling took place there. After about two years the state police got wind of what was happening, and sure enough, two state police cars showed up one Sunday afternoon. They walked into the bar to determine what the situation was, and they found what they came for. Gambling taking place all over the room. They wanted to know who the owner of the bar was, and Rossi told them that he was. One trooper continued to question Rossi as to why he was allowing all this gambling to take place in his bar because he had a liquor license, which could be revoked if he was convicted of promoting gambling on the premises. Rossi told him that it was an innocent stag party, and it was all meant to raise money for the groom like any other stag party that takes place all over the Mohawk Valley. One of the troopers wanted to know who the stag party was for, and Rossi told him it was for Jack Brown. The next question was, where was Jack Brown? Rossi told him he didn't see him anywhere, but he might have gone outside to smoke or go buy more food or whatever the case may be, but he was there somewhere, and the party was to raise money for him. Stag parties with gambling were a common occurrence in those days but not so much anymore with the opening of casinos. Both officers bought Rossi's story and left. The truth be known, it was no stag party. It was a regular occurrence just for the sake of gambling. As for Jack Brown, there was no Jack Brown. Rossi's dog's name was Jack, and he was brown. The two state troopers went for it hook, line and sinker. Soon after that, the gambling stopped and likely moved somewhere else because word had gotten out that there was a lot of illegal gambling taking place in Frankfort at the Grand Prix on Orchard Street on Sunday afternoon. Eventually, people would get arrested, and rather than take that chance, the gambling just moved to some other location in Herkimer, Utica, New Hartford, or somewhere else. It never stopped, and it's never going to stop.

"As always with gambling, there is the gambling itself and various scams associated with the gambling swirling around the actual gambling. There was a simple scam that probably went on for three years before the bookie taking the bets caught on. Rossi called it "PP," and evidentially, it is the oldest scam in horse racing. It took place on Orchard Street, Monday through Saturday night, from mid-April to mid-October, about three or maybe four nights a week. In those days horse racing in general and specifically at Vernon Downs, a local standardbred track for trotters and pacers located in Vernon, New York, about thirty miles southwest of Frankfort, was a huge attraction. Vernon Downs would draw at times four thousand people on weekend nights to bet horses. The track is located on Stuhlman Road in Vernon, New York, about a mile from Route 5. On the corner of Route 5 and Stuhlman Road, there was a pay telephone, a long-ago common sight, which probably doesn't exist anymore due to the advent of cell phones. Pay phones were phones that could be found in various locations. Many years ago, the cost of a five-minute call was 10¢. Then it went up to 25¢ for a three-minute call. When what are now rudimentary cell phones came along, slowly pay phones and booths began to disappear. Now and then I do spot one but rarely. I doubt if the one in Route 5 and Sthulman Road is still there. Frank "Chico" Sanders, one of Rossi's best friends, would drive to Vernon Downs to watch the first race. When the first race results were official and Frank knew the winner, for example horse number one, he would quickly drive to the corner on Stuhlman Road and Route 5 to call Rossi from the pay phone there and tell him the winner of the first race. In horse racing what is called the daily double, at that time at least, was the winner of the first race coupled with the winner of the second race to make a payout. Again, if you know the winner of the first race is number one and the second race hasn't run yet, you could guarantee yourself a winning daily double by taking the winner of the first race and betting that horse with all the horses in the second but only when making the bets with a bookie."

I asked Johnny if he knew the name of the activity he just described, and he told me that he did not.

I began to explain. "Horse players call that a "front wheel." One bet which you have your money on is a guaranteed winner because you know the winner of the first race and have it bet with all the horses in the second race separately. Even though you don't know which horse wins the second race, you have a winning daily double. In that you have all the combinations of whatever horse is the second race winner bet with the winner of the first race, and you already know the winner of the first race. In effect, an automatic daily double payout. At the track you can't bet like that, because once betting is closed for the first race, daily double betting is closed also. Rossi would then, after Chico's phone call, call a local bookie and make the front wheel bet. The bookie, not knowing about Chico's phone call, would take the bet, making Rossi a guaranteed winner of the daily double. There was also another way to guarantee yourself a daily double winner, but it was more risky. If you could, with the drivers involved in the second race, "fix" the race so that horse number one, for example, in the second race is the winner. Then a bettor could use the same process and do what is called a "back wheel." Again, if you know the assumed winner of the second race by way of a "fix," the bettor could then bet, for example, number one in the second race with all the horses in the first race while daily double betting was still open, thus, as the name indicates, betting backward. Again, time for the back wheel was also a factor because once betting closed for the first race at the track, daily double betting also closed. A back wheel was clearly riskier than a front wheel because in the front wheel, the first race was over and the winner was official. The back wheel was dependent on a fix, which may or may not happen, and time to bet while daily double wagering was still available. Goodness, I sound like I know an awful lot about these obviously underhanded practices. With a front wheel 'all the bets would have to be made with an illegal bookie.' In the back wheel all the bets could be made legally at trackside and these days at Off Track Betting, but the bets had to be placed prior to daily double betting closing time. Still, the second race had to be fixed, which entailed more risk because those involved with the fix might agree then not go along once on the track racing. Everyone involved might not agree to the fix at all, and a whole myriad of potential issues can arise. Either scenario has an illegal component to it too.

"There was another possible way you could lose, not so much the bet but money on the bet. For example, if the horse that wins the first race is a two to one favorite and only pays $3.50 for a $2 wager, the bettor then places bets in a front wheel on number one, the official winner of the first race, which you already know. The bets would be on one/one, one/two, one /three, and so on. If the bettor placed $2 on each combination times eight combinations or the number of horses entered in the second race, he would have to wager $16 in combinations to cover all the horses individually in the second race. The plan is good so far, yet there is still room to go wrong. If the winner of the second race then proves to be a favorite and only pays out $4 with favorites winning both the first and second races, the daily double payout might only be $12. The bettor's front wheel made a $16 investment to cover all the combinations but only wins back $12. There is a four-dollar net loss. A winning bet but a loser in terms of the money it cost to make the necessary wagers and the money that gets paid back. It also can work the other way, which is what the gambler is looking for. If a twenty to one horse wins the first race and gets front wheeled with another twenty to one horse winning the second race, the daily double payout might be $800 minus the assumed eight horses in the second race $2 wager to cover all the potential daily double combinations there is, a $784 net gain. That is a winner for sure but no guarantee that it will happen. In the front wheel, at least, if the first race winner was a favorite and the payout a small amount, the bettor could choose not to bet the daily double at all for fear that the second race winner would be a favorite also. In turn making the daily double payout was possibly not enough return to warrant the money that would have to be placed to cover all the bets in the front wheel. Even when the gambler thinks he has the advantage, he really doesn't. That's why they call it gambling. The bettor would still have the option of not placing the front wheel bet if he knows the payout of the first race winner is small. Yet for an addicted gambler, especially a horse player, the likelihood of him not placing a front wheel bet, already knowing which horse won the first race, is very small. With knowledge of the official winner of the first race in hand, a real gambler is going to likely bet, usually depending on the degree of addiction, a large amount of money in the hope that the second race winner will be a long shot and with full knowledge of the fact that the daily double payout could be less than the amount wagered. As the saying goes, "It's the nature of the Beast."

"The first race at Vernon Downs was at 7:30 p.m. and the second race usually about 7:55 p.m. By approximately 8:00 p.m., the official results of the winners of races one and two, along with the payouts for win, place, show, and with the daily double payout were official. The winning ticket holders could then cash their bets. Beginning usually about 8:03 p.m., a local radio station WIBX would broadcast a live report from Vernon Downs with the first and second race results, the daily double results, payouts, and the like. Many, I mean many people in Frankfort, were betting that daily double and listening in the house or in their car to WIBX for that daily double result. Right after the radio broadcast, local bookies would begin to make payouts to their bettors. Whether they won or lost, people would then bet more races on the card for that evening. The only problem was that you could not get anymore race results until the next morning when they were printed in the sports section of the *Utica Observer Dispatch*. With no more information available in regard to winners or losers until the next morning, that mostly usually ended the bookies' business for the day.

"Yet as sure as the sun came up the next morning, the gamblers in Frankfort were busy picking, for certain, their Vernon Downs winners again. At least they hoped so.

"All true. All local.

"Yet there is a much larger historical context that spreads out all over the world for three millenniums. That is why it is called gambling…"

*****

With Carol and my wedding anniversary being August 12, typically this time of year we take a short three- or four-day trip not too far from home to have some fun. In the past we have visited places like the Thousand Islands, New York, or Atlantic City, New Jersey, to visit some sites, have dinner in different restaurants, and just enjoy ourselves. August 5, the last time John-John and I met, we agreed to take some time off while Carol I do some roaming. We also agreed that when we meet again, we would continue to discuss the history of gambling on a larger historical scale than on Orchard Street. Johnny and I both reveled in hearing the history of all the gambling that has taken place on Orchard Street and its environs from all those years ago. We would get back to the topic soon enough.

This year Carol and I decided to travel to Western New York to a location named Letchworth State Park. Carol had been there before and told me that it's beautiful and is often called the Grand Canyon of the East. In the past, when vacationing, I had been known to miss my intended location by maybe a block or across the street, but this time, I was way off the mark. As we drove toward Western New York and Letchworth State Park, I soon realized that I had gone about eighty miles west of Letchworth for lodging. Goodness. I wasn't even in the right county. With that realization, we quickly reassessed our plans. Instead of Letchworth, we visited Lockport, New York, where our accommodations were, which is a truly historic locale on the Erie Canal and then to Niagara Falls State Park. It turned out to be not a bad trip after all. Lockport, thus the name, has some of the biggest locks along the Erie Canal. What was truly impressive is the engineering. To raise and lower the water through likely five different levels in a stretch of three miles was imposing, to say the least. The numerous inlets and outlets for the locks to control the ebb and flow of the water due to rain or drought is amazing. The canal was begun in 1817 and fully completed in 1825 and was considered at the time an engineering marvel. Engineering that is common today obviously dwarfs the Erie Canal. Yet in light of the time period of construction, the canal is a majestic site to behold even to this day.

Engineering? What can be said about the natural engineering of Niagara Falls? The force of nature flowing over that cataclysmic gorge is astounding. The noise and the swirl of the water are deafening. The constant mist covering everything with billions and billions of beads of water for eons is beyond description. Although I have been to Niagara Falls numerous times on both the US and the Canadian sides, it never fails to impress me. The falls are thunderous and powerful, beyond description. I am certain that Letchworth State Park is a natural wonder too but to exceed the power and beauty of Niagara Falls is high bar to get over. Come to think of it, Niagara Falls for a thirty-third wedding anniversary trip was a pretty good mistake after all.

Next year's plan is to visit Watkins Glen, New York, for the NASCAR weekend and attend the Bowling at the Glen race on Sunday. Then Letchworth State Park on Monday, returning home on Tuesday. That shouldn't be an issue, in that we have been to Watkins Glen many times and, for that matter, Carol many years ago lived in the Finger Lakes Region.

It would seem by then I should at least be able get in the right county.

As Carol and I were driving to the falls, we came upon an American tradition that has almost disappeared now. We stumbled upon a fully functioning five-screen drive-in movie by the name of the Transit Drive-In. Neither Carol nor I had been to a drive-in movie in probably fifty years, and sure enough, purely by accident, here was our chance. The existence of drive-ins in this country is as American as apple pie. Carol and I both quickly recalled when we were kids, there was in this area about five drive-in movies. There was the Kallet Drive-In in New Hartford, Schuyler Drive-In, in Schuyler with three screens, the Rome Drive-In, another whose name escaped both of us by where Whitesboro High School is now, and still another in Little Falls. At one point, in the 1950s and 60s there were over five thousand functioning drive-ins in America. Unfortunately, that number has dwindled to about four hundred. It seems now that the movies themselves are not what keeps the remaining drive-ins in business, but rather what keeps them open are the dollars generated by the concession stands. Without the concession stands, most of them would not be in business today. Carol and I also recalled when we went to the drive-in with our families, we would go in our pajamas due to the fact that the movie started at dark, and we probably wouldn't get home until eleven o' clock or later. More likely than not, we would be asleep long before that. To make it convenient for our parents, we would go to the drive-in in our pajamas, and all they had to do then was put us in bed. I'm ready to wager that almost everybody reading this sentence had the same experience as a child. The Transit Drive-In was still showing double features, another American tradition long gone.

It was Carol's turn to pick the movie. She decided on *Bullet Train* starring Brad Pitt. The other screens were showing *Top Gun: Maverick*, *Thor: Love and Thunder*, and *Minions: The Rise of Gru*. Carol decided on *Bullet Train*. Bad choice. The funny parts of the movie were funny; the rest was pretty much bad. If I had known that *Bullet Train* was as bad as it is, I would have picked the *Minions*. Who knew? At least I would have been entertained instead of falling asleep watching *Bullet Train*.

After two nights in the Niagara Falls Lockport area, we continued our trip to Oswego, New York, so that I can donate copies of my first book *Ruthie Deeply* to the Alumni Office Library and to Oswego State's main library book collection housed in the Penfield Library. We have numerous family members that are Oswego State alumni including myself and my brother-in-law Bob Pacific. My father-in-law, Nick Ciufo, met my mother-in-law, Therese Fitzgerald—Therese being born and raised in Oswego—when they were both students at the college. Due to that fact Carol still has a dwindling number of relatives alive in town, we tend to make trips to Oswego on occasion for weddings as we did two weeks prior to this trip and, unfortunately, at times funerals. We go there so Carol can visit what is left of her mother's family and so I can wander around town and reminisce about my college days. Again, this year on our way back from Western New York, we made our second stop in Oswego in about two weeks. While there we made the traditional visits to Carol's cousins, Rudy's Fish Stand, a Lake Ontario legendary eatery, the Ferris Wheel, which was the most popular college student hangout along with Buckland's at the time I was a student, of course, to watch a beautiful sunset on Lake Ontario and walk along the lakefront. Whenever I'm in town, I always make a point to purchase a mixed cold-cut sub or a meatball sub for my brother-in-law Bob at his favorite sub shop, the Oswego Sub Shop. There are some famous Oswego State alumni, other than Bob of course, such as a Al Roker of the Today show who was a college acquaintance; Steve Levy and Linda Cohn, famous broadcasters on ESPN; and Ken Auletta, longtime novelist. Arguably the most famous of all is Jerry Seinfeld, but there is a caveat. Seinfeld never graduated. He quit college before he graduated to pursue a career in comedy, which in the end turned out to be a pretty good choice. I lived for two years in Scales Hall, which was the same dormitory Seinfeld lived in for two years. We were there together when I was a freshman, and he was a sophomore. I didn't know him, likely did see him, but I was a friend of his roommate, another student by the name of Larry Watson. I met Larry through a mutual friend by the name of Lamont Glass. Larry, Lamont, and I among others had lunch together many times and often were found in the student lounges studying, watching TV, or just doing the college dormitory thing.

When I went to the Oswego Sub Shop to get the mixed cold-cut sub for my brother-in-law, the owner, an elderly man by the name of Bob, was working. The menu in the sub shop includes the Al Roker Sub, the Steve Levy Sub, and the Rhonda Cohen Sub, just to name a few. As I made my order and discussed with Bob that Al Roker was a college acquaintance of mine but Steve Levy and Rhonda Cohen were younger than me, the topic turned to how Bob still had contact with Steve Levy. Bob continued to tell me this story of how Levy came to the shop about two years ago, which he often did when he was in the area to visit with Bob and have a sub. Levy wanted to know why Al Roker got more publicity out of his namesake Oswego sub than he did. Bob explained to Levy how it was a business decision in that Al plugged the Oswego Sub Shop more than Levy did, thus Al got more publicity out of his namesake sub than Levy. Bob believes that Steve caught on quickly because not two weeks later, Bob was watching a Syracuse University football game in which Levy was doing the commentary. A Syracuse player broke through the line and was sprinting down the field about fifteen yards ahead of all the defensive players. As Levy described the play, the ball carrier was sprinting down the field so fast and so far ahead of everyone else that he was running clear to the Oswego Sub Shop. When Bob heard that comment, Levy's Oswego Sub Shop currency shot through the roof quicker than that Syracuse University ball carrier sprinting down the field.

While listening to Bob's telling of the story, I had an idea. I asked Bob how I could get a sub named after me. He applied the same business protocol to me as he did to Steve Levy and Al Roker. If I could generate publicity for his Oswego Sub Shop through the channels I had available to me, he would consider naming a sub after me. A connection was made. I explained to him how I recently published my first book and was working on my second. I could, as I just did, write the Oswego Sub Shop into my new book, thus generating publicity for his business, and he in return would name a sub after me. Bob agreed, and the deal was closed. As *The King of Orchard*

Street progresses to its finish, there are numerous situations where the Oswego Sub Shop, the city of Oswego, Oswego State, and Carol's family fit well, not so much in the context of Orchard Street but rather in the context of my life from age eighteen right up to now with over thirty-five years of being married to Carol. Only time will tell how it all works out for Bob, the Oswego Sub Shop, and me, but there is Bob and the Oswego Sub Shop's first plug for sure.

I hope Bob, the Oswego Sub Shop, and I all live long enough to consummate the deal and to see the Vincent Palmieri Sub on the menu board in the shop.

With that, the first installment of our collective histories is written.

After that somewhat misdirected but fun trip to Niagara Falls, John-John and I continued our discussion of the larger-scale history of gambling other than on Orchard Street.

We start with the Bible and the crucifixion of Jesus. The Bible records, "And when they had crucified him, they divided his garments among them by casting lots." Indeed, Roman soldiers were at the foot of the cross gambling for Jesus's clothes or what was left of them, and I cannot imagine there being much left. I told John-John that *lots* is an ancient term for dice, which he had never heard before. Apparently, the soldiers felt the only fair way to divide up the clothes was by gambling for them well over two thousand years ago. Gambling certainly has a long sordid history. Gambling for whatever was left of a just murdered innocent man's clothes, which was most likely rags after the horrible death Jesus had just endured? Vile, to say the least, but unquestionably gambling.

Gambling, also called betting or gaming, is using the value of something and wagering it on an outcome to make more of that something, or taking a risky action in the hope of a desired greater result. There are three elements of gambling: consideration—the amount you bet, risk—the chance that your bet is right, and prize—what you receive, hopefully larger than what you risked. Those three elements are the essence of any gambling. In certain types of gambling, the outcome of the bet is known almost immediately like which horse crosses the finish line first or where the ball stops on a roulette wheel.

Other types of bets take longer. For example, a futures bet where your bet at the beginning of the NFL season that the San Francisco 49ers or the team of your choosing will win the Super Bowl. Whether the bet is a winner or not is not determined until the end of the NFL season about six months after placing the bet.

Gaming, as used in that context, is legalized gambling specific to a location or type of betting. That context allows the creation of gambling commissions such as the Nevada Gaming Commission. The commissions allow gaming companies to operate within their boundaries because it's sanctioned and it's legal in that area. With the advent of the World Wide Web, computers, and cell phones, gambling has gone to an entirely new level. Online gambling is a major international market estimated to generate about $400 to $500 billion a year in business just on the legal side.

Even prior to "they divided his garments among them by casting lots," in prewritten history, dice had been discovered in Mesopotamia likely dating back to 3000 BC. The dice were apparently based on something called Astragali, a form of divination that used dice specifically marked with letters or numbers. The actual purpose of these "dice" has never been clarified, but at some point they moved from being used for divination to a gambling device.

Chinese and Japanese history also indicate some of the earliest known forms of gambling. In China, betting was common on fighting animals, lottery games, and dominos. Pai-gow poker is noted in China in the tenth century with playing cards traced back to China and Japan in the fourteenth century. Modern poker games also derive from a game played in Persia in the seventeenth century. The first casino operated in 1638 in Venice, Italy. The preferred form of gambling in Great Britain, horse racing, goes back for at least four hundred years. Gambling has been popular in the United States for centuries dating back to the cowboys in Nevada, North Dakota, South Dakota, and California. In 1876 frontiersman Wild Bill Hickok was shot and killed playing poker at a saloon in Deadwood in the Dakota territory by Jack McCall who was later hanged for the crime. Although gambling was suppressed by law in many areas of the United States, by the twentieth century it was universally outlawed.

Yet it developed and continued to spread as a very popular illegal activity and spawned the rapid growth of many illegal organizations, specifically the Mafia.

Religious organizations either outlawed gambling or allowed it in a heavily controlled environment. In the long run, attempts to control gambling have proven mostly futile. Parts of the world have developed it into a whole business of tourism where people travel from place to place to gamble in locations such as in Las Vegas; Monaco; and Macau, China.

Laws are now mostly written in an attempt to control gambling by other methods. Most often by attempting to be certain that gambling devices are statistically random to prevent the manufacturers/owners from making high-value payoffs and keeping the probability of payoffs in small amounts to minimize people's interest. In other words, utilizing the theory that the likelihood is that the bettor will lose more money than earn, thus minimizing the desire for people to gamble. The idea runs along the same lines as insuring your home against destruction by fire, water, and the like. The insurance policy is a wager that if your house were to be destroyed, the insurance payout would be sufficient to replace it. Yet clearly, it is in the homeowner's best interest to prevent that destruction from occurring.

Over the past three millenniums, the major religions have also played a role in gambling. The ancient Hindu poem "Gambler's Lament" testifies to the popularity of gambling among Vedic people. The poem is a monologue from a repentant gambler about the ruin his addiction to dice brought upon him. Certainly, a forthright indication of the popularity of gambling in India during the Indian Iron Age. Judaism frowns heavily on gambling, even disqualifying a professional gambler from testifying in court. The Catholic Church's position is that there's no moral impediment to gambling so long as it is fair and all gamblers have an equal chance of winning. If there is no fraud and the participants do not know the outcome of the gamble, the Catholic Church clarifies that it is a reasonable form of entertainment, and the church is not opposed to it. The opposition in the Catholic Church is to minimize the negative effects of gambling such as loan-sharking, prostitution, corruption, and general immorality.

The Catholic theologian Saint Thomas Aquinas felt that gambling should be forbidden when the bettor is underage and not able to consent. Aquinas urged viewing gambling through the lens of social consequences.

Blaise Pascal, a French mathematician, philosopher, Catholic theologian, and the long-ago creator of Pascal's triangle, which delineates the odds of a specific number appearing on a roll of two dice, advocated for strict control of gambling. Protestantism has varying views of gambling. Some denominations forbid or discourage gambling, while others urge full participation. Gambling is opposed by Protestant denominations such as the Mennonites, the Church of the Lutheran Confession, the Southern Baptists, and the Assemblies of God. The Jehovah' Witnesses and the Church of Latter-day Saints expressly forbid gambling. Islam has many different interpretations as to the practice of gambling. According to Sharia Law, *maisir* is expressly forbidden in that the participation is based on an immoral inducement brought about by the wishful hopes of the gamblers that they will create a gain from chance but not from productive activity and never anticipate a loss. Muslim jurisprudence describes gambling as chronic and generally harmful to any Muslim. Generally speaking, to a practicing Muslim, maisir is forbidden.

Modern betting systems have been created in an attempt to beat the odds, but there is no mathematically assured version of winning. One such system is card counting whereby the player can memorize the cards that have been played and to some degree predict the next card. Casinos minimize that advantage by using multiple decks of cards to the extent card counting becomes literally impossible. Another system called column betting is where a bettor sets a target profit and then calculates the bet size they have to make to achieve that profit level. That system plays into the fixed profits form of gambling in that a bet is placed according to odds to create a specific profit. The same amount is wagered on each selection hoping that the bigger odd selection wins. The Martingale System, originally developed in eighteenth-century France, consists in doubling up the next bet on a losing bet and reducing winning bets by half. That system is based on a loss-averse mentality. At best, it improves the odds of breaking even, but the purpose of gambling is not to break even. It can also result in severe and quick losses.

There are numerous negative consequences to betting. Addiction to gambling varies your brain chemistry to the same compulsion that drives people to drug and alcohol abuse, which are often associated with gambling too. Most problem gamblers experience feelings of helplessness and anxiety due to the losses they incur. Others look to gambling as a way to create revenue to pay debts and medical expenses, which rarely, if ever, happens. Of course, it is true that gamblers exhibit a number of cognitive and motivational biases that distort their perceived odds of winning. They have a preference for desirability bias, namely a tendency to be overoptimistic about a future outcome as a result of their desire for that outcome. Gamblers can also exhibit a mental process called reluctance to bet, whereby they make what is called a hedge bet to protect against the bets they have actually placed being losers. With a hedge bet, the bettor places their original bet and then places another bet on the opposite side of their first, in the hope that if they lose their first bet, they make it up, at least to some degree, with their win on the hedge bet. Gamblers also look at what is called a ratio bias in that they prefer to bet worse odds drawn from a large sample, like one out of one hundred as opposed to better odds, one out of ten in the hope of a big win. That ratio bias is what lotto, Mega Millions, and Powerball wagers are based on.

With our review of the history of gambling on both the Orchard Street level and the worldwide level some sixty years ago and three thousand years ago respectively concluded, the discussion turned back to our latest gamble. Who is the King of Orchard Street?

We both were back on track, so to speak, to attempt to answer that question immediately.

John-John ran off with a pertinent memory to both of us.

"How old were you when I shot you in the head with the BB gun? I bet we were about six and eight. We were in your grandmother's backyard looking at my new BB gun when I stepped back, aimed it at you, and pulled the trigger. The BB hit you in the forehead and bounced off, but you started to cry and ran into the house.

I ran with the gun into my aunt Nina's house and told her what had happened. She could not believe that I had done it. She wanted to know if I hit you in the eye, was there any bleeding, and about ten other questions in ten seconds. I told her that it didn't look like you were hurt, but I was very scared that I had really injured you. Was I ever frightened. It scares me to talk about it even now. With a cracking voice I told my aunt that I didn't mean to hurt you. There was nothing intentional. It just happened, completely accidental. My aunt brought me over to my house to inform my mother, who asked the same questions and was even more appalled that I did it than my aunt. My mother told me that if you were seriously hurt, my father would tear me to shreds and that I better pray that you were okay. I think my mother then went over to talk to your mother and make sure that you were not injured. Your mother assured her that you were fine. It was just an accident and not to be worried. When my mom came in the door, I was a wreck. What a huge weight off my shoulders when she informed me that you were good and your mother told her not to worry. In a second I was off the hook with my mother, my father, and your mother too. Thank God no injuries and no family problems in mine, yours, or between them. The next day we were back to the same old shenanigans, like it had never happened."

From my side of the situation, there was no real harm, but I do remember the incident vividly. My mother wrapped a bandage around my head, which made me feel like the toughest kid on Orchard Street and even way back then a strong candidate for the King of Orchard Street.

John-John continued. "That was not the last of the potential problems, though. The next one was when I got your thumb caught in the bicycle chain. We had flipped my bike over to lubricate the chain to go faster. As I was spinning the sprocket, you were putting the oil on. Again, we were in your grandmother's backyard. You put your thumb too close to the spinning sprocket, and it got caught in one of the teeth of the sprocket with the chain over the top of it. There was no way to pull your thumb out. Our only choice was to spin the sprocket all the way around from the top, where your thumb was caught, to the bottom of the sprocket, where your thumb would come out, because the chain was no longer holding it in a tooth of the sprocket. Of course, it hurt, especially when I started spinning the sprocket. Eventually, your thumb moved from the top of the sprocket to the bottom and was freed up. I remember your thumbnail being mashed up and bloody, but you got up and ran into the house. Next, I had to go tell my mother about this one. She was more astonished than the BB gun situation. Same questions rolled off her tongue. Where were you? Was there blood? How bad were you injured? Instant replay from the BB gun incident.

"Once more, my poor mother had to go over to see Rosie to be certain there was no real problem with injuries or families. Once more, I waited breathlessly for her to come home. Once more, in a second, I was off the hook."

Again, from my side of the bike-chain event, there was no real harm. My thumb was a little bloody for a day or two. Eventually, my thumbnail turned black and fell off, but a new one quickly grew back.

Still, I now had to show John-John that right up to this sunny day in the summer of 2022, my thumbnail and cuticle never grew back as typical as the rest of my fingernails.

I was never destined to be a hand model anyway.

While talking about hands and hurting them, the topic of trains came up again in the sense that by playing around trains, you could get killed, lose an arm or leg. Only God knows what could happen.

John-John took up the story again. "I still think jumping on those trains was the most dangerous thing we did, and we did it all the time. One afternoon, unbeknownst to us, with my mother and father watching, Alex Rosemyer, Johnny Kipper, Joe Candella, and I hopped on a train that was parked behind Corrado's Mill. Each one of us was hanging on a separate boxcar. My mother and father were screaming at us to get off the train, but with it starting to move, we didn't hear them and didn't realize they were watching us. What we didn't know was that the train had just unloaded and was about to pull away. As we are hanging on, it started to move and headed west. As it got farther and farther outside of town, the train began to pick up more and more speed. I could feel it moving faster, and I was getting scared, so I jumped off. Johnny Kipper saw me get off, so he jumped off next. Alex was still holding on, and the speed of the train was continuing to rise. By now the train was probably one-half mile west of where we climbed on. Alex jumped off, but Joe Candella was still on. We were all yelling to Joe to jump off, but he didn't budge. The train was a mile out of town, by what we used to call the Black Bridge, and three of us were chasing it, trying to get Joe to jump off. Finally, he jumped. We all ran along the tracks to find out if he was hurt, which, thank goodness, he was not. Now, we all wanted to know why he didn't jump off when he heard us yelling to him that the train was going faster all the time and would not stop until the train station in Utica about ten miles west. With a befuddled look on his face, he asked us how he was supposed to hear us when he was deaf. All three of us looked at each other with an equally befuddled look on our faces because we all had known him since birth and were all well aware that he was deaf. What were we thinking about?

"Joe used to constantly repeat this tongue twister he knew:

> One smart fellow he felt smart,
> Two smart fellows they felt smart,
> Three smart fellows they felt smart.

After that experience, none of us felt smart.

"As we walked back east to Orchard Street, I really didn't feel smart, especially when I saw my father running toward me. Like lightning, I quickly figured out he must have seen what we were doing, and I was really going to be in trouble for this one. I had gotten away with shooting you in the head with the BB gun and getting your thumb caught in the bicycle chain, but my chances were very small to get away with this one. My father grabbed a hold of me by the arm, gave me a few whacks on the butt, and one or two in the back of the head. He told me that if I ever did anything like that again, I wouldn't be alive to see the next day and that he would likely spend the rest of his life in jail, but that was the price he would have to pay. It was all out of love and his desire to keep me safe, but enough was enough. He had had it with me, and I knew it. Kid-level trouble was one thing, but this time my life was at stake. I don't think I ever saw my father that serious in his life. I got that message loud and clear. That entire situation calmed me down well, and I started finding more positive circumstances to be connected to.

"Soon after the incident with the train, United States Attorney General Robert F. Kennedy made a visit to Frankfort for a campaign stop as he ran for the United States Senate representing New York. He was in a convertible with the top down, sitting on the top of the back seat, smiling and shaking people's hands. I stuck my hand out. Robert grabbed it and shook it. I was astounded. I had just shaken hands with a United States Attorney General. Robert F. Kennedy had shaken my hand. Very impressive for a ten-year-old, and my admiration for him grew even more from there.

"When I walked home north on Railroad Street, there was a guy who would show up on the corner occasionally to sell candy apples for 10¢ each. I had about 13¢ in my pocket and bought one as I had done so many times before, but this one was not like any I had previously purchased. The apple was sweeter, and the candy coating was thicker and redder than I had ever seen. The best candy apple I ever had in my life. I wonder if United States Attoney General Robert F. Kennedy had anything to do with it.

"The summer came to a close soon after the visit by Kennedy. School opened, and things on Orchard Street got more into the everyday routine with school open and winter fast approaching. It was a long, hot summer for my father and me. Still, all was well. When the spring with summer right behind came, I was determined to stay out of trouble. Alex had an excellent suggestion. Why don't we get a job? Great idea on two levels. First, hopefully a job would keep us occupied and out of trouble. Secondly, we could earn money. As luck would have it, at the time there was a huge strawberry farm in Schuyler owned by a woman from New Jersey. It turned out to be a very good season for strawberries, and because they rot quickly, she needed a lot of people to pick them fast. They would then be loaded on a truck, again quickly, be shipped to New Jersey to be sold in the grocery stores, all these before they rotted. A truck would come by on Orchard Street in the morning and pick up people who wanted to work and return them back later that afternoon. Alex and I decided that was the job for us. The picking rate was about 6¢ a quart. The owner had probably fifty people picking for eight to ten hours a day. The women would set up workhorses with a sheet of plywood stretched between two horses, one stand for each person picking. As you picked your quarts, each picker would bring their quarts over to your stand and accumulate them. If the picker was really fast and their stand was filled up, the owner would count your quarts and give you a ticket so that there was room to put more quarts as the day passed. At the end of the day, for the number of quarts you picked, she would pay you. It really worked well in that you got paid every day and in cash. After about a week Alex and I got fast at picking these berries and earning money. As I was busy picking one morning, evidently Alex was arguing with another kid in the patch about something. At one point as they were both walking back to their stand to place their quarts, Alex had heard enough. While the other kid was talking some nonsense, Alex picked up a quart of strawberries grabbed the other kid by the back of his head and squashed the whole quart of strawberries in his face. While this was happening, one of them kicked over an entire stand of quarts. The owner saw this happening and started screaming about how they were costing her a lot of money and that she wanted them out of her strawberry patch. She told them if you fight, you had to get off her property. I think Alex had enough of her too. He called me, and the two of us walked out of the patch. Basically, the first job either one of us ever had, and we both got fired. The woman would not pay us for what we had picked, which wasn't much early in the day, because Alex and the other kid in the scuffle had kicked over an entire stand of quarts.

Being that the patch was about five miles west of the North Frankfort bridge on Route 5, our issue now was, how do we get home? I asked Alex how far he thought we were from home and what we were going to do. With no other choice, we began to walk. It must have taken us almost two hours to walk home, but again we had no other choice. Back then there was no cell phone to call anyone, and most people only had one car anyway, which the father usually drove to work in the morning. That scenario quickly ended our strawberry picking careers.

Thinking back, I bet that other kid never ate another strawberry in his life, and if he did, it was likely jam. Strawberries all squished up."

Coincidentally, one of Carol Palmieri's most enticing desserts is strawberry shortcake made with cake, not biscuits. I think I will ask her to make strawberry shortcake for dessert tonight. With the strawberries really squished up.

Uncle John

I had always been fortunate enough since I was a child growing up for my mom and dad to afford a vacation at least once a year. That, coupled with the fact that we owned a camp in the Adirondack Mountains for over fifty years, which always provided my family with a permanent vacation option. At times in my youth, the vacations were mostly to New York City and Philadelphia. Yet we also frequented Lake George in New York, which Thomas Jefferson called "the most beautiful lake in the world" numerous times, and Saratoga Springs. We would camp at Pine Lake in NY every weekend and for at least two full weeks in the summer.

As I grew older, during my college years and up until the time I got married in 1989, vacations were always on the agenda. During four years of college, I went to Florida probably six times, four of them during spring break. After graduation from college, I still continued with trips to Atlantic City in New Jersey, New York City, and once or twice more to Florida. Even though I was now an adult, my dad still owned the camp at Pine Lake, and when my parents weren't using it on weekends, often my friends and I would. There were numerous times, when I was a teacher and off from work in the summer, that friends and I would go to Pine Lake for a week or longer if their vacations permitted.

Once I got married and prior to owning a home and having children, Carol and I made trips to Las Vegas on three different occasions; to Kingsport, Tennessee, to visit her girlfriend Lisa Wright; numerous trips to Maine and New Hampshire; and even twice more trips to Florida. Once we built our house and started having children, we were still fortunate enough to vacation at least once a year, sometimes two or even three times.

As a family, we made trips to New York City; Boston; Washington DC; Maine; Las Vegas; Disney World in Orlando, Florida; Lake Placid in New York; and the Finger Lakes region of New York. On numerous occasions, we traveled to Savannah and Tybee Island in Georgia, even going so far as Maui and San Francisco at other times. Now that my son and daughter are adults with good educations in high-demand, well-paying fields, they mostly take vacations on their own or with friends. There had been a few occasions in the past three or four years that I was still lucky enough to have my children interested in vacations with Carol and me. That is a blessing that I hope continues.

The main vacation that Carol and I take begins in early January and usually ends in mid-February to milder-climate areas, then upstate New York. We still continue our twice yearly trip to Maine and during the summer to various locations in upstate New York such as Niagara Falls, the Thousand Island region, and Watkins Glen. In February 2021, Carol and I traveled to San Francisco, then drove south on the coast to Palm Springs, and then northeast to Las Vegas. While in California, we made side trips to Pleasanton, Pebble Beach, and Pasadena to name a few. While in Nevada, we spent time in the Valley of Fire State Park, Henderson, Hoover Dam, and as any good tourist does on the world-famous Las Vegas Strip. Upon returning from California and Nevada, we were home for a week and then departed again for Palm Coast and Saint Augustine, Florida. From

Saint Augustine, we then drove north a to Tybee Island, Georgia. This year 2023, we have decided to return to Florida and Georgia, leaving most likely on December 29 and returning sometime in mid-February or later, depending on how long our money lasts. This trip, like all the others, is solely for pleasure, but there is a small yet important business aspect to it. We will depart Whitesboro to stay overnight in Rocky Mount, North Carolina, then proceed south to Palm Coast, Florida, to meet with my uncle John Iocovozzi to provide him with an opportunity to make his case as the possible King of Orchard Street. I am betting it will turn out to be a very interesting proposition.

After leaving Uncle John's, we will drive twenty miles south and I-95 to Daytona Beach to meet with Richard Sassone, another potential King of Orchard Street, and provide Richard with his chance to contend for the coveted title too. Although, it may be a small part of the entire trip, there is the business aspect to it, but shenanigans are still the driving force. After our time with Richard, Carol and I will again proceed on I-95 South to Key West, Florida, for a week in a luxury hotel for guaranteed shenanigans. From Key West, we will drive north to Orlando to meet Alaina and Noah for a few days at Disney World. This year 2023 is the fiftieth anniversary of the opening of Disney World in Orlando. I am not sure of the specific day that Disney opened its doors, but I am sure that while a freshman in college, I made a Spring-Break trip in February 1974 to Fort Lauderdale, then Daytona, and a side trip to Disney. That timeline puts me in Disney World when it was newly opened for just about a year.

At that time, Disney World was the only park. There was no Epcot, Hollywood Studios, or Animal Kingdom; it only had the Magic Kingdom. That was so long ago that Disney had not yet made their admission structure a flat-rate fee to attend all the sights in the park. The customer would purchase books of tickets for what I believe was $21 for the most expensive book. The attractions in the park were rated as A, B, C, or D. Depending on which book you bought, there were a series of A coupons, then B coupons, C coupons, and so on. Naturally, the first group of admissions that the average tourist used were the A coupons, the best rides, then proceeding to use the B, the C, and last the D. The inherent problem was, once all the A and B tickets were gone, the remaining C and D were for the least entertaining attractions. What would happen for the average tourist, myself included, was the customer would then be forced to buy more A and B coupons, which again disappear quickly causing you to go back and buy more A or at least B. The entire scenario continually drove up the cost of admission to the park throughout the entire day. At some point after that, February 1974 until the next time I went to Disney World in about April 1987, Disney decided the best approach was a flat-rate fee, which provided the customer with admission to all the attractions. Yet Disney being Disney, the corporation found another way to continue to drive up the cost of admission. The last time I was in Disney World was in 2002. If a customer wanted to lessen their wait time for a particular attraction, it could be done but for an added fee to enter the attraction through the Lightning Lane. Having not been inside any of the parks since 2002, I understand now that there are added fees for just about everything you do, continually driving up Disney's bottom line. When COVID became an issue for the world, Disney set up protocols to prevent the spread and eventually closed for about a month.

When we did go to Disney this year, I purchased for Alaina and Noah two-day Park Hopper passes so that they could attend any park they choose. The admissions were expensive, to say the least. Attached to those admissions are numerous other conditions. For example, the customer must decide which park they want to attend on a given day and then make a reservation at a specific time to enter the park. Far too many caveats for me, especially in terms of the cost of the admissions.

I will take back the old days when I was a college student. I walked up to the ticket booth, bought the most expensive coupon book at $21, and walked in the park for a long enjoyable day. No other conditions attached other than if I wanted to buy more A and B tickets, which was at my discretion. I know Disney is a lot of fun and a huge draw especially, for families, but now at age 68, I have nowhere near the patience to meet all the conditions required to enter Disney World or any other of their theme parks. I give Alaina, Noah, and anyone who has the patience to visit Disney World nowadays a great deal of credit because it takes patience that I certainly don't have, especially when viewed in the context of the cost of an individual admission. I think of many families and their children that would love to vacation at Disney World but just cannot afford it, sad to say the least.

In the end, I hope to use my time in Orlando to sit by the hotel pool, possibly do some shopping and find the quietest place on the grounds. That, at least, was my first intention, but in the long run, Disney did hook me into buying two one-day adult passes but only to the Magic Kingdom. I must say, Carol and I did enjoy ourselves perhaps due the cost of each admission. Yet speaking only for me, I did force it a bit.

After those five days at Disney World, we will drive north to Saint Augustine for lunch and some sightseeing. Then to Tybee Island for two weeks, to really enjoy an environment that fits my purposes. While on Tybee, I'll spend most of my time walking on the beach, sitting on the pier at the end of what is now known as Tybrisa Street but is Sixteenth Street. Tybee is the perfect laid-back southern environment I enjoy or as the locals call it "Tybee time." My time on the pier and beach is consumed talking to and checking on the daily catch of the numerous fishermen who dot the pier throughout the day and not much else.

Truly the most enjoyable part of those days is to watch, in the words of Otis Redding, "the ship's roll in, and then I watch them roll away again, sitting on the dock of a bay wasting time."

Otis left his home in Georgia. I left mine in New York.

The antecedent to all that pleasure is business first with King of Orchard Street hopefuls Uncle John and Richard Sassone.

After a long treacherous drive from Rocky Mount, North Carolina, to Palm Coast, Florida, in a blinding rainstorm—and I do mean blinding—Carol and I finally checked in to our hotel in Palm Coast. We drove the entire length of the storm from north to south for over eight hours. The storm was so severe that I could not read the license plates on the cars twenty feet ahead of me while driving no faster than thirty-five miles per hour. What strikes me as ironic was that probably 25 percent of the vehicles do not adjust their driving at all because of the tricky conditions. In fact, it seems at times they drive even faster. One theory I have heard is that with the proliferation of SUVs, the height of those vehicles allows the driver to ride above the fray and is less limited in sight, allowing for more speed. That sounds like a possibility but not enough of one for me to warrant what is still a risky practice. I did something on that trip that I rarely if ever do in that I pulled off I-95 South in Saint Marys, Georgia, to take a break from the storm for a few minutes. I had to because of the traffic and weather conditions, which were exceptionally intense. As scary and stressful experience as I had ever witnessed while driving all the across 3 states, 8 hours, and 544 miles.

When we finally did get to Palm Coast, the first order of business was to phone Uncle John to inform him that we had arrived and we would see him the next morning. The second order of business was to thank God for getting us to Palm Coast safely and to pray for the safety of those still on I-95 South as I could see and hear the traffic behind my hotel still moving along at dangerous speeds in terrible weather. After that drive, I pray for the safety of people traveling every chance I get. The third order of business was to order a Chinese-food delivery, go to bed early, have breakfast the next morning, and be at Uncle John's, ready to start by 9:00 a.m.

Carol and I met all those requirements and were at Uncle John's on time the next morning. When we arrived at his house, Uncle John and Aunt Cookie were waiting for us with open arms. We shook hands, exchanged hugs and a few words, then we quickly moved in to one of their spare rooms in order to delve deeply into the King of Orchard Street project.

Uncle John decided the best way for him to remember his life on Orchard Street as a child, some eighty years ago, was to lay out the geographic setup of the street or, as I suggested to him, "the lay of the land."

He agreed and began. "Orchard Street is located on the north side of the village of Frankfort, running east and west between Main Street, the New York Central West Shore Railroad line, and the Mohawk River. On the west end of the street is Rankin Dairy, and on the east end is the lumberyard of the Union Fork and Hoe Company. Rankin Dairy is a milk-producing plant with the Union Fork and Hoe company making shovels, rakes, pitchforks, and about any type of manual farm equipment imaginable to be shipped all over the world.

"Farmers brought their milk to Rankin Dairy every day starting at about 5:00 a.m. The raw milk was in big cans on the farmers' truck and would be dumped from the cans to even larger vats in Rankin's milk station. The raw milk would be processed for fat content, allowing the farmers to be paid in cash on the spot accordingly. From the vats, processing would begin to refine the fresh milk for bottling, making cheese, and eventually distributing them to stores all over central New York. Next to the milk plant was a large barn that was used to store ice that was cut from various ponds all over the area during the winter months. The ice was then sold in the summer to people that were fortunate enough to own an icebox, which was an early form of a refrigerator. We had an icebox and most of our friends did too, but there were many households that did not.

"Alongside the dairy, there was a skim-milk plant. When the skim milk was run between two big rollers, it came off the rollers in a very thin sheet that could then be pulverized and put in barrels. When the rollers got stuck, the resulting product was not fit for sale. Many times the workers would wind the sheet of pulverized milk on a stick and give it to the kids in the neighborhood for a treat, and what a great treat it was. That was the kind of world we lived in. It was safe, and people were happy to help one another. Kindness was, as you say, 'the code.'"

I had to add, "Russell Marchione also told me the story about the rolled milk on a stick. Amazingly, he gave the same description as you. They were delicious, a real treat. They were likely a penny each, and most times, the workers gave them to kids who were in the neighborhood. That genre of a practice is the crux of the King of Orchard Street lifestyle."

"Do you think anybody lives like that anymore, Uncle John?" I asked.

His eyes got a forlorn look in them for a second. He thought about it for another second, then replied flatly, "No."

In the two or three seconds that elapsed between my question and his reply, I could see the movie reels of his over ninety-year life running through his mind. When in his life and where—I have no idea, but the reels were running. I bet those reels in his mind could all run in less than twenty minutes.

Life and time certainly have an aberrant ingredient to them, and I could tell by the look, for those few seconds, on my dear uncle John's face, that he also was wondering about those aberrant ingredients.

As I was too.

Uncle John picked up with the milk plant again. "In the plant, they had a huge boiler room that was always full of coal. They kept the boiler running all the time to provide heat for pasteurizing the raw milk the farmers bought in every day. The room was filled with coal all the time. After all, the raw milk needs to be warmed up. We would help ourselves to the coal if the right time line were to show up. If it didn't, we would make it the right time line. One way or another, we would have enough coal to keep our houses warm. That extra free coal, along with what my mother purchased, enabled us to stay warm all winter. I didn't then, and I still don't now, consider it stealing, more like surviving. In the end, how much coal did we consume? The milk plant was always able to write off their coal purchases as a business expense anyway.

"Walking east along the railroad tracks, there was a dump. It started out small, then got big as the years passed. The dump was located on the north side of the railroad tracks sloping downhill toward the canal. The residents would daily bring their trash and drop it in the dump. There was no NYSDEC in those days. It was simple. Every household had trash to dispose of, and there was a dump on the block. Easy. No fuss, no muss, and your household trash was gone in a second. I have no idea who owned the land the dump was on, probably George Corrado, but whoever did own it didn't care if we all dumped our trash there because no one ever stopped us.

"Corrado's Feed Mill was quite a big building and operation at the time. When the farmers brought their milk to Rankin Dairy to sell, they would get paid mostly in cash, but some preferred to get paid monthly. With the money in hand or due them, they proceeded next door to Corrado's to purchase supplements, specific grains, and whatever else they needed to keep their cows healthy and producing milk at full capacity. The two businesses, Rankin Dairy and Corrado's Mill, kept each other going strong for over fifty years—a perfect business relationship if there ever was one, or as they say these days, a B2B relationship. Now that I think about it, it was the perfect B2B2B relationship between the farmers, Rankin Dairy, and Corrado's. I bet no one in the modern day has thought of B2B2B business relationships. I just coined the phrase, didn't I?"

We both got a big chuckle out of that and got right back to Uncle John's story.

"There were two guys who worked at the dairy that I specifically remember. One was Jimmy, and the other one was Howard. About ten people worked at the dairy, but those two guys I remember clearly. As kids, we used to wait for the workday to end and watch the employees either walk to get a bus on Main Street, or if they were fortunate to have one, get in their cars and drive home. The reason we waited for them was when they came out the feed mill with all the powder from the dried grain floating around in the plant, they would look like Santa Claus covered in white fluffy snow. In the employees' case, what covered them wasn't snow but light-colored grain dust. For a group of kids, that was very amusing, and we would laugh like hell about it.

"My mother, once in a while, when she had extra money, would walk over to Corrado's to buy fresh flowers that they would sell in the summer. There again is the beauty of the way we lived. Even though my mother didn't have a husband—because my dad died young— and she had seven children to raise, she still managed to buy fresh flowers for the table to make our home a nice place for raising her family, which she was doing alone. As George Corrado got older, he handed over the daily operation of the mill to his daughter, Mayme Hosney; and her husband, Paul. The Hosneys also put in a store to sell shovels, rakes, and other hand-powered farm implements, most likely purchased from the Union Fork and Hoe Company located on the east end of the railroad tracks with Corrado's located at the west end of the same spur less than a mile apart. Not a big shipping price there and another B2B2B business relationship that never left the block. As kids, we used to love to go into the store and see the baby chicks they sold, which they kept in a light bulb–warmed incubator. During Easter, it was an especially a big thrill to go in the office to see the chicks. Many people had chickens in those days, and the mill sold a lot of them quickly."

That statement struck me more quickly than the one on Corrado's selling the chicks.

I blurted out, "Goodness, Uncle John, I forgot all about the baby chicks. You're twenty-four years older than me tomorrow, as a matter of fact, and I did the same exact thing when I was a child. It was a huge thrill for all the kids on Orchard Street, in my time there too, especially at Easter, to walk in the mill office and see the baby chicks in the light bulb–warmed incubator. Likely it's the same incubator that was in the office when you were ten years old, and the Hosneys were very good about letting us walk in and out of their office unannounced."

I had, in effect, a portrayal of Obi-Wan Kenobi's famous quote, "I felt a great disturbance in the Force."

I also felt a great disturbance in the Force right there in Uncle John's spare room on Princess Ruth's Way in Palm Coast, Florida. Was that a sort of metaphysical time warp that we just flew into and directly out of in a split second? Yikes! What a recollection for me that has been moored in my brain somewhere for about sixty years, and Uncle John just broke it loose with that statement. The vagaries of time were alive and breathing in that room. What cobweb did that just clean out? Overall, a first-rate one.

At that point, I had to take a break.

When we began again, Uncle John started discussing a good friend of his whom I never heard of. "Around the corner on Tisdale Avenue, on the north end of the street, I had a very good friend by the name of Tommy Papa. I believe his father's name was Sandy, but I have no recollection of him. Maybe Tommy's dad was dead, or his parents were divorced. I don't recall, but I never knew him. The Papas lived next door to Corrado's warehouse. At about eleven years old, Tommy fractured his leg in a few places, a bad break to be certain. My brothers, a few other friends, and I took it upon ourselves to build a cart for Tommy. We could wheel him around on it, so he didn't have to stay home. We would take turns wheeling him in it. Even if he couldn't play catch, basketball, or just run around with us, he could still be part of the gang. Among my brothers, the Pileggis, and the Tubias—all big families—we took very good care of him for, I bet, three months as his leg healed. Once more, there was the code we all maintained. We were all in the same boat and helped one another in just about any way we could as individuals, families, children, and adults.

"Our house sat between the Tubias and the Falcones, and the movement between families was constant. On the west side of my dad's house, the Tubia side, was a garage. In front of the garage, above the black-topped driveway to drive in to the garage itself, my father constructed a big pipe frame to grow grapes or, as the old-timers used to say, "uva." He ran strings from the west side, the Tubia side, of the framework over the top to the east side. Then he planted small grapevines at the foot of the strings on the west side to allow the vines as they grew to follow the strings over the top of the pipe structure, then down the east side of the structure to the ground. I am not sure if he knew exactly what he was doing or just took a guess, but I suspect he knew perfectly well what to do with it because by the end of that first summer, those six-inch vines he planted in the spring grew clear up from the west side over the top to the east side as he had planned. By early October, we had so many grapes we didn't know what to do with them. Of course, the attitude was to share them with the neighbors, and everyone was happy we did. Before you knew it, everyone was making grape jelly, wine, grape-seed oil and even grape pie. Those wonderful aromas filled the entire block for two to three weeks. As the years passed, those grapevines, after being cut back each fall to their original six-inch size, flourished more and more as did the process of sharing their bounty with our neighbors. I think all that goodwill flourished more than the vines did themselves because of those little six-inch grapevines.

"Behind our garage, on the north side, my father also built what we called a shanty or as it is called now a shed. My father kept all his gardening tools in there—shovels for his garden along with snow shovels for the winter, rakes for both dirt and leaves, hoes, a wheelbarrow, just a lot of hand tools that he used all the time. At first, our house was big for the size of the family, but as the years passed and my parents had more and more kids, it got a little tight. Then as we all grew up, got married, joined the military, or relocated, the room in the house got to be more and more. I was born at the end, so for me, there was always plenty of room. My mother had seven children, but she was pregnant ten times. She lost the first three right off the bat. After those letdowns, my father wanted to adopt, but my mother would have none of it. She told him it would take time, but everything would be fine. After the third loss, she had seven healthy children over about a twelve-year stretch. Great come back, I would say. My sister Flora was the first to marry, marrying Jim Favat. They lived upstairs in my house in the same apartment you grew up in.
"When we were kids, we would go to a farm near Hamilton or Clinton, New York, I don't remember which, to pick beans. It must have been Clinton because the ride from Frankfort was short. Maybe it was Clinton near Hamilton College or Hamilton, New York, near Colgate University. I can't remember, but we went there to work. The farmer would send a truck to pick us up about six in the morning. When my mother could, she would come with us. I think for a lot of reasons. First reason was to keep an eye on all of us, second to make certain we were being treated fairly by the farm owner, and last to make some extra money. The point I am making is, on one, I remember very hot August day, we were all riding home in the back of the truck. I don't know how, but my mother got wind that my sister Flora had given birth to a baby girl and named her Verna. As we drove north on Tisdale Avenue, the Addolorata Society was just starting their festival parade from their shrine on the corner of Tisdale Avenue and Orchard Street, then proceeding east to turn left

on Railroad Street, then right to their grounds on Sheldon Avenue. The driver of our truck was waiting for the parade to move east so that he could drop us off where he picked us up, which was coincidently, in front of my mother's house, likely because my house was in the middle of the block. As we waited, I could see that my mother was getting restless. I don't know if you are aware of this, but she was a midwife and delivered I bet 50 percent of the kids born on Orchard Street during her short adult life. I also bet she intended to deliver Verna, her first grandchild. As fate would have it, she decided to go work with us that day. When the truck finally did stop in front of our house, I never saw my mom move so fast. She was off the back of the truck and bounding two steps at a time up the stairs, to what eventually was your apartment, like a jackrabbit. I can see her as if it happened yesterday. I don't know what my mother would have done if it were a week, that she worked on the farm. If that were the case, my mother would have gotten back to Frankfort by hook or crook. That's the way it worked, no second-guessing. That Verna—she was beautiful from the day she was born with dark hair and big dark eyes. The woman was beautiful from the day the sun first rose on her.

"Most times, everybody—all my brothers and sisters—went to pick beans. My mother would help us put together our bedrolls like the cowboys used. We would pack clean clothes, and off we would go for the week. Kids from all over the region would come, entire families just like us. We would stay for at most a week, but some kids would stay all summer. My mother would never go for that. She felt bad that we had to go for the week, but that is how we made money. When we came home on Friday, my mom gathered up all our clothes and bedding to wash. On Monday, we would be ready to go with everything clean. We slept in small shacks that were lined with beds. The shacks were nothing fancy, but they served the purpose. They were a little tight, but we managed. There would be cookhouses outside the shacks that the farm hired to feed us breakfast, lunch, and dinner. Again, the food was not fancy, but it served the purpose. There was plenty of food, and no one was ever hungry.

"We worked in the fields picking from about seven in the morning to four or four thirty in the afternoon. It was hot, hard work, but we had to earn money somehow. I think we were paid 11¢ a bushel. When we filled a bushel, we would bring it up to a stand and would be issued a ticket, then grab a new bushel and go out to start picking again. Thinking about it eighty years later, it was fun with all my brothers, sisters, at times even my mother, and I was working hard on the farm or at home but always in one another's company. My brother George, God love him, was always the best at everything. He could pick more beans in the shortest time than anybody on that farm, young or old. That guy just had it working for him all the time in everything he did."

I responded, "Funny you should say that, Uncle John. I remember years ago you told that when Uncle George first moved to the Landings in Savannah and held parties at his house inviting many of his neighbors—be they old cotton money, fruit money, lawyers, doctors, or whatever—that they were shocked when he told them stories as to how he grew up as a child. A large family, with a deceased father, not much money, picking beans and doing about anything to make a living. Those old four- or five-generation monied Georgia families couldn't believe that was where he came from. When he would invite you to the parties, his kids, specifically Kevin and Kim, would ask you if you thought their dad would start telling bean-picking stories."

Typically, you replied, "You can bet on it."

Almost prophetically, after Uncle George had a few scotches in him, the bean-picking stories would flow out as easily as the scotch flowed in, much to the bewilderment of his genteel Southern guests.

I could see that Uncle John had "the flow" now and continued. "All the blocks of Orchard Street had large families residing in almost every house. The Falcones, the Tarrises, the Carusos, the Tubias, and others all with seven, eight, ten or more children in each family. The street teemed with kids. As my family got larger, we needed more room, so my father decided to build a wraparound porch on the front of the house. The street was paved, but from the edge of the street to the front door of our house were wooden planks because the village had not put in sidewalks yet. The purpose of the planks was to walk on when it rained to cut down on the mud getting in the house. My father put the porch on the front for more room and to get closer to the edge of the street again to alleviate the mud problem. When we laid those planks down, as did other houses, the street looked like an old cowboy town you see in the movies. My dad hired a carpenter from Herkimer, Mr. Macrena, I think, to build the porch. Macrena was a little short guy, but he could work like a horse. He measured everything up and cut it then, my father and he nailed it together. They did a great job because all the while we lived there, as did you, I never knew that porch to move an inch. They both worked on it in the early evening and on the weekends. In about three weeks, they had it done. It really did resolve both the mud and living-space issue. Eventually, when the village put in sidewalks, we were close to the road, but in those days, there was very little attention paid to setbacks. Most places likely didn't even have those laws on the books yet. It was your property, and as the owner, mostly you just did what you wanted to do with it.

"Moving east after Falcones' house was the Tarrises, then Zito's Restaurant. Bars couldn't serve alcohol on Sunday before noon, but many customers wanted to drink earlier than that. Zito's had a big dining area to the left of the bar. After dinner hours, they would clear out the tables for dancing with live music. On Sundays, when the women went to church, the men went around the back of Zito's building, where there were two doors. The door on the left entered the bar, and the one on the right entered the dining room. Mr. Zito would keep all the lights off in the bar and sit in the back of the dining room away from the windows with one light on waiting for customers. Beginning about 8:00 a.m., the men would start to show up at the back door to buy alcohol. Mr. Zito would be happy to serve them legally or not. He was a businessman trying to make a living no matter what the laws said. My dad could walk through Falcones' and Tarrises' backyards to get to the rear door of Zito's without walking on the street, which is exactly what he did. Everyone would go to the door and order a roll and a cup of coffee. There was no roll, and the cup of coffee was a shot. I remember the first time my dad called me over and said, 'Johnny, I want you to taste something.' He gave me a little sip of whiskey, which I didn't like and then a little sip of beer to chase the whiskey down, which I did like. The Zitos lived upstairs of the restaurant with their two children—Jack whom we called him "Bullet" and his sister, Marion. A small family by Orchard Street standards.

"My mom and dad were good friends with the Internicolas who lived next door to Zito's Restaurant. Mr. Internicola was maybe a little over five feet tall, and we always called him Shorty. I think his real name was Nick, but I am not certain. His wife's name was Peppina, and she was even shorter than him. They had five kids—Theresa, Nick, John, Anthony, and Nappy. For that matter, I am not certain what Nappy's real name was either, but I think it was Norfield or something to that effect. I was the best man in Anthony's wedding. These people were really short, like the tallest one was pushing it five feet, five inches. Still, every one of them was a great person, and I will never forget any of them. Something happened way back then with the law, and somehow Nappy was involved. To keep him out of jail, he had to move to Kansas City to live in a secure facility of some sort for a short period. Whatever it was, Nappy was young and made a mistake getting involved. He served whatever the punishment was, got released, and spent the rest of his life in Kansas City as fine a citizen as anyone else. I remember seeing him in the Valley now and then, probably visiting family, always dressed in red Kansas City Chief's clothes. He made a mistake, although I don't remember what it was, but I bet mostly as a result of being young and immature. We all make mistakes. You own up to it, pay the bill, and move on. Nobody's immune."

That statement from Uncle John connected to a story of mine. "I agree 110 percent, Uncle John, and I must tell you what happened to me about fifteen years ago with one of the Internicolas. For many years, Joe Papa was my mechanic. When he sold his business to build Stewarts in Frankfort, I moved east on Main Street to do business with Jerry Crimmins for about as long as I did at Papa's. When I built my house in Whitesboro, I continued to do business with Jerry Junior, but then it got too hard. When Jerry Junior took over the garage, he stopped opening on Saturday morning, which many times was when I would bring my car in for work after our Kiwanis meeting. Then my wife, kids, and I stopped having dinner on Monday night at my father's because as he got older, and it was too difficult for him to cook dinner for ten people, which again was a time when I dropped my car off at Jerry's to be worked on. After all those years and now being a resident of Whitesboro, I began to do business with Village Motors in Oriskany at the recommendation of a friend by the name of Pat Marthage. As the years went by, I also became friends with Matt Shannon, the owner of the Village Motors, his family, and the employees. After close to fifteen years of doing business with Village Motors, on one occasion, I asked one of the body guys that I only knew by his first name, Neil, what his last name was, to which he replied, 'Internicola.'

"That set the entire discussion in going in an expected direction. I wanted to know who his dad was. I wanted to know if he was from Frankfort. I wanted to know if his dad was from Frankfort, specifically Orchard Street. I wanted to know if I told him about my first book *Ruthie Deeply*, much of which takes place on Orchard Street. I asked if I ever told him the story about his grandfather, Mr. Internicola, the five foot one you mentioned earlier, how every time I walked by his house at about five or six years old on my way to Sam Talerico' s store, Mr. Interncola would ask me in broken English 'Whatsa you' name.' Then give me a few pennies to buy candy at Sam's store and on the way back home again ask me, 'Whatsa you' name?' Which going in both directions, I would tell him.

"When I got home, I would ask my mother why he kept asking me my name. To which, she would reply, 'He's an old man and an old friend Just tell him your name.'

"I continued with many other questions for Neil. Neil replied with some nos but mostly yes. The point being, here was a third-generation family friend from Orchard Street right under my nose for fifteen years, and I had no idea. My connection to Neil was instantly made thicker, deeper, and richer, all stemming from the 1930s on Orchard Street in Frankfort right up to the day Neil and I had our conversation in 2011 and still continuing to today as we work our way through *The King of Orchard Street*.

"It's a long continuous two-family progression stretching for almost a century now."

Uncle John fully disclosed that he really liked my story by the way he snickered at me as I told it. As quickly as I finished the story, he launched into a discussion of his father and cars.

"My dad had a car that was massive. It had enough steel and chrome on it to make about three of today's cars. That thing was a weapon on wheels. When my brother Vince got old enough, my father would let him drive it to Herkimer. It was a Willys—Overland Whippet—and it was huge. My brother, my cousin George DiCamillo, and Nicky Internicola would push it out of the driveway, then push it east on Orchard Street to get the speed up so that my brother could pop the clutch to start the motor. Once it was started, George and Nick would jump in. My dad worked very hard. I never knew exactly where he worked, but he went to work every day. The reason I say he worked very hard is that, he generated enough money to own a house with a garage and owned a car too. I don't think anyone else on the street had all three other than my dad. The others may have had a house but many rented. Usually the house, if they owned it, didn't have garage because very few on the street had a car, which would indicate, compared to everyone else, that my father was financially in good shape. At times, I would go with him to Joe Valero's garage in Herkimer for gas or have the car worked on. Many times, I think we went just to hang around the garage and get the news of the day. The feeling, at about ten years old, of driving in our own car with my dad at the wheel, hanging out in Valero's garage with full-grown men, knowing very few people were lucky enough to own a home with a garage and own a car, I felt right there like not only the King of Orchard Street but the King of the World for all to see."

Coincidentally, at approximately the same age in the mid-1960s, I had the same inkling. The differences being, I was riding in a convertible Cadillac. Joe Cristiano was driving. Verna Favat was in the passenger seat. I was in the back seat, and we were on our way to A&W Root Beer in East Utica.

The more things change, the more they remain the same. As it says in Ecclesiastes 1:9 (KJV), "The thing that hath been, it is the thing that shall be."

Now that the topic of money came up, Uncle John continued. "After my dad died, without his earnings, we struggled to a degree. Always keep in mind there were seven kids in the house and my mother to feed, dress, keep warm, and all the other everyday living expenses. My dad always worked, but there was a short period when he was still alive that he was out of work, and we couldn't pay our light bill. My father was a registered Republican, but the Democrats were in control of Frankfort's political structure at the time. Someone suggested to my father that he change his party to have a better chance at getting a job. With the light bill still being a problem that needed to be cleared up, one afternoon, my mom was standing at the kitchen sink with the small knife in her hand cleaning some vegetables. Someone knocked at the door, and when she answered it, the guy told her that he was there to turn off the power and would have to go down to our basement. My mother was having none of it. She, in no uncertain terms, told the guy that if he went down those stairs, he would never come back up. Whoever he was got the message. The guy spun around and was off that step on his way south on Litchfield Street in less than two minutes. I'm not sure if my father changed his party or not, but I think he did because the next week, he got a job working for the village. You must do what you must do to make it work, politics included.

"When I was born in 1932, the Great Depression had taken hold in America and was spreading quickly. I don't think anyone had any inkling of what was about to happen over the next ten years in the United States, especially in terms of the federal government. I was too young to remember a lot about those days, but as I grew up, by the time 1942 or 1943 rolled around, things had gotten better as a result of the US moving to a wartime economy. In the interim, one way or another, my mother kept us together. Isn't that always the case in adversity the mother glues it together somehow? Well, probably not always the case but in most cases anyway.

"To this day, my mother made the best bread I ever tasted. She would bake thirteen loaves a week. Why the number was thirteen, I have no idea. Maybe she was thinking a loaf and a half of bread per person per week was enough for the week? I am not certain why thirteen loaves, but what I am certain of is, that bread was the best I have ever eaten to this day. The finances were tough, but we all worked somewhere, doing something, then pooled our money and kept everything paid in full. Come to think of it, having seven kids in the family was, in our case, a good thing. We had seven pairs of hands to work and pay bills. Our strength lay in our numbers, and somehow we made it work.

"Another guy that often comes to mind when I think about Orchard Street in those days is Frank 'Bull' Zaffarano. Frank always wore a cowboy hat, which we all got a big kick out of. Obviously, we weren't in Texas, but apparently, Frank thought we were. Bull even went so far as to start a band, which he named the Cowboys. They would play in the restaurants in Frankfort and throughout the Valley. When serving dinners was done, dancing would start usually around ten in three or four different establishments that had live bands on the weekends. Usually, the Brass Tack, Grippe's, and few others would have live music, thus keeping the Cowboys and a few other bands popular in the area for many years. The Zaffaranos had a big family that ran all over Orchard Street also.

"About five houses east of us were Joe, Angelo, and Mary Aiello, who were also our close friends. Angelo was involved in music, and Joe was a battlefield commission in World War II appointed to the rank of captain for his bravery under fire. He was truly a war hero, and after World War II, he became known in Frankfort as Captain Joe. For many years, Joe was the owner of Western Auto on Main Street. His sister, Mary; and adopted son, Donnie, worked in Joe's store their entire lives. Carmen and Tom Ruffalo had a grocery store two doors east on the block from Aiello's house. The store had the best sausage around. When my uncle Joe Dee Sr. would come from Saugerties, where he lived for many years while working for the NYSDOT as a civil engineer, on the train to visit my mother, she would wake me up early to go to Ruffalo's store and buy fresh sausage. She knew the sausage was ground fresh every day, and her brother loved it. She would fry that sausage so that it smelled throughout the entire house and block. God, that brings back wonderful memories. The Ruffalos would put the purchase on her bill, which she would send me back later in the week to pay. My mother would have me buy four or five pounds, two or three to cook and one for her brother Joe to take back home with him. The sausage was less than 10¢ a pound. Actually, I think it was about eight, which would put the price of four pounds somewhere around 33¢. The Ruffalos operated their store the same way we all lived—fairly, honestly, and with no nonsense. Fairly? Honestly? No nonsense? Not in this world today. Could the world ever use some of those concepts now? Some? All of them to an enormous degree?

"The amount of activity that occurred every day on that five small block of Orchard Street was impressive. The entire street was less than a mile long from end to end. On the east end of the street was the lumberyard for the Union Fork and Hoe Company, another grain mill GLF Corporation and big roundhouse for New York Central Railroad trains. On the west end of the street was Rankin Dairy and Corrado's Mill. Scattered between those far ends were Billis's Hotel, Zito's Restaurant, Ruffalo's Grocery store, and going a little south on Litchfield Street was Puzze's Restaurant and the Argonne Grill. That's ten businesses in that five-block stretch of less than a mile.

"The Fork and Hoe being the largest employer, followed by New York Central Railroad, Rankin Dairy, and Corrado's Mill, there was probably five hundred jobs just on that street. Between the Union Tool and the New York Central roundhouse, I bet three hundred people were employed in those two businesses.

"In the morning and really throughout the day when people were working at the various companies, the street was full of cars, trucks, and people walking from their jobs to have breakfast, shop at Ruffalo's Grocery store, walk to the bank on Main Street, or whatever they were doing. The activity was nonstop. The residents of Orchard Street, with all those big families, were in constant motion also. Orchard Street was a beehive of activity as if you were in a big city. Many of the men came to work early—at least, I bet they told their wives that—but they also knew very well the trick at Zito's bar to get a coffee and a roll. The workers had the coffee-and-a-roll ploy down as well as the male residents of Orchard Street did on Sunday morning. Precisely like on Sunday morning, the workers would go to the back door to Zito's to find Mr. Zito waiting for them. Alcohol couldn't be served between 4:00 a.m. and 8:00 a.m., but there was money to be made, and Mr. Zito was going to make it. New York State liquor laws be damned, especially in the case of the New York Central Roundhouse workers. They were at Zito's well before 6:00 a.m. Many of them having to be at work by 4:00 a.m. to turn the trains around that were now moving into the roundhouse from traveling overnight.

"As cars became more affordable for the average person, people traveling by train dropped off dramatically. Up until that point, the train was the main form of transportation for both people and products. As the Great Depression started to weaken, along with cars becoming more affordable, many people who formerly traveled by train were now able to afford cars. My uncle Joe Dee, as we talked about earlier, came to visit my mother by train, but a few years later, like many others, he was able to afford a car and would drive to see her.

"Trains still came in and out of the roundhouse all day and night, only now they were mostly used for transporting goods rather than people. Eventually it got to the point that the roundhouse was no longer even necessary. Train ridership was down to nothing, and product transportation was being done more and more by airplane and tractor trailer. With the advent of the interstate transportation system, most products were soon transported by tractor trailer, and the railway system was slowly becoming nonexistent. Right there on that microcosm of Orchard Street, we witnessed the evolution of transportation in America from the Erie Canal to trains, from trains to tractor trailers, and eventually to airplanes. New York Central Railroad in the late 1930s decided that train transportation was becoming more and more obsolete, and the company needed to tear down the roundhouse. After they disassembled the wood housing of the roundhouse and disposed of it, there was a lot, and I mean a lot of steel still on their property—the entire turntable, which must have been fifty feet in diameter; the tracks running into the building; tracks that were stored in the roundhouse; and the small what resembled a forklift-type vehicles that they would drive up to the side of the locomotive and push with to spin around the train on the turntable. All that had been disposed of. I couldn't make a guess as to how many tons of steel there were in and around the roundhouse.

"New York Central's problem then became how to dispose of all that steel. It was too big, heavy, and costly to be loaded on trucks and transported for disposal. The company decided the best way to dispose of it was to dig a big hole and bury it. Environmentally, it probably wasn't a bad idea because the steel came from the ground as iron ore and been refined into steel. If the company buried the steel, eventually it would rust and seep back into the ground. After all, the ground is where it came from. Once they finished burying all the steel and closing the operation on Orchard Street, someone somewhere came to the conclusion that the buried steel could be dug up and resold to various companies in the area to be reused.

"When the word spread throughout Orchard Street, Frankfort, and beyond that all the steel was buried, people started to come from all over the area to dig it out of the ground. As they dug it up, they would pile it with this pile belonging to one person, that pile belonging to another, and then another pile belonging to a third person, and so on. Throughout the day, flatbed trucks would pull in with scales on the bed to weigh the steel that each person had in their pile and pay them in cash for it, recycling on a small scale long before the scale of recycling today. My brother George always being a businessman, Nicky Internicola, and myself saw opportunity there. We, like many others, began to dig our share of steel out of the ground to sell.

"As we were digging one day, there were two or three guys, maybe thirty or forty feet away from us, digging also. As my brother Nicky and I started to pull a big piece out of the ground, the other guys started pulling the steel they had located out of the ground too. As we both started getting it out, we came to the conclusion that it was the same piece of steel, probably a thirty-foot long piece of track. A big money piece for sure. When that became evident, one of the other guys walked over and told us that the piece of steel we were both digging out belonged to him. My brother George told him that it certainly did not, that it belonged to us because we had been digging it out of the ground just as long as they had been. The other guy continued to insist that it was his, and I could see my brother was losing his patience. After a few minutes of going back and forth about the steel, my brother told him that he had two choices. Choice 1 was that the steel belonged to us, and my brother was going to beat the daylights out of the guy to prove that it belonged to us; or choice 2, we could finish getting it out of the ground together, and when the truck came to buy the piece, we could sell it and split whatever money we got paid for it. The other guy thought about it for a second and then decided his best choice was number 2—work together to get it out of the ground, sell it, and split the proceeds. My brother agreed, and we worked as a team to get that piece out of the ground. When we finally did, it was big to the point I didn't think it was going to fit on a truck. In the end, I think we sold the piece of steel we had all dug out of the ground for 67¢, which would be 33¢ for us, and 33¢ for the other guys leaving a penny to still be split. A penny, a single penny. In the United States, there are no half pennies. The question then became how do we split that other penny. Split a penny? That's an indication how little money there was around and how much a penny was worth. There we were trying to split a penny. Again, my brother George always the businessman, wanted the transaction complete so he could be on his way to dig up more steel and get paid more money. Finally, my brother told the other guy to keep the penny, the half penny that belonged to us was a tip. The other guy and his friends went off very pleased, and we continued to dig up more steel.

"The money we made digging up the steel helped us pay our bills, but we often found that we needed more money mostly to pay for coal to warm our house in the winter. As far as food was concerned, we could do expense wise because we all had gardens, and we all shared what came from each other's gardens. Everyone canned food for the winter so that we could stretch meals. We had to make it work. To pay our taxes and utility bills was not a problem. Most times, the problem was coal for heat in the winter. My mother would buy coal or later fuel oil from Murtaugh's Fuel Company on Railroad Street. In any event, any way we could find to get access to more coal or save money on heating, we did. There were times when you might be sleeping in bed with three blankets and a jacket on, but one way or another, we kept warm all winter. To augment our coal consumption, when trains would deliver to Corrado's Mill, Rankin Dairy, or the Union Fork and Hoe Company, coal that was piled too high on the boxcars would fall off the train as it moved along the tracks and when they would dump the boxcars into the coal bins at the businesses, many times some of the coal wouldn't fall in the bin and would spill out onto the ground outside the bin, that gave us our chance to access extra coal so that we didn't have to reorder from Murtaugh's. Once or twice a week, we would walk along the tracks from behind Corrado's Mill east to the Union Fork and Hoe and collect in a bushel or bag any extra coal we found lying along the tracks. Once we got that coal home usually at night, we would also check the coal bins near the boilers at Rankin Dairy to collect the coal that had not fallen into the bins when the boxcar full of coal was dumped. We never thought of it as stealing, especially along the tracks, because it fell off the train by itself. Perhaps it was stealing from the bins at the various businesses, but again, we weren't taking it out of the bin directly. It was the coal that never got in the bin. It was not stealing. It was survival. I don't think there was ever anything more to it than that.

"Your dad used to tell the same story about walking along the tracks to pick up the coal that fell off the trains along with the coal that missed the bins, but he and his brothers went even further. At some point, they pulled the bottom board off the coal bin thus allowing coal in the bin to spill out from the bottom, which they soon collected up and brought home to burn. They would bring a hammer and a few nails with them to pull the board off, help themselves to the coal, then nail the board back on to prevent anyone from noticing the board had been tampered with. They brought with them an old refrigerator, which they took the door off and turned over on its back to load the coal in to drag home. The door of the refrigerator they also flipped on the front, used it as a sled in the winter. Certainly, reengineering at a high level of proficiency. I suppose if you look at it, that likely was stealing, but how much could they actually have stolen? Again, more like survival, and the company that owned the bin took a tax credit for the coal as an expense any way.

"Mary Nicolette, who lived at the far-east end of Orchard Street whose house we would walk by on our way back home, after we followed the tracks and collected coal, had two magnificent black walnut trees growing in front of her house. As kids, we looked up at those trees in admiration. They were beautiful. As the years went by, the trees got bigger and bigger to the point they were encroaching on her house and might someday would have fallen on the house if they weren't controlled. Mary saw the potential problem and hired a tree cutter to come to her house and take them down. As we were walking home one morning, the tree guy was discussing with Mary a price and when he would have a chance to cut down the trees before they fell on her house. The two or three of us walking back home with our coal bags and stopped to ask Mary why she was going to cut down those beautiful trees. She filled us in that they had gotten too big, and they were a danger to fall on her house. The guy who was looking to take them down for Mary then explained to her that both of the trees were black walnut, a rare, expensive, and difficult tree to grow. The walnuts that fell off the tree, which we would collect and crack open, contained these sticky black nuts that we fished out with a knife and ate. They were delicious. We knew they were walnuts but not specifically black walnuts, and were they ever good. If you check out recipes for fancy desserts, many of them contain very costly black walnuts. The trimmer went on to tell Mary that he had a guy who would cut the trees down at no cost to her if he could keep the wood. Of course, Mary thought that was a good idea, and she would be glad to give him the wood as payment for cutting the trees down. Mary then asked the first tree trimmer what the other guy would do with the wood. He explained that he would make the black walnut into gun stocks, tables, chairs, and different types of furniture, but mostly, he would use it to make gun stocks. He would sell the stocks to manufacturers, like Remington Arms in Ilion and Savage Arms in Utica, to make high-end collectible guns. Mary agreed to have the other tree trimmer come to her house to evaluate the condition of the trees, and if the guy agreed, he could cut them down at no cost to her but the price of the lumber, then it would be a done deal. Over the next few days, Mary came to an agreement with the tree trimmer about the black walnut trees. Once he got there and started to work on taking the trees down, we watched over the course of probably a week how he meticulously cut off each branch of the tree until he had it down to the trunk and then even more meticulously cut the trunk into the size pieces he wanted. I'll bet he took those pieces of black walnut home and made some beautiful tables and gun stocks. I bet those trees are protected now because they take so long to grow that they are rarely cut down anymore. I've had a pretty large collection of guns my entire life as you know. I would have loved to own a gun with a black walnut stock from those exact trees. Unquestionably, a piece of local history that I could bond to for life.

"That reminds me of the hunting that we did along the banks of the Mohawk River, in the Flats running east and west of Orchard Street and along the old Erie Canal bed. I was very good friends with Frank 'Pop' Spina, who was probably your high school social studies teacher. One afternoon, when we decided to go frog hunting and while walking alongside the canal bed, we spotted a large group of bullfrogs jumping in and out of the water from the bank. We scooped them up, dressed them out, and recovered their legs. We brought them to your grandmother, who breaded and fried them to make Frank and I a big frog's leg lunch. Although we weren't hunting with a gun, it still played out into a delicious lunch.

"When we walked home from the east end of Orchard Street to the west end with our bags full of coal, frogs, or whatever, we would find all kinds of ways to get into mischief. One morning, when we got back home and dropped off the coal we picked up along the tracks, I was following my brother George back to the playground on the corner of Orchard Street and Railroad Street. The day was icy and very slippery as I recall. When we got to the playground, the fence on the west-side end didn't have a gate into the playground. Rather than walk around, my brother decided to just climb over the fence, and I followed suit. George got over the prongs on the top of the chain-link fence and jumped down to the ground. I wasn't so lucky. I got up to the top of the fence, but when I tried to jump off, my sleeve got caught on one of the prongs running along the top. A prong also caught the side of my hand and wrist resulting in a six-inch-long gash. After all those years of sitting there through the winter, summer, spring, and fall, of course, the prongs and really the entire fence was rusty. My jacket was caught, and I couldn't jump down to the ground. While I am hanging there bleeding, someone—I don't know if it was my brother George or not—ran across the street and called Carl Kipper. Carl was in the North Side School gym playing basketball and came running out in shorts, sneakers, and a jersey. He sprinted over to the playground from the other side of the street and lifted me up so that my jacket sleeve would unhook from the prongs. He never even brought me home, rather he carried me directly to Dr. Frank's office on Main Street. Carl was a good man and a war hero because he gave his life for his country while in the Navy during World War II. When Carl got me to the office, Dr. Frank took one look at my hand, wrist, and bloody jacket knowing immediately that I had a deep laceration. George had his nurse clean it up so he could figure out what to do. By that time, by way of the Orchard Street grapevine or my brother, my mother heard what happened, and she showed up at Dr. Frank's office. I remember George telling my mother that I was lucky because I had not hit a vein or artery, which would have been a lot more trouble, but it was still bad. He told my mother that he would take care of his little cousin and make sure it didn't get any more complicated than it was. He gave me a script I would imagine for an antibiotic and tetanus shot, then sent me home with instructions and an appointment to come back. It took a while for it to heal, and I still have a long scar. It was a very scary incident for an eight-year-old boy. Good thing that Carl Kipper thought quick and brought me directly to Dr. Frank's office because, with all that bleeding, it could have been a lot worse.

"It is amazing how the New York Central Railroad and the Union Tool Company were able to use the area surrounding Orchard Street to make their businesses profitable. On the railroad companies' property, about two hundred feet west of my house, they built a big pumphouse from which they would pump water out of a well that was so deep it hit what was part of the Mohawk Riverbed long ago and then pumped the water into the boilers on their locomotives to boil and create steam to power their trains. The water was also pumped west to the lumberyard of the Union Tool Company and then up through pipes to large sprinklers, which sprayed water on the logs stored in their lumberyard to keep the logs from drying out. The logs would be then cut into ten-foot-long, three-inch-by-three-inch-square sticks, then cut in specific lengths, spun on a lathe, and used to make handles for rakes, shovels, and hoes. They were simple manufacturing jobs for the employees but still manufacturing jobs. The companies used the resources that they had available right on the block to keep the expenses down for their production thus increasing their profits. Very smart business decisions when you consider maximizing what they had available to them. Those two companies, along with Corrado's Mill and Rankin Dairy supplied a lot of jobs and money to many families for generations. Without them, I can only imagine how many families would not have been able to prosper. Unfortunately, all that opportunity no longer exists because companies first moved out of the United States and now are completely offshore. People, families, and spin-off businesses thrived for a century or longer right on Orchard Street and in the entire village because of those four or five small corporations. Small companies that made big opportunities for so many people rarely exist in America any longer. Working at any of them may have not been the best job in the world, but it is a paycheck every week. Rarely were there any layoffs. Benefits were probably minimal, but it was better than nothing. I can only imagine how many houses, cars, groceries, and college educations were paid for by those small neighborhood businesses.

"There was another small stone-crusher company just over the bridge that my grandfather, father, and my brother Vince all worked in at various times. Most of the employees, like my father, walked over the bridge in the morning to their jobs, worked all day, and walked back home at night. Everybody came home dirty, dusty, and tired, but they had a job—again, good, steady employment that put a paycheck in your hand every week. They were very hard and dirty work but steady work—simple manufacturing jobs but again manufacturing jobs. You don't see that anymore. Everything is massive corporations and conglomerates that all expect bachelor's and master's degrees, which obviously limits a lot of people. Those high-skilled jobs are where the money is made. Everything else is a fifteen- or sixteen-dollar-an-hour, low-skill, low-wage jobs. With expenses being as high as they are, it becomes very difficult to make ends meet with that type of low-pay position. At least when I was growing up, maybe an individual didn't make much money, but your expenses were low too. As long as you worked, saved, and used your head, you could live a decent life. That's not the case anymore."

We stopped to do some research on labor and pay statistics to verify what Uncle John postulated. As sure as the day is long, he is correct. The statistics are not encouraging.

The research that Uncle John and I did shows that global outsourcing has reached $92 billion with US being approximately 66 percent of the total or $62 billion, and 59 percent of companies doing outsource cite cost as the biggest factor in outsourcing. It is done by companies of all sizes—small, medium, and large. The US does the most outsourcing at 66 percent with the United Kingdom being second at about 48 percent. After cost, the next biggest factor in outsourcing is talent shortage. As manufacturing increases overseas, it generates a need for more white-collar labor in the US but not blue-collar labor. White-collar labor generally requires a college degree, which many people are not able to afford. Offshore outsourcing is often done to avoid US disclosure laws and paying US taxes. Note that 20 percent of all US manufacturing is now done in China. Recently, some companies have been leaving China for more favorable business environments in other countries, but China is still the leading production center in the world. Most international outsourcing occurred between 2001 and 2009. The major concerns with offshore manufacturing are environmental harm and human rights.

In the last five years, the United States had lost five million jobs. Most of the lost jobs were employees without college degrees and workers of color. Manufacturing peaked in the United States in 1969 with about 7.5 million manufacturing jobs. The most significant loss in manufacturing jobs was between 2000 and 2017.

Uncle John and I began to discuss the local situation with manufacturing jobs over the past forty to fifty years, and again, the same outflow of manufacturing employment became evident. In the early 1950s through the 1970s, Univac, makers of the first ENIAC computer, a general-purpose electronic digital company had a massive manufacturing plant stretching across the border between Utica and Frankfort. In the late 1970s, Univac completely left Utica and Rome for the tri-city area of Tennessee with a massive PILOT, or payment in lieu of taxes plan, whereby the county waives the companies' property taxes usually for a period of ten years because of a promise from the company to develop and enhance their area. Univac, as in the case of many large corporations, stayed in the tri-city area for ten years until their PILOT benefit ran out after building an entire manufacturing entity there. Univac then relocated to Manassas, Virginia, for another ten years due with another PILOT plan in hand, then disappeared from computer manufacturing in 1986. A General Electric plant, of which the area had three, at the corner of Bleeker Street and Culver Avenue in Utica was at one point the largest manufacturing site of transistor radios in the world. In the mid-1980s, GE left this area, completely moving many of its local jobs to Syracuse. When AMD Corporation discussed building a chip manufacturing plant in Marcy, New York, General Electric expressed an intention to relocate about one thousand jobs from Syracuse back to Utica and Rome. When the deal to bring AMD to the area fell apart, General Electric promised to bring some jobs back, but that promise never came to fruition to the best of my knowledge.

Smaller yet very prosperous companies such as Chicago Pneumatic, a high-performance manufacturer of power tools, air compressors, generators, and hydraulic equipment for professional industrial applications closed their plant and moved to South Carolina in 1996. Remington Arms was established by Eliphalet Remington in 1816 near the site of where the Remington plant still stands today. In the 1940s through the 1980s, Remington employed up to three thousand people working three shifts, at times, seven days a week. The current status of the company is well under one thousand employees with 70 percent of the factory no longer in use. At Remington's levels of highest employment, the Ilion Police Department had to place an officer at the exit from the factory parking lot when the first shift ended to control the traffic of employees leaving work and coming in to work for the second shift. Remington recently ran an ad looking for employees, but the rate of pay in relative terms from the 1980s is about half of what it was during the high-employment years. A defined pension plan that thousands of Remington employees had access to over the past fifty years was replaced by a 401K.

Mohawk Data Sciences was founded by Schuyler's George Cogar in 1964. Mr. Cogar invented a process that could transfer data from a keyboard on to magnetic tape directly thus making obsolete the former data-entry process of entering information into a computer by way of punch cards. The Union Fork and Hoe Company, founded in Columbus, Ohio, in 1890, also had another large plant in Frankfort but left the area and returned to its roots in Columbus, Ohio, in the late 1980s. There was a day as unlikely as it seems now in the Herkimer and Oneida County area you could quit your manufacturing job at one company and literally walk across the street and get a better manufacturing job at another. Recently, a Craftsman plant in Fort Worth, Texas, closed completely with a promise to keep their manufacturing in the USA as much as humanly possible. The jobs in Texas were transferred to South Carolina at least for the time being, but their permanence remains to be seen.

Nevertheless, after all that negative loss over the past fifty years, there are some bright signs. Recently, General Motors, US Steel and Intel have moved some manufacturing back to the United States, albeit to a small degree. All the outsourcing has led to unforeseen costs, delivery issues, the need for supplemental services, and additional staff that have led to shortfalls. On a local level, Wolfspeed recently built the single largest silicon carbide chip manufacturing foundry in the world in Marcy, New York. Silicon carbide chips can operate at much higher voltages, temperatures, and frequencies than traditional silicon-based semiconductors. They are a better choice for use in electric vehicles, solar power conversion, and 5G wireless phones. Micron Corporation has pledged to build a one-hundred-billion-dollar manufacturing site in Syracuse, New York, over the next twenty years. That investment being possibly the largest manufacturing investment ever made in United States history. Some bright spots locally and nationally are beginning to show, but it is unclear if the United States will ever get back to its largest degree ever as the leading manufacturing country in the world. The increases are still far outweighed by the decreases, but there is hope for the future.

The research we did ended, and Uncle John returned to the fond memories of his youth.

"Alice Billis, who ran the Billis's Hotel after her dad died, was my mother's close friend. The hotel was built during the heyday of the Erie Canal for the canal workers to be able to eat, drink, and rent a room for the night. Alice had a son by the name of Mitch, who was a famous artist, whom I believe, lived in Maine for many years producing artwork that was well-known throughout the world. One of Mitch's close friends was Teddy Murray. Ted owned three or four paintings that Mitch did for him. I don't know what happened to the paintings after Ted died, but I bet they are worth quite a sum of money now. Mitch was another regular everyday guy born on Orchard Street who had a lot of talent and made a name for himself.

"Another, was a close friend of mine by the name of Donnie Merle. When Donnie was in the military stationed in Europe, to keep himself occupied, he signed up for an intramural basketball league. One of the other players who was on his team, I believe his name was Bob Pettit, whose father was a basketball coach at Louisiana State University. Donnie was a good solid basketball player from the day he was born. I think he was the first one on Orchard Street to nail a bushel basket on his garage that we could use as a hoop to shoot baskets. Donnie spent every day shooting baskets in the driveway of his house. He could be heard dribbling that basketball over the entire street all day long, and he could shoot as they say "the lights out." When he was released from the military, Donnie returned to Frankfort, and his European teammate returned home to Louisiana. Bob told his father about Donnie. Bob's father saw potential based on his son's recommendation and made a trip to Frankfort to talk to Donnie and, in the end, signed Donnie to play scholar basketball at LSU. Even in the 1940s and 1950s, that was huge college sports at LSU just as it is today. Think in terms of Shaquille O'Neal, Pete 'Pistol' Maravich, DJ LeMahieu, and Leonard Fournette. Donnie was a starter at LSU all four years he played there, and for many years, he was in the top ten or fifteen all-time scorers, really a super athlete and later an important businessman. He eventually lived in Canada—I believe in Montreal, where he was an editor and writer for various newspapers, and if my memory serves me correctly even the *National Enquirer*. Again, a regular guy from Orchard Street who made a big name for himself in both college sports and after the business world. Two excellent men who both started out on little old Orchard Street.

"Good heavens from little old Orchard Street."

Those evocations melted into us both like the balmy Florida weather. In the blink of an eye, Uncle John started again.

"Even though there were a lot of legitimate businesses on Orchard Street, there was also some illegitimate activity taking place beyond gambling and noncompliance with the liquor laws. There were situations that I heard of but never actually saw where people were smuggling illegal aliens from Italy into the United States by way of Canada. Not that the people coming in were dangerous criminals, I imagine some were, but most were coming because they already had family here and didn't want to go through the lengthy process of becoming an American citizen. By way of a few connections and payouts in the US and at the Canadian border, they were able to circumvent the immigration laws and get into America with less wait time than usual. Once they were here, they blended in with the rest of the population and became ordinary citizens like the rest of us. If anyone ever asked them for a passport, it would have been a different story, but much to their luck, no one ever did that I know of anyway. I understand many of these people settled in Frankfort and the Mohawk Valley in general but never made any problems.

"One illegal activity, which I know did take place two or three times a week, was running bootleg alcohol between Frankfort and Rochester. One guy in particular whom I remember was called Two Gun Sam. I don't remember exactly who he was, but especially during Prohibition, illegal home-brewed liquor was being transported from Frankfort to Rochester to supply illegal bars. Sam's job was to ride shotgun on the deliveries to ensure that the trucks carrying the alcohol weren't hijacked. Like the Wells Fargo agents on the stagecoaches that were assigned to protect the money, gold, or valuables that were being transported. Even after Prohibition ended, it was cheaper to buy the illegal booze, plus the purchases didn't show up on your bill from the liquor distributors, which is how the government keeps track of your liquor sales to generate a sales tax bill every quarter. In the bar business, it's the oldest trick in the book. The trucks would leave Rochester about one o'clock in the morning for the two- to three-hour trip to Frankfort. Then would load the booze and try to get it back to Rochester by about seven in the morning. Two Gun Sam's role was to ensure that the entire transaction went off without a problem. A young man from Rochester named James DiGiovanni, who eventually became Uncle Jim DiGiovanni, was one such driver. At times, because of bad weather, vehicle breakdown, or other reasons, the drivers from Rochester would stay in Frankfort to sleep, then return well-rested early the next evening to make another liquor run. Next to my grandfather George Dee's house on the corner of Litchfield Street and Orchard Street on the east side of his house lived Jim Kipper. Jim had an extra room in his house that he would rent to the truck drivers from Rochester if they needed to stay overnight. On one occasion, when Jim DiGiovanni stayed overnight, he was fortunate enough to meet Aunt Jenny Dee, who lived next door to the Kippers with her mother, father, brothers, and sisters. Jim DiGiovanni was a smart man because he recognized a good woman when he saw one. After dating for a while, Jim was making the trips back and forth from Rochester to Frankfort and purposely staying overnight at the Kipper's. Eventually he got enough nerve to ask Aunt Jenny to marry him, to which she consented. After they married, they moved to Rochester and lived there until they died both well into their eighties. It was a lifelong marriage that had its beginning, buying, transporting, and selling illegal liquor brought from Frankfort to Rochester.

"There was another scam, which again I heard about but can't prove, that involved fire insurance. Many people in the village of Frankfort had attachments built on their houses for other family members to occupy as their families got larger, marriages took place, and grandchildren were born. People also had good-size sheds built behind their houses for storage, to house chickens and other uses. As you know, the Frankfort Fire Department is on the south side of Frankfort, and there was a railroad spur that ran behind our house parallel to Orchard Street east to west effectively splitting the village into a north side and a south side. Again, nothing I can prove, but evidentially there was a practice whereby people who lived on the north side of tracks would purposely raise the insurance coverage on their houses, sheds, interior possessions, and their overall property. By observing the time of day that the trains arrived in Frankfort to make deliveries to Corrado's Mill on the west end of the spur and the Union Tool Company on the east end, the schedule quickly became apparent. When the boxcars would be stretched across Railroad Street from east to west preventing any traffic from moving north and south on Railroad Street, all traffic proceeding on Railroad Street across the tracks from the north side of the village to the south side would be halted while the trains loaded and unloaded. The loading and unloading process could take fifteen to thirty minutes. While the loading and unloading occurred, no vehicle traffic could travel from the south side of town to the north side. Do you see the theory here? If by chance there was a fire on the north side of the village with the Frankfort Fire Department being on the south side of town, the pumpers couldn't travel north on Railroad Street to the fire scene until the train was moved. The perfect storm? Under some circumstances? Perhaps. Paint the picture. Raise the value of the insurance on your property, wait for the train that usually runs on schedule to block Railroad Street that runs north and south through the village. Then by a stroke of bad luck, have a fire on your property on the north side of town with the fire department on the south side of town forcing the fire department to have to wait until the train could be moved to get from the firehouse on the south side to the north side where the fire is located. Double the bad luck now. Maybe? I could never verify any of it, but that is the rumor I heard many, many times as to the way it was done.

"As the old saying dictates, 'Every rumor begins with a grain of truth.'

"Along with close relatives, we had living on Orchard Street, like Aunt Josie DiCamillo, we also had more distant relatives within walking distance on the same block. The Tamburros and the Franks—both distant relatives of ours—lived on the east end of Orchard Street, with our house being on the west end. Joe 'Sonny' Tamburro and I being both cousins and friends spent countless hours together tearing up Orchard Street, in a good way, of course. Sonny always had a problem with one eye, but that didn't slow him down one bit. There were many nonrelatives but close friends like the Marines, the Ingros, and the Maneens, also in the neighborhood. Even though we all inhabited this wonderful little niche, there were still people who decided Orchard Street wasn't for them and moved to various parts of the United States. Bert Frank, a relative also, somehow got connected to a job working in the airplane-manufacturing industry in California and moved there after marrying to live in California the rest of his life. Of course, Uncle George, Uncle Tony, and I made the move to Georgia for business opportunities. Most people stayed in the area even after they were married and had a family, but there were a few who did leave and found success in other parts of the United States.

"There were also individuals who had no connection to Frankfort but worked on the surrounding blocks of Orchard Street and loved it. One in particular that I remember was Mr. Sheckle, who was a music teacher at North Side School. He really loved music but loved teaching kids music even more. The district budget for music was not very big, but many kids expressed interest in it mostly because of Mr. Sheckle's enthusiasm. It got to the point there were not enough instruments for every student. Mr. Sheckle, if that was his name, took it upon himself to buy and repair instruments so that he could provide them to the many students who wanted to learn to play music. He taught my brother Vince how to play the coronet, and he was good at it too. The only condition Mr. Sheckle had was if the student decided to drop music, they had to return the instrument to him directly so that he could then provide it to another student. He was trying to make it possible that every student who wanted an instrument had one. You don't find many teachers like that anymore.

I'm sure there are some, but I bet not many. Mr. Sheckle brought a dynamic to Orchard Street that would not have existed if he didn't get so many kids interested in music. The guy did a superb job. He would have the band practicing in the parking lot behind the school, on the playground across the street and even marching in the street. The entire student body, the parents, and the residents in blocks around the school loved him.

"I made a big mistake one day when my mother asked me to help her get something out of the basement. I didn't want to do it right then because I was playing with my friends. The more she insisted that I help her right then, the more I resisted, to the point she made me very angry. I don't remember exactly what I said, but it wasn't very nice, and I think I swore at her once or twice too. Big mistake. She let me go on doing what I was doing and never said another word. I thought I was off the hook and that was going to be the end of it. Big mistake. When my father came home, she quietly told him what I had done and said. The quiet, discreet conversation that she had with my father lit his fuse. I was in the street playing baseball with my friends, a telephone pole being first base, and a chalk square being second base, so on. When my father came out of the house, he whistled and waved his arm for me to come over. I knew I was in trouble. He grabbed me by the collar and started giving me a good beating with his belt. I think he forgot about the buckle on his belt, and I even got hit with that a few times.

"He kept my mother on a pedestal. He had a passionate love for her that never waned for one second, and she deserved the degree of devotion that he gave her every day. My mother was a very kind, quiet woman who didn't say much but would help anyone she could. She was very pretty, not tall but classy in everything she did. I don't know if she even realized the beating that my father was giving me. When she did, she came running out of the front door of our house wiping her hands on her apron and telling my father that it was enough. By the time my mother was outside, I had gotten the message anyway. That was the first time and the last time I ever spoke to my mother like that. I can't stress enough that my dad treated her like gold, and if there was anyone in the world that deserved to be treated that way, it was her. She raised seven children in effect by herself, and none of us were ever short of anything. The most important thing was that she loved every one of us unequivocally, helped us in any way she could, and taught us right from wrong every day. What else could we ask for? If any of my brothers or sisters were sitting here with us right now, they would tell you the same thing. If anyone in this world ever had a mother who was a blessing to them, my mother was that person for every one of us. It was never easy for her, but she had a knack for making a good life for all of us as difficult as it was at times for her, and she did it for the most part by herself, with a smile on her face all along.

"Vinny, I tell you, love conquers all.

"As kids, we all competed against one another, but when push came to shove, we helped one another in any way we could. We were always competing as to who was the tallest, the strongest, the fastest, or who could catch the most fish, just about in any way we could compete. Yet if a problem came up, as much as we competed, we banded together. There was an incident I remember when a candy truck was making deliveries to one of the stores on Orchard Street. When the driver went in the store, we noticed he would left the bay of the truck open. My brother George, Rossi Caruso, Chico Sanders, and one or two other kids on the street saw their chance. While the delivery guy was in the store, using Rossi as the lookout, we literally took every single box of candy off that truck. When the delivery man left the store and realized what happened, we were long gone. We stashed all the candy on the ledge going to the basement of Peleggi's house, and it was a lot of candy. Of course, the deliveryman went to the police. I think Bob Cavanna was on duty, and he came to Orchard Street to assess the situation. In the time it took the delivery guy to drive one block south to the police station and the police to drive one block north to Orchard Street, everyone had developed amnesia. Nobody knew anything about candy. Nobody even saw a delivery truck. We all had no information. No matter how many of us Bob questioned, no matter how he asked the question, nobody knew anything. Talk about circle the wagons. We left the candy in Peleggi's basement until the next day and then started passing it around. We had Baby Ruths, M&Ms, Snickers, packages of gum, Bazooka Joe bubble gum, about every candy imaginable. We shared it with the whole street. There was so much it lasted for two days before it was all gone. Was it wrong? Probably, but the delivery guy should have known better than to leave a truck full of candy open on a street with probably fifty kids under the age of twelve. It was an accident waiting to happen, and sure enough, it happened. Kids will always be kids.

"That bond together lasted through every situation whether it was competitive or cooperative. For many years, there was a football, basketball, and baseball coach at Frankfort High School by the name of Ken Patrick. Mr. Patrick and one or two of his friends on Saturday afternoon and sometime on Sunday also would get together for lunch and a few beers at Puzze's. The thing they really liked was the limburger cheese sandwiches. That cheese smelled to the heavens. Two or three of them would sit at the bar and eat their lunch. Of course, someone would see them walk into the bar, and that was our cue. In a period of about five minutes, there would be a bunch of us out in the street racing each other from pole to pole, a pickup basketball game would start by whichever telephone pole was nearest with a bushel basket nailed to it. We would start playing touch football, throwing passes, and so on. Someone would show up with a bat and ball, and a baseball game would spring up all of us trying to impress Mr. Patrick as to who would be the next starting pitcher or quarterback at Frankfort High School. It was competition, but it was clean, fun competition. That same bond stuck us together throughout our entire lives. Whether Mr. Patrick knew about it or not, he was affecting us in a positive way by getting us to compete against one another, not cooperate like the candy-delivery incident but, in this case, compete. My brother Vince played on his football teams for years, Frank and Angelo Reina played on his football and basketball teams, and the Licaris had players on all his teams. Even if Ken was only watching out of the corner of his eye while he was relaxing with his friends having lunch and a drink, I think he was paying attention to us all. I also think, in the end, it paid off for him because he always had competitive teams in whichever sport for a lot of years."

I must add, "I ran into one of my son's football coaches from high school the other day at a church festival. His name was Kevin Scranton. Kevin also happens to be a neighbor of Tommy Della Posta. Tommy was born and raised in Frankfort but moved many years ago when he got married to Deerfield. In any case, Michael always felt that Kevin was the best coach he had in any sport at any level because he cared about his players in that he would warn them about cold weather and to come prepared for it because he didn't want anybody sick when the team might need them. In any case, as with Ken Patrick, year after year, having strong teams, the same scenario took place with Whitesboro Football for likely two decades. The feeder programs from Whitestown Pop Warner to Whitesboro Modified teams right through to Junior Varsity and Varsity level teams was unbeatable. For a twenty-year stretch from the mid-1990s to well past 2010, I don't think I saw Whitesboro lose a total of fifteen games and, God forbid, maybe one or two at home. It is amazing how in small towns all across America and big cities too, sports programs both boys and girls can be successful for long periods just by a few strong coaches keeping their finger on the pulse, so to speak, to facilitate years of high-quality sports programs by way of feeder systems. Be it Ken Patrick in the 1940s in Frankfort, Tom Schoen along with Kevin Scranton and others in Whitesboro in the 1990s, or the massive soccer locator systems in Europe, it works. As with everything, times change, but if it ain't broke, don't fix it."

We got off track there, but we were soon back to Uncle John and the King of Orchard Street.

His story continued to peel back the layers.

"We had another game we used to play that was based on Leapfrog. One player would stand next to a telephone pole with his arms wrapped around it. The next player would bend over and wrap his arms around the first player's waist. The next in line would bend over and wrap his arms around the second player's waist, then the third player would do the same, and so on for usually seven players. One player, normally the lightest and the fastest, would move back from the line of bent-over players, approximately ten feet to get a running start, then leapfrog off the back of the last bent-over player as far as he could to land as far down the line as possible. We would form teams with one team on one side of the street and the other team on the other side to compete as to how far the jumper could get down the chain of bent-over players. At times, the chain was seven or eight players long, and the jumper could get to the fourth or fifth up player in the chain. We would keep score as to which team went the furthest up the line in a specified number of attempts. As I have said, the competitive and cooperative aspect of our relationships were equally as strong in both directions, and we all knew it.

"There was always a group of homeless men living on the north side of the railroad tracks toward the west end of Orchard Street. Keep in mind that I was growing up at the tail end of the Great Depression, but many people still had no work. We used to call these homeless man hobos. Apparently, they would jump on the trains and just ride them wherever the train was headed until they got caught by the security and thrown off or decided to get off themselves. A small version of what is now called a Tent City, where homeless or displaced people are often housed, sprang up behind Corrado's Mill where Moyer Creek runs into the Mohawk River. One name in particular that I remember was John Peach. I don't know who he was, but he was there for years. I think a lot of these men had drug and alcohol problems also. They would fish in the creek, hunt rabbits or squirrels or whatever they could find, usually not with guns but with snares and traps. Whatever they caught that day, they would eat. To fish, they used twine tied to the end of a stick with a grappling hook, a safety pin, whatever they could find to snag carp, suckers, or at times, a turtle. Fires were lit twenty-four hours a day for them to cook and keep warm. As the winter approached, one by one they disappeared, most likely for warmer climates, but each spring, they reappeared. The whole thing was unfortunate for them. They never really bothered anybody. They just kept to themselves and tried to survive. They must have had access to marijuana because we could see them smoking something, but it had a different smell than tobacco, which they also smoked. As they smoked hand-rolled, most likely, joints to a small butt, they would put it out and toss it in the weeds. As each spring came, those butts that they tossed in the weeds, which had seeds in them too, would germinate, and marijuana would start to grow. This went on for years to the point the patch of marijuana directly behind Corrado's got big, probably twenty feet by twenty feet. When the state police somehow came to the realization that it was marijuana patch in July or August, a few state troopers would show up and burn the entire patch. We had no idea why the state police were there and what they were burning, but eventually we caught on that it had to be something illegal growing. I never found out for certain, but we could smell that unique marijuana odor from whatever it was the state police were burning and the hobos were smoking. Looking back now, my guess is that it was marijuana. It seems as if those hobos weren't as disconnected from society as we thought they were. Or possibly that is why they were disconnected. In either case, they were ahead of their time.

"I have very specific time memory in my young life when I was seriously worried for my brother Tony as was my mother. As a child, Tony developed pleurisy, which is an inflammation of the tissue that lines the lungs and chest cavity. My mother was very strong at holding us together as a family through thick and thin, but still I could tell she was worried about Tony. My brother as a child experienced chest pain, difficulty breathing, unexplained weight loss, and had severe back pain. He was the youngest, and we could all tell that something was wrong. Being a mother of seven, my mom struggled to keep us all healthy, and we usually were, but Tony wasn't doing good. On one or two occasions, she brought me with her and Tony to Dr. Frank's office to have him examined. I could tell as we waited in the office that she was a nervous wreck. Dr. Frank would examine Tony, then lay him on his stomach, and make a single incision in his back through which you would insert a tube. Then with a small pump attached to the tube suck fluids out of his lung cavity. The fluids put pressure on his lungs and didn't allow them to expand to full capacity when he was breathing causing pain. After the treatment, within twenty-four hours, Tony would be back to normal, but in the meantime, my mother was stressed out to the maximum. Then maybe a year or two later, the situation would reoccur causing major stress again. I don't know what my mother would have done if my brother Tony we're permanently sick or even died. She struggled every day to make everything work out in one way or another, which, by the grace of God, it usually did. I think my brother, if it hadn't turned out well, it would have really been the straw that broke the camel's back. Fortunately, Tony eventually grew out it, and our life as a family went on every day. The bonds of family and friends on Orchard Street held us and every other family together no matter how bad things got. Those same bonds have sustained me as I turn ninety-one years old tomorrow, through sickness, health, cooperation, competition, even life and death."

After that observation, the symposium ended for both of us.
Right there.
Simultaneously.

Richard

After three days with Uncle John and that horrendous drive from Rocky Mount to Palm Coast well in the rearview mirror, it's time for Carol and I to "saddle up" for the southern end of our excursion to Key West. Before we get to Keys, we have a scheduled stop in Daytona Beach to interview Richard Sassone concerning his chance at being the King of Orchard Street. From Palm Coast to Daytona Beach is a short twenty-five miles. I am familiar with the Daytona Beach area from my spring break years in college, Daytona being our on-the-way-home stop from Fort Lauderdale. Although I haven't been to Daytona in close to fifty years, I am happy to be going again. In those college days, after about twenty-eight hours of straight driving, switching drivers on and off all night, we would arrive in Fort Lauderdale. Usually after three nights in Fort Lauderdale, we would start back north for a four-night stay in Daytona Beach, then home. Fort Lauderdale was very nice, but the beach was narrow, and it was much more expensive than Daytona. Daytona Beach was wide to the extent the city then allowed people to drive their cars on the beach. The historic bandshell had live, free music literally all day and into the late-night hours. During the day the beach was packed with spring breakers, and at night the bars and restaurants overflowed with those same spring breakers. Everyone there was there for the same reason—to party—and there were girls all the way from Ormond Beach to Daytona Beach Shores. A perfect location for a large group of twenty somethings from the cold, snowy Northeast and Midwest to have some fun. There may have been some studying going on but not much that I could verify.

Richard's house is in a perfect location, a few miles from the interstate, another two miles to the speedway, and another four miles from The World's Most Famous Beach, Daytona Beach, Florida. With the aid of a GPS, we were at Richard's house in less than an hour after leaving Uncle John's. Rich's house is in a typical Florida neighborhood, likely built in the 1980s with block after block of ranch-style brick homes. It couldn't have been any easier for us to locate him. Once we got to his house, I went to the front door and knocked. Immediately, Richard answered and told me he had some bad news. That both he and his significant other were sick. They had tested negative for COVID and more likely than not had the flu. He told me that he called and only got voicemail on which he left messages. I wanted to know what number he was calling, and he told me it was a seven-three-six number, which is the landline at my house, and no one ever answered. I asked why he hadn't called my cell phone because I told him I was traveling, but he didn't think I gave it to him. When he checked his cell phone contacts, as luck would have it, there was my cell phone number. Richard never thought to scroll past the seven-three-six number to my cell number. Not wanting to force the issue, I asked him what he thought was the best thing to do. Rich told me that the choice was mine since I had traveled a long way, and whatever I wanted to do was fine with him. I suggested that we do the social distancing. Carol and his wife could sit in the living room ten to twelve feet apart, and he and I could go in a separate room and sit six feet apart. We can all wear masks, maintain social distance, not shake hands, and use the protocols that we have all grown accustomed to over the past two years. Richard agreed to try it. After a brief introduction to his significant other, Carol and Joanne sat in the living room while Richard and I went into the kitchen all the while keeping six feet apart at the kitchen table.

From there Richard began his chronicle as the potential King of Orchard Street.

"I was born on Orchard Street in 1943 and lived there with my father; my mother, the former Theresa Nicolette; my younger brother Ronnie; and my aunt Mary. Our house wasn't very big, but it was enough room for all of us. In fact, it was cozy and made for a very nice family life with my aunt and mother in the house in that there was always at least one female present creating a warm atmosphere as only a woman can. Our house was right next door to Ruffalo's Market, which to this day made the best fresh sausages I have ever tasted. Across the street from us was Smizzi's and a name you may have heard before, a guy called Two Gun Sam. I don't know where the name came from exactly, but it was Two Gun Sam. Also, on the south side of the street resided the Carusos, Moroccos, and on the corner the Maneens. The Spinas also resided on Railroad Street. All very good people coming from very strong families. Those families and numerous others were the glue of the neighborhood. They are what made Orchard Street a unique place to live. I'm sure you've heard others say the support and appreciation of all the different people living on the block was stunning. In the morning when we all attended North Side School, the procession of kids walking to school would begin on the west end of Orchard Street and proceed east with the group getting larger and larger as it went. As the crowd walked past each house, two or three kids would join in, depending on the age of the kids and the number in each residence as the group went. By the time we got to the end of west of Orchard Street to cross Railroad Street to the North Side School on the corner, there might have been fifteen to twenty kids in the group. At times the group would get so large that we'd have to split into two and walk on each side of Orchard Street. Other times we didn't bother to stay out of the street and walked right down the middle like a parade.

"We all attended North Side School until sixth grade, then we moved from North Side to Sarah Piper School on the corner of Third

Avenue and Frankfort Street. The walk to Sarah Piper from home was now eight blocks instead of being half a block to the North Side School. Yet the same situation occurred as when we walked to Sarah Piper. As we got closer to school, the crowd of kids walking would grow until we got to the school. In the winter we would climb up and down the snowbanks on our way, throw snowballs at each other, and have a great time. Then we would do it again on the way home after school. I don't recall there ever being any problems among us with anybody fighting or getting angry. We were just a group of us walking over to school. We had fun, laughed, joked, shared homework, and talked about what we watched on TV. Boys talked about girls, girls talked about boys, and all the things that kids do when they find themselves in a safe environment. I find it ironic that the North Side School is now the Frankfort Village Offices and Police Department and Sarah Piper, which was demolished and replaced by Saint Mary's School, is now the Town of Frankfort's offices. Both buildings started out as schools and eventually repurposed into government buildings. I find that amusing and ironic at the same time. We all attended Sarah Piper for seventh and eighth grade and then went to Frankfort High for grades nine through twelve. The walk to school went from half a block to the North Side School to about eight blocks to Sarah Piper and then close to mile to Frankfort High. Obviously, the walk was getting longer and longer for the kids who lived on the north side of Frankfort. It was great fun to the point looking back now I wish the walk to each school was even longer yet. Eventually, as more people got cars, their parents would bring their kids to school, not like you see today, though. At times parents would even let their high school children with driver's license borrow their car to get to school. When the Frankfort schools started to centralize with Schuyler is when bussing started. If you resided in the village, you were required to walk no matter where you lived in the village. Bussing was only from West Frankfort and Schuyler. If you're lucky enough to have a car or your parents let you drive theirs, that was big-time cool. It became an entirely new dynamic to drive to school. It was so cool to have a car.

"It seemed like good luck just shined on us every day in everything we did. Most of the days in school revolved around academics, of course, but the biggest aspect of school for myself and most of my friends was sports. Frankfort High School was the original brick building built, I think, in 1927. It was the school that my mother and father went to. With the school district centralizing with Schuyler, there was a need for more room than the original building had, so in mid-1950s the size of the original school was doubled with the addition of a new wing that stretched from Sixth Avenue to Eighth Avenue, and beyond if you include parking lots and athletic fields. The Frankfort School District became an amazing thing for us in that it had gotten so big. We went from two-floor North Side School to double the size Sarah Piper, to bigger the original Frankfort High then with the addition to the high school probably four times bigger than what we originally attended in the North Side School. An immense jump in size of the schools we attended over a period of about ten years. We were all very impressed. We felt like we were going to some large college or university, but it was really just good old Frankfort High. Excellent feelings of attachment and belonging emanated from those schools every day. Then after school, when we returned home to Orchard Street and our own homes, those feelings only multiplied. That attachment and belonging were reinforced no matter where we went. Fortunately for us, we never were threatened or intimidated anywhere. Not at home, in school, church, or in the village. Actually, the opposite was true. Everywhere we went we were accepted and protected. A blessing for us that kids today don't have. Kids are threatened and intimidated everywhere now—in school, on the street, at home, online, you name it. There are school shootings, shootings in grocery stores, in malls, at the beach. Drugs are everywhere, highly addicting drugs, runaways, human trafficking, and child pornography. Horrible situations that used to occur, if at all, only to adults now happen to kids daily. By the grace of God, we had none of that. We had the opposite. We had safety. We had protection. We were never threatened. Maybe once in a while, someone would punch someone else in the nose over a girl, but then it was over. The people involved shook hands, and we were back to being friends the next day.

"I always focused well on academics while in school, but the thing I really was there for was sports. I was very active in football and then basketball as was my best friend, Jim Alsante. I see Jim now and then if I'm in the Frankfort area, or he visits in Florida but not very much. He was by far my best friend. We played on the same sports teams, went to each other's houses for lunch and dinner, and really spent a lot, if not all, of our time together. A few years back I went to my sixty-fifth class reunion and was happy to see many of my classmates. Unfortunately, time has taken a toll, and there are not many of us left, but when we were in high school, it was a pretty good mob. There was very little arguing or infighting. It was mostly just having fun day in and day out. What I wouldn't give to have those days back again. Those young days were a huge plus for all of us."

Richard appeared to be running out of gas a little likely because he was not feeling well. It seemed like a good place to shift gears. We began to discuss the Daytona Beach area historically and by way of my recollections visiting the area when I was a college student.

As we search the Web, we find an interesting narrative slowly peeling back for over a three centuries of Daytona Beach history.

I said to Richard as I searched the web, "This is an old city on a site poised for success. Daytona is fifty miles from Orlando, ninety miles from Jacksonville, two hundred miles north of Miami on the eastern edge of the Atlantic Coast with easy access to those locations, and many others. The 2020 census indicated a population of approximately seventy thousand inhabitants. Daytona Beach, Deltona, and Ormond Beach have a combined population of six hundred thousand residents. No wonder this is called the Fun Coast, but I have always known it as The World's Most Famous Beach or The Spring Break Capital of the World. Along with the famous beach, it is also historically known for the hard-packed sand that allowed land speed racing long before stock car racing became famous here. The title the Capital of Speed caught on in 1903 when two men argued over who had the fastest car and decided to settle the argument by racing on the beach. History doesn't record their names or who won the race, but local lore has it that was the start of racing in the area. Cars are still allowed on the beach with much more strict parameters than in the long-gone past of land speed racing. The original Daytona Beach Road Course was on highway A1A South Atlantic Avenue until Daytona International Speedway was built in 1959. Daytona Speedway is also the corporate headquarters of NASCAR. The Daytona 500 also known as the Great American Race or the Super Bowl of Stock Car Racing is the kickoff event of the NASCAR season. The Coke Zero 400 is also held in August with Bike Week in March, Biketoberfest in the Fall, and the 24 Hours of Daytona in January. One of my cousins from Savannah, Kevin Iocovozzi, has owned classic cars for many years and has come to Daytona for the 24 Hours of Daytona and to drive a lap or two around the track for a long time. He told me recently that it has gotten so expensive that he doesn't drive laps anymore and comes to watch the race only. Is there anything anymore that hasn't gotten so costly that most people can no longer afford it?

"Still, the history of the region goes back long before any of that. The Timucuan Indians were the first inhabitants living in fortified villages. Through disease, war, and enslavement by the Europeans, they moved into extinction as the decades passed. The Seminoles, descendants of the Creek Indians from Georgia, frequented the region and took a much more aggressive stance than the Timucuan in terms of the Europeans, fighting two wars and eventually chasing many European expeditionary armies out of the area. Also, The Kings Road, in use from 1763 to 1783, the main thoroughfare north and south from Saint Augustine through Daytona to an experimental colony in New Smyrna, was often under control of the Seminoles, further disrupting European efforts to control the region. Eventually, through disease and enslavement, the Europeans took full control and quickly established a slavery-based plantation economy with the main products cotton, citrus, and rice. In 1787 Samuel Williams received a land grant from the Spanish king after Spain regained Florida back from the British at the end of the Revolutionary War. The area, known as the Orange Grove Plantation, was situated on the west bank of the Halifax River, north of Mosquito Inlet. Williams was a British loyalist from North Carolina who fled following the Revolutionary War, to the Bahamas, due to fear of retaliation by the new American government against British loyalists. When Spain reopened Florida to non-Spanish immigrants, Williams returned to the area with his land grant in hand and immediately developed a plantation economy built again on slavery, cotton, rice, and tobacco. The area grew rapidly and became very prosperous. At some point, most likely due to the advancing Seminole warriors during the Second Seminole War, Williams abandoned his plantation, and it was burned to the ground, most likely by those same fierce Seminole warriors.

"Sounds much like *Gone with the Wind* with those imaginary Union forces taking control of Atlanta and in the end chasing Scarlett, Rhett, along with Tara into the fictional pages of history. The real advancing Union forces almost prophetically chased the entire plantation-based southern economy into the factual pages of history. Only, in the case of Daytona, it was the Seminoles, not the Union Army and Samuel Williams, not Scarlett O'Hara. I'm guessing, but I would think there are many similar stories to Scarlett's as historical fiction and Samuel's as historical nonfiction all across the South as the slave-based southern economy fell apart under the withering onslaught of the Civil War.

"After the tumultuous era of two Seminole Wars, then the Civil War, the Daytona area remained quiet until 1871 when Mathias Day, a business tycoon from Mansfield, Ohio, purchased the former Orange Grove Plantation's 3,200-acre plot for $1,200. You're a retired accountant. That price is about 35¢ an acre. What a buy! Day then built a hotel and resort in the area that flourished for a short time, but in 1872, due to financial troubles, he lost his title to the land. The residents of the area decided to name the city in his honor and incorporated it in 1876. Ten years later the Saint Johns and Halifax River Railway reached Daytona, only to be purchased five years later by Henry Flagler who made it part of his Florida East Coast Railway. By then three separate towns had developed Daytona, Daytona Beach, and Seabreeze, which all merged into Daytona

Beach in 1926. The consolidated towns were quickly dubbed The World's Most Famous Beach. Prior to that, at the turn of the century, auto industry pioneers located an ideal place to test their products. No place other than the smooth, compacted sand of Daytona Beach. Official motorcycle and car races began in 1912 with famous land speed racers making at least one trip a year to Daytona to test cars along with other new automotive innovations that were rapidly evolving. Land speed racers such as William Vanderbilt set an unofficial record of 92.30 miles an hour, only to be challenged by Barney Oldfield, Henry Segrave, and Malcolm Campbell who would repeatedly visit the beach and attempt to forcefully push the record higher. Other racers such as Frank Lockhart in his Stutz Blackhawk and Lee Bible and his Triplex Special soon arrived in Daytona. Land speed racing continued until 1935 when the record was set at 276.81 miles an hour, ending Daytona's land speed racing days. The era of racing was far from over but rather was just beginning when March of 1936, the first stock car race was held at the Daytona Beach Road Course in the present-day town of Ponce Inlet. William Franz Sr. created NASCAR in 1959 at the famous Daytona International Speedway, which was built to replace the beach course. Franz's dream was to take cars directly from the assembly line and put them on a race track to determine who built the best, fastest, and most durable automobiles. Again, cars are still permitted on most of Daytona Beach but with a maximum speed of ten miles per hour. A massive speed downgrade from the land speed racing era of William Vanderbilt, Lee Bible, and Frank Lockhart in his Stutz Black Hawk.

"Still, it is big-time fun to motor north and south on the beach as part of a rich history that is still being written for The World's Most Famous Beach.

"As I recall Daytona Beach from my college days, it was a big party that stretched for miles in both directions, spread out over a four-month period. We would come in mid-February and sometimes again in April when the weather could still be a little chilly, but it was better than Oswego, New York. The entire beach area was a party every day and well into every night. One of my best memories is of that Coquina Clock Tower as part of the beach bandshell area and the entire oceanfront complex of kiosks, concessions, and changing facilities. The name Coquina Clock Tower comes from a local material, coquina rock, of which it is built as was the bandshell. The oceanfront is now listed in the National Register Historic Places as an entertainment, recreation, community development, and architectural landmark.

"I see the beach has had redevelopment with the Marriott Convention Hotel, overtaking much of ocean park, demolishing the pavilions, the octagonal bathhouses, most of the shops and game rooms. There is some remaining ocean view seating, but most of it is gone. I understand that the Coquina Clock Tower has also been renamed to Sir Malcolm Campbell Clock in honor of a famous auto speedster who set numerous world and land speed records. Campbell Street was renamed in memory of Dr. Martin Luther King. I never knew the bandshell and clock tower were started in 1936 and completed in 1937 by the Great Depression's Works Projects Administration. An amazing effort in such a short time. The first concerts held at both landmarks went on all day and long into the night. When we came to Daytona for spring break in the mid-1970s, I believe the concerts were free, but for $2, you could purchase a VIP pass, which was basically seats in the first ten rows. The action was farther back than that.

"The bandshell and clock tower along with the Atlantic Ocean as a backdrop are often stopovers for presidential candidates and their wives as they campaign through Florida. The beach makes for a picturesque venue to connect with young voters and display for the candidate their comprehension of the issues young people care about. MTV Spring Break held broadcast concerts at the bandshell for many years. I am not certain if that programming is still available, but it was a popular show for years. At times I, too, watched it mostly for nostalgic reasons. The uniqueness and history of oceanfront park coupled with the architecture of the bandshell, the beach houses, the clock tower, the ocean as the backdrop with palm trees waving in the breeze engendered for me an appearance as if in North Africa or Middle East. The coquina stone edifices gave an appearance, although I have never been to either place, of what I imagine

Alexandria, Egypt, or Algiers with their medieval casbah motif might look like. Alexandria and Algiers are located on the Mediterranean, and Daytona on the Atlantic. I venture any of them can invoke an equally as impressive sentiment in any individual."

Richard seemed to gather his strength again and set about chronicling another King of Orchard Street tale.

"'The Two-Gun Sam' guy whom I mentioned earlier was a player in a reportedly accurate incident that has taken on a life of its own for as long as I can remember. The way I got it from my grandfather was a rich depiction, but I have no idea if any of it is true. Apparently, some well-connected individuals had control of the area in terms of gambling, prostitution, and other illicit businesses of which Sam had a degree of involvement. Someone, I don't know who, crossed these individuals and had to be, shall we say, eliminated. The men involved in the elimination were high level and much too powerful to be held responsible for anything. They were "too big to fail." Someone else had to "fall on the sword" as Saul did in the Bible. The body of whoever they eliminated was found on the railroad tracks, causing it to appear that someone who lived in the area of the tracks was the perpetrator. The proposition made to Sam was to allow himself to be convicted of the crime and sent to jail. In return, a guarantee was floated that while Sam was in prison, he would be taken care of on the inside as would his family on the outside until he was released and once he was released, if ever the deal would be maintained, until Sam and his spouse were deceased. The scene was literally set up to point at one person, Two Gun Sam. I would assume payoffs were made to the right people. Some information would show up, and other information would disappear, but in the end the data would point only to Sam. Although Sam was not directly involved, collectively everything would implicate him. Evidently, Sam went for the deal and spent many years in jail. How much of any story is true, I have no idea, but that's the way the narrative was related to me. The facts of the story are now lost, or if it ever happened at all, it cannot be verified. Yet if it did happen, I would think some kind of deal was made because one hundred years or more later, here you and I sit, still discussing the whole alleged—and I stress alleged—occurrence. That makes me think that somehow, somewhere there is a degree of truth to the story, but as I said, it is all lost now."

I mentioned to Richard how I had heard different stories of whoever this "Two Gun Sam" guy was, but he was no one I ever knew. In any case, the stories I had heard from various people, including another potential king of Orchard Street, painted a very colorful picture of who he was and what he did, to put it euphemistically.

Rich went on. "There was a similar situation that occurred when I was ten or twelve, part of which I know to be true. One family in Frankfort had a close relative who died, most likely a grandfather or grandmother. This person was known to keep a lot of cash and valuables in his house. Funeral customs had changed in that the wake of the deceased was no longer held in their home but rather at a funeral home. After a two-day wake, a Mass of Christian burial was held for the deceased at the church where the deceased was formerly a parishioner. When the family left deceased's home for the final wake and Mass, someone I don't know who, saw a perfect opportunity. As the family returned to the home of the deceased after the burial rite, they found the house had been robbed. The stress level for the family soared. Apparently, they had every intention of calling the police so that the crime scene could be preserved and evidence gathered. One family member who also came back to the house after the burial explained that calling the police was not necessary and that the whole situation could be resolved without law enforcement intervention. After the family left the home of the deceased, whoever suggested not to call the police did some intensive research, and within forty-eight hours, all the stolen property was miraculously returned and beyond what would have been stolen. The police were never called at the request of one of the family members, and the situation was rapidly resolved. How it was resolved I have no idea, but whoever the perpetrators of the theft were, they were persuaded that they had made a mistake and all the property should be returned to the family including a homage. There are times when things just work out like that usually because someone knows the right people in the right places. The only aspect of the occurrence I can be certain of was the family's house was robbed while they were at the funeral Mass. How the valuables got back to the family I really don't know, but the story has had traction for a long time. As in the case of Two Gun Sam, here we are decades later discussing both incidents, which makes me doubt they were beamed down from the Starship Enterprise.

"I have a lot of good memories of the Favats, Verna, Matti, and of course, Joe. Joe and my brother Ronnie wore a groove in the sidewalk walking back and forth between our two houses all day long. If Ronnie wasn't at the Favats' house, Joe was at our house. They would switch between each other's houses for lunch, dinner, and at times even breakfast. They were very close. I remember Verna always had a smile on her face and was so pretty. Matti was my age, and I thought the world of her too. When we graduated from eighth grade, all the boys had to wear white jackets, and all the girls had to wear pink carnations. I thought that was so cool. I remember sitting there thinking, as the graduation ceremony progressed, that all my classmates, me included, sparkled in that gymnasium light. Why I would think anything like that I really don't know. It must have been the ambiance overwhelming my senses. Strong sentiments that have lasted my entire life. I remember your mother, father, you, and your sister living upstairs from the Favats' in an apartment for many years. We all got along so well. All the Carusos with nieces, nephews, children, and grandchildren in and out of the house all day long. Joe Ingro and Tommy Stone wore a groove in the sidewalk on the other side of Orchard Street from my house with the constant back and forth from Ingro's to Stone's. The Kippers and the Maneens had big families. It really was just constant interaction and a lot of fun. The environment was very safe and conducive to family life.

"In the early evening, people would leave their own homes and make the rounds on the street, stopping to visit with anyone who might be outside. They would check out each other's gardens, sit on each other's porches, and gab. The only purpose being to enjoy each other's company. The respect we had for each other just overflowed. Most of the respect came from the fact that we were all in the same boat. No one was rich, but no one was poor, and we had what was most important. We had homes, families, food on the table, and respect for each other. If the world suddenly started to live in that same environment as the microcosm that we were able to enjoy, most problems would disappear. I doubt if it would ever happen, but that's the kind of goal we should all set for ourselves. At eighty years old, tomorrow being my birthday, it is something I can only hope for, and it all revolves around one universal concept—respect.

"We really didn't have to go anywhere other than Orchard Street and the Village of Frankfort to have fun, but there were experiences my brother and I had on many weekends that I have appreciated throughout my life. Oddly, those experiences didn't occur on Orchard Street but rather in New York City, and they were amazing. My dad worked for the railroad in the freight yard at the east end of Orchard Street. He made many friends who were conductors and engineers as they ran their daily routes from New York City to Buffalo. Plus being an employee, when he traveled on the trains, he would be eligible for a discount. On numerous weekends, from when I was maybe seven to eleven, my father would get free train tickets to New York City on Saturday morning, then back home on Sunday night. My dad, brother, and I boarded a train to Yankee Stadium, arriving at about eleven in the morning, and checked into our hotel, which, if I remember correctly, was the Stadium Hotel that has since been knocked down and was only about two blocks south of Yankee Stadium. We could walk to the stadium just in time for the afternoon game. It could be the Yankees versus the Indians, the Boston Red Sox, or whoever. After checking in at the hotel, we would quickly get over to Yankee Stadium to buy our tickets. I can't imagine how much they cost, but they were likely cheap, and my dad bought whatever was available at the on-site box office. I'm guessing maybe a dollar apiece if that much. We would catch the game in the afternoon, then walk back to our hotel picking up dinner on the way.

The next morning, we would repeat the process or take another train to Brooklyn to see the Dodgers game or Upper Manhattan to the Polo Grounds to watch the Giants against whoever they might be playing, be it the Pirates, the Reds, or any team for that matter. Again, my dad would get us the best tickets available. We might have seats in the bleachers or good seats, but he always made the best deal he could. We would eat lunch in the stadium, the usual hot dogs, pretzels, ice cream, peanuts, whatever we picked out. Peanuts were 10¢ a bag, hot dogs were 20¢, soda was a nickel, and a beer may have been 20¢. What a way to live. We soaked up the whole atmosphere of the food, the noise of the crowd, the New York City skyline as a backdrop—an amazing, unique experience on a regular basis that I will never forget. The Brooklyn Dodgers, Ebbets Field, the New York Giants, the Polo Grounds, Yankee Stadium in the 1950s and 1960s—think of the nostalgia there. I saw some of the greatest players on many occasions. Joe DiMaggio, Mickey Mantle, Yogi Berra, Pee Wee Reese, Roy Campanella, Duke Snider, Willie Mays, and many others of the most iconic players ever. How fortunate were my brother, father, and I? These guys are baseball legends, and I was right there at the game with my brother and father for many weekends. Sometimes it would be both Saturday and Sunday games. Other times it would just be Saturdays. Still at other times it would just be Sundays. One way or another, we would be there for a game, or two, and be home in time for bed and school the next day. The Giants and the Dodgers both left New York City in 1957. I was born in 1943, so the years when we went were the magic years of baseball from about 1948 to almost 1960. How many people got that chance? Food, free transportation, and practically nothing for admission. The nostalgia factor for me is overwhelming. Watching all those future Hall of Famers along with the four-hour train ride with my brother and father. In a sense, the train ride was the best part of the trip. I know I will never get those opportunities again, but I am grateful that at one time I did have them on numerous occasions. Those trips were another aspect of my larger Orchard Street life that I cherish every day."

When Rich told me that he had been to the Polo Grounds and Ebbets Field, my interest immediately surged.

I rejoined. "Richard I never met anybody who can say they've been to either stadium let alone both. The Dodgers and the Giants both moved to Los Angeles in 1957, and I was born in 1955, so there was no chance for me to get to either. I have been to both Yankee Stadiums numerous times beginning as a Little League player in 1964 up until this summer at the new Yankee Stadium, which is only across the street from the old Yankee Stadium and still has the same address, East 161st Street. Do you remember, after the city of Little Falls built Veterans Park, the Little Falls Mets franchised from 1977 to 1988 as a class A New York Mets farm team in the New York-Penn League? The New York Penn is also one of the oldest minor leagues in America. From 1979 to 1982 I purchased Little Falls Mets season box seats on the first-base side. There were four seats in each box with the season being sixty-four games, thirty-two at home and thirty-two away. With four seats in each box for thirty-two home games, it was over one 120 total admissions if my math is accurate. I paid $89 for the season tickets being 128 admissions exactly. You're an accountant. Consider that price, about 70¢ a ticket. How can you go wrong? The kicker of it was if you didn't use the tickets for the box at the designated game, they could be used for general admission at any time during the remainder of the season. As sweet a deal as a person can get.

Wally Backman played second base for the Mets and later played for the Twins, Pirates, and I believe, the Phillies too. He still works for the Mets as the manager of one of their farm teams on Long Island. Bobby Valentine, who later was the head coach of the big-league Mets, was the first-base coach for Little Falls. Bobby used to walk on the diamond sideline of the first-base coach's box when there was a break in the action, with his arms out, balancing himself as if on a tightrope. Valentine also managed the Mariners and, I think, the Twins too. John Elway, two-time Super Bowl winner, president of the Denver Broncos, MVP, and Walter Payton Man of the Year in the NFL was also signed as a pitcher by the New York Yankees, playing a season with the Oneonta Yankees. To the right of my box at Veteran's Park was the injured players box for the visiting team. I had no idea who John Elway was at the time, but after he became an NFL starter and I saw him on TV, I realized that on five or six separate evenings he was sitting in the box next to me. We talked throughout the game with Elway being not much younger than me. We seemed to have a lot in common and enjoyed ourselves fully. If I had known how famous he was to become, I would have got his autograph and bought him a hot dog.

"I have been to Shea Stadium, the original home of the New York Mets, which is now next to the Mets' new home Citifield alongside the US Tennis Center and the famous Unisphere sculpture at the site of the 1964 World's Fair, which I mentioned earlier. Many years ago, I attended a Philadelphia Phillies versus Pittsburgh Pirates game at Veterans Stadium in Philadelphia on the corner of Broad Street and Patterson Street just off the Atlantic City Expressway. In 1991 I went to a Toronto Blue Jays versus Yankees game at the SkyDome in Toronto, which is now called the Rogers Centre. In 1999 my family and I went to a Toronto Blue Jays versus the Cleveland Indians game at the Rogers Centre also. The unique thing about that trip was that the outfield wall of the stadium had a hotel attached to it whereby you could watch the game from your hotel room. My wife, children, and I went to the game and stayed in the hotel to watch the game from our room. We ordered what was called the Ballpark Buffet from room service, which consisted of pretzels, hot dogs, peanuts, and beverages enough for four people. After the game, the stadium allowed fans to enter the field and run the bases. In that we were technically not in the stadium but rather in the hotel, and I didn't want to miss the chance to run the bases, we had to find a way into the stadium quickly. We walked around the other side of the stadium from the hotel, and I commandeered four canceled admissions—keep in mind this is after the game—from patrons exiting the stadium. Using those canceled tickets and some American dollars, I convinced the security to allow us in even though we were never in the stadium so to speak but rather the hotel. My wife videotaped while my children and I ran the bases. I'll have to look for that video. I have it home somewhere. I've been to Legends Field in Tampa twice, the first time in about 1996 and have a video of rookie or second-year player Derek Jeter, Jorge Posada, Paul O'Neill, and other players of that era doing their pregame loosening up drills. While in the Legends Field, we got lost and got on the first elevator we saw. My wife, my son in a stroller, and I got in the elevator and pushed a button thinking I was going to go to the first level. In reality, it was an employee-only elevator. When the door opened, I was in some office with Reggie Jackson talking on the phone and one of George Steinbrenner's sons talking to a coworker. They politely asked us to leave, which we did and proceeded to the gift shop where George Sr., surrounded by security, was talking with two women he evidentially had known for many years. He was telling them to pick out anything they wanted in the store and it was on him. I have a video of my son at about four years old while I'm holding him reaching over and tapping George on the shoulder. Really very cute and very accidental.

"I have also been to Holman Stadium at Dodgertown in Vero Beach, which I think is the best venue for spring training. The complex is surrounded by golf courses, and the beach is nearby too. The players have to walk from the clubhouse on the other side of the grounds to Holman Stadium, passing through all the fans who line the sidewalks, making the players very accessible for autographs and pictures. I've seen him in numerous games at NBT stadium home of the Syracuse Mets and many years ago went to two Rochester Red Wing games at Innovative Field, which was originally in Frontier Field. In February 2019 my wife, daughter, and I attended a Minnesota Twins versus Pittsburgh Pirates game at LECOM Park in Bradenton, Florida. We had excellent seats on the third baseline. Not expecting it to be as hot and sunny as it was, we all got pretty good sunburns but ate a lot of ice cream to keep us cool. You can't beat South Florida for that warm, sunny weather all year round. I also attended a Phillies game in Clearwater at BayCare Ballpark in 2000. Sometimes I think that those spring training facilities are better than the actual Major League parks because there is not as much security or pressure, making the players more friendly to the fans who in the end are the people who sign their paychecks. At least that's been my experience. After all that, my point is, you going to both the Polo Grounds and Ebbets Field is something I have never known anyone to do."

That fact begged some research.

We quickly discovered an abundance of information regarding both the Polo Grounds and Ebbets Field.

Beginning in about 1880 the original Polo Grounds was one of three stadiums that was built and demolished through about 1963. The original Polo Grounds opened in 1876 and was demolished in 1889 and, as the name indicates, rebuilt for polo. The first stadium was in Upper Manhattan between 110th Street and 112th Street on the north and south, with the east and west bounded by Fifth and Sixth Avenues just north of Central Park. It was converted to a baseball stadium when it was leased by the New York Metropolitans in 1880 in effect then becoming the second Polo Grounds. That structure remained until 1889. The third Polo Grounds was built in 1890 and renovated after a fire in 1911 and became known as the Polo Grounds, that building being the one historically referenced as the Polo Grounds. The stadium was in a section of Manhattan known as Coogan's Hollow. It was bathtub-shaped with short left and right field walls but a deep center field. Bleachers were eventually put on either side of the batter's eye, those bleachers being cigar-box-shaped and uncomfortable. The large outfield was cut down to some degree when a rope fence was erected behind which carriages and later automobiles could park. The entire bleacher construction formed willy-nilly seating arrangements but did contain a large outfield area that could be used for many purposes. Although it was the home of the New York Metropolitans and the New York Giants, the last Polo Grounds was generally referred to as the home of the New York Giants. The Polo Grounds also went by the name of Brotherhood Park around the turn of the century to reflect the creation of Major League Baseball's first union, the Brotherhood of Professional Baseball Players. The overall area was bounded by rail yards, and a bluff also served as home of the York Yankees from 1913 through 1922 and the expansion team New York Mets in the 1962 and 1963 seasons. Each of the four versions of the ballpark hosted at least one World Series with the fourth version hosting the All-Star Game in 1934 and 1942. The third Polo Grounds also served as the home of the New York Brickley Giants for one game in 1921, and the New York Giants played home games there from 1925 through 1955. The New York Titans, later the Jets, of the American Football League played their and the league's inaugural season in 1960 at the Polo Grounds with the Jets staying until 1963.

 Other events at the Polo Grounds included soccer, boxing, and Gaelic football. The final pro sports event at the Polo Grounds was between the New York Jets and the Buffalo Bills in 1963. With Shea Stadium opening in 1964, the Polo Grounds was replaced as the home of the New York Mets and the New York Jets. In that same year, 1964, the Polo Grounds were demolished over four months and eventually became a housing complex.

Images of baseball at the Polo Grounds show up originally in about 1882. The New York Metropolitans, an independent team of roughly Major League–level players, was the first professional sports team to compete at the Polo Grounds in 1880. At about that time the Metropolitans' owners had a chance to bring the team into the National League but instead organized a new team named the New York Gothams that soon became known as the New York Giants. Most of those players on the Gothams were from the Metropolitans and the Troy Trojans. The stadium was divided into two parts—eastern and western field for the Metropolitans and the Giants respectively. The Polo Grounds hosted its first Major League Baseball team in 1883 as the home of both the Metropolitans and the Gothams. The two-field setup proved unworkable because of the poor surfacing of the western field. Other issues arose quickly. When two teams played at the same time, the fans in the upper deck of one field were able to watch the game in the other field. Home run balls hit in one field landed in the diamond of the other field as did foul balls, obviously leading to confused players. Attempts were made to rectify the problems but proved to no avail. The Metropolitans eventually moved to the Saint George Cricket Grounds on Staten Island in the mid-1880s.

In the early morning of April 14, 1911, a fire of an undetermined origin swept through one grandstand, completely burning out the wood and leaving only the steel uprights in place. A large portion of the outfield seating was saved from destruction, and Giants owner John Brush decided to rebuild using only concrete and steel. Brush rented Hilltop Park from the New York Highlanders during the reconstruction. Progress rebuilding the Polo Grounds moved along quick enough in that it was able to reopen just two and a half months later, becoming the ninth concrete-and-steel stadium in the majors and the fourth in the National League. The unfinished seating areas were rebuilt during the same season often while games were in progress. Whatever wooden bleachers survived were retained as is with gaps between them and the newly constructed fireproof bleachers. The Giants were able to persevere through the turmoil and in 1911 won the National League Pennant. The team renamed the structure Brush Stadium in honor of their owner John Brush as evidenced by the 1911 World Series programs. Oddly, the name did not stick, and with the demolition of the old wooden bleachers in the 1923 season, the nickname "The Bathtub" took hold along with the original name The Polo Grounds. Soon the Giants became the choice of the city in terms of professional baseball. From 1913 to 1922 the New York Yankees sublet the Polo Grounds from the Giants when their lease on Hilltop Park expired after the 1922 season. When the Yankees built Yankee Stadium directly across the Harlem River from the Polo Grounds, that construction spurred the Giants to expand the capacity of their park to remain competitive with the new Yankee Stadium. Yankee Stadium contained more desirable seats than the Polo Grounds for baseball. However, the Polo Grounds, due to its shape, was better suited for seating at football games. Highlights of the early Polo Grounds were Roger Connor's home run over the right field wall onto 112th Street that set the record for home runs by a single player, which Babe Ruth would eventually break in 1921 and Henry Hank Aaron would break again in the 1974. The stoic "shot heard around the world," a walk-off home run in 1951 that decided the National League Pennant between the Giants and their crosstown rivals, the Brooklyn Dodgers, is generally considered the most famous occurrence at the Polo Grounds. Willie Mays's over-the-shoulder catch against Vic Wertz in deep center field is also considered one of the most iconic plays in baseball with Mays's immediate spinning around and making a long throw to second base, thus holding the runners at first and third.

    Two tragedies also occurred at the Polo Grounds that to this day have never been repeated. On August 16, 1920, Cleveland Indians shortstop Ray Chapman was hit in the head by a pitch from Yankees Carl Mays. At that time batters did not wear helmets, and Chapman died twelve hours after he was hit at 4:30 a.m. on August

17. Chapman remains the only player to have ever died directly from an injury sustained during Major League Baseball game. On July 4, 1950, Bernard "Barney" Doyle of Fairview, New Jersey, was killed by a stray bullet while in his seat waiting for a doubleheader between the Giants and the Dodgers at the Polo Grounds to begin. Doyle was killed about an hour prior to the start of the first game. A young boy later confessed to having shot a pistol into the air from his rooftop located about 1,100 feet from where Doyle was sitting, striking and killing the spectator.

The Giants' final years in the Polo Grounds proved to be anticlimactic, especially when compared to the "Jewel Box" ballparks that had been recently constructed all over America. The biggest issue was the overall condition of the park, which was never well maintained. While the Giants owned the stadium, James and Harriet Coogan owned the parcel of land on which it stood. Unfortunately, the area around the stadium also began to deteriorate in the 1950s. Both of those factors, along with others, restricted ticket sales even when the Giants played well. In 1954 the Giants only sold 1.1 million tickets compared to 2 million for the Milwaukee Brewers even though the Giants won the World Series. Those factors combined with the football Giants leaving the Polo Grounds for Yankee Stadium in 1955 made for a deadly combination at the Polo Grounds. The 1956 season for the baseball Giants proved disastrous with the team spending most of the time in last place, causing a further decline in ticket sales. Ironically, Giants owner Horace Stoneham, who was not nearly as wealthy as other owners, with the Giants being his sole source of income, had no money for stadium upkeep and was forced to lay off the stadium's maintenance workers to stay afloat.

A lack of parking, especially with the advent of the car, kept fans away along with the fact that the entrance onto the field was through the center field gates, making a problem even when the stadium was not at full attendance. Frustrated with the Polo Grounds being obsolete and dilapidated with no maintenance staff or any prospect of it being renovated, Stoneham considered having the Giants become tenants of Yankee Stadium in the Bronx or moving to another stadium that could have been built by and be the property of the city.

After both of those plans fell apart, the Giants announced in 1957 that they would relocate to San Francisco, California, at the end of the season, following their longtime rival, the Brooklyn Dodgers, to the West Coast. The Giants were always proud of the fact that they had won five World Series titles at the Polo Grounds. A fact that can never be denied. For nearly ten years the stadium sat vacant until the newly formed Titans, the present-day New York Jets, began to play there in 1960 followed by the expansion of Mets in 1962. The Mets used the Polo Grounds as a temporary home until Shea Stadium was built in 1961. New York City eventually claimed the land under the Polo Grounds in eminent domain for the purpose of condemning it and building a high-rise apartment project there. The Coogan family who owned the property fought this effort until settling in 1967 in the city's favor. On September 18, 1963, 1,752 fans showed up to watch the New York Mets play the last game at the Polo Grounds against the Philadelphia Phillies, with the Phillies winning five to one. The Polo Grounds later that fall played host to an exhibition game of the Latin American All-Stars managed by Roberto Clemente, featuring the pitching of Juan Marichal. The final sporting event at the Polo Grounds was December 14, 1963, when the now renamed AFL team, New York Jets, lost to the Buffalo Bills nineteen to ten.

It is reported in 1963 that Mets manager Casey Stengel, who had bittersweet memories of his playing days at the Polo Grounds, went out to the mound to talk to his pitcher Tracy Stallard, whose greatest claim to fame was giving up Roger Maris his sixty-first home run home run in 1961. Stengel reportedly said to Stallard, "At the end of the season they're gonna tear this joint down. The way you're pitchin' the right field section will be gone already."

The Polo Grounds were demolished in 1964 beginning on April 10 with the wrecking ball painted to look like a baseball. It was the same one that had been used four years earlier to tear down Ebbets Field. The wrecking crew wore Giants jerseys and tipped their hats to the historic stadium as they began the demolition process. With a crew of about sixty workers taking four-and-one-half months to level the field, it is rumored that the Cleveland Indians bus passed the Polo Grounds while in town to play the Yankees as the demolition was taking place. Indian player Dick Donovan, spotting the rubble, remarked, "Boy, they must have had a helluva a game there last night."

All that now stands in the place of that magical site for baseball is the Polo Grounds Towers, a public housing project opened in 1968 and managed by the New York Housing Authority.

Ebbets Field was located in the Flatbush section of Brooklyn beginning with groundbreaking on March 4, 1912. The stadium opened in 1913, but with baseball becoming more popular every day, it eventually almost doubled in size to accommodate over thirty-two thousand people. In 1949 the field was bounded by Bedford Avenue, Sullivan Place, along with Cedar Street, renamed McKeever Place in 1932, and Montgomery Street. In 1908 Dodgers owner Charles Ebbets began acquiring lots until over the years he owned the entire block. That section of Brooklyn was at one time a garbage dump nicknamed "Pigtown" because of the many pigs and goats that could be found eating there and the stench that they created in the area. The street was full of old houses and shanties with farm animals wandering freely throughout the neighborhood. The cornerstone for Ebbets Field was laid on March 4, 1912, made of Connecticut granite with a time capsule placed inside containing newspapers, baseball cards, telegrams, and almanacs. At a cornerstone ceremony, Charles Ebbets predicted that the stadium would be ready by September 1, and Brooklyn would win the National League Pennant in 1913. The park's construction was not progressing as quickly as planned when it was announced that Ebbets had sold shares in the team to Steven and Edward McKeever who made a fortune in contracting and were able to speed up the construction of the park even withstanding an ironworkers' strike. Ebbets sold 50 percent of the team stock to cover cost overruns and makeovers. That sale led to slowing down of the decision-making process as construction progressed. Fortunately, by early 1913 the stadium was finished with local newspapers praising it as "A Monument to the National Game" and boldly predicting that it would last two hundred years. Ironically, it only lasted forty-seven.

The first game between the Yankees and the Dodgers was played on April 5, 1913, when thirty thousand fans attended and five thousand were turned away due to lack of seating. A second game was played on April 7 in front of only one thousand fans due to very cold weather. Upon opening, it was soon discovered that a flagpole was never erected, no one had a key to the bleachers gate, and the press box was never included in the scope of construction. Concrete bleachers extended along the third baseline to the outfield, but there no seating in the outfield. The right field wall was fairly high with the street immediately on the other side. Fenway Park and Tiger Stadium opened just prior to Ebbets Field and were often compared to Ebbets small, intimate configuration, not in a flattering manner, prompting some writers to dub Ebbets a "cigar box" or a "bandbox."

The early Dodgers were also called the Robins, named after their longtime manager Wilbert Robertson who coached the team to National League Championships in 1916 and 1920. Seating was expanded in the 1920s, a boom time for baseball, with the second deck and field seats along both sidelines. The first night game was played on June 15, 1938, with thirty-nine thousand people squeezed in without an inch to spare, let alone a seat. By the 1940s a large scoreboard was installed in right field. After much early success, the team slid into a two-decade long decline until promotional wizard Larry MacPhail was brought in. Then due to MacPhail's wartime induction into the military, player development genius Branch Rickey was hired. Rickey was able to use his farm system savvy to build success year after year, and the moniker "Dem Bums" quickly became a thing of the past. The Dodgers were soon a contender every year. After many winning seasons, the Dodgers found themselves victims of their own success due to a stadium that could never seat more than thirty-five thousand people comfortably, the constraints of the neighborhood, and the many fans who had moved to the suburbs in Long Island or New Jersey, being unable to locate parking space on game days and nights. When Walter O'Malley obtained ownership of the Dodgers in the 1947, he announced plans to build a domed stadium at the Atlantic Yards site in Brooklyn, the current location of the Barclays Center, after a large market was scheduled for demolition. The city building commissioner Robert Moses refused to help O'Malley secure the land and instead wanted the Dodgers to move to a city-owned property in Flushing Meadows, Queens, the future site of Shea Stadium and now Citi Field. O'Malley refused informing the city that his team was the "Brooklyn Dodgers not the Queens Dodgers." After his plans fell through, O'Malley started to flirt with the idea of using his political leverage to move the Dodgers to Los Angeles. In the end, O'Malley and city building commissioner Moses could not come to an agreement, and O'Malley decided to move the team to Los Angeles. During their last two years at Ebbets Field, again due to parking constraints in the neighborhood, the Dodgers played several games in Jersey City at New Jersey's Roosevelt Stadium, a tactic used by O'Malley to try to force the building commissioner to acquiesce and allow a new stadium to be built in Brooklyn. Once the Dodgers committed to leave for Los Angles, O'Malley also urged Horace Stoneham, owner of crosstown rival, the New York Giants, to move to San Francisco. After the Dodgers left Brooklyn, there was a twilight phase in which Ebbets Field occasionally hosted high school-level games and a handful of Negro League games featuring a team formed by Roy Campanella. In one of those games, Satchel Paige made a guest pitching appearance. The demolition of Ebbets Field began in February of 1960, more than thirty years after the Dodgers left Brooklyn. Federal judge Constance Baker Motley in the Southern District of New York called the Dodgers' relocation to Los Angeles "one of the most notorious abandonments in the history of sports."

Today the site of Ebbets Field is a large apartment complex aptly named the Ebbets Field Apartments with Middle School 320 on the same block renamed as the Jackie Robinson Intermediate School. A street sign that once stood at the corner of McKeever Place and Montgomery Street at the site of Ebbets Field sold at an auction in 2014 for $58,852.08.

Quite rich histories for two sites that only one person I've ever known in my life, Richard Sassone, to have been to. Especially in the glory days of the Polo Grounds, Ebbets Field, and Major League Baseball.

After that discovery process, we got back to Richard's King of Orchard Street chronicle and explored many true-to-life circumstances.

Richard picked up with a story about the many older men who inhabited Orchard Street.

"On the corner of Railroad and Orchard Street, there was a gas station. I think the building is still there, but it it's been empty for as long as I can remember. Many of the old-timers would gather there to play cards. They played pitch and pinochle. In am guessing they were gambling but not to a great extent. It was mostly socializing, and if you got lucky, you might even make a few bucks. Never anything high stakes that I saw, but I imagine at times you could win some pretty good money if Lady Luck was with you. There was also a pool hall on Main Street that my father used to work at sometimes on weekday nights. I don't remember who owned it or exactly where it was, but they had three or four pool tables and pretty much the same guys who played pinochle in the gas station were the ones who shot pool too. I'm sure there was some gambling taking place and illegal bookmaking but again nothing to any big extent that I was aware of. Illegal bookmaking is generally a victimless crime anyway. A group of old Italian guys socializing and having some fun was all it really was. I don't remember there ever being any alcohol or trouble in either place. I used to go at one time or another into both places and never felt any type of intimidation or fear. If these guys had been there hanging out with their wives and kids, it would have been more of a family event than anything else. They were there consistently having fun. It was a good Orchard Street environment—very friendly, maybe a little risky but nothing menacing. The pool hall in particular would sell candy bars, soda, coffee, and that sort of thing. Kids, even at times, women would go in and out during the day. At the gas station I don't remember anyone pumping much gas or working on many cars. It seemed like more of a social club than anything else. I'll say again, never a risky or dangerous environment, which was the overall atmosphere on Orchard Street even with four bars lining the street.

"As usual in any environment, there always has to be someone who causes problems. One guy in particular—I think his name was Philly—drove an old beat-up Plymouth, and if my memory serves me correctly, he was pretty much an alcoholic. None of us ever really knew what his problem was, but he was mean to us for no reason. We were a bunch of kids just hanging around being kids, and this guy was nasty to us. He would swear at us, call us names, and make all sort of vulgar statements. I think he was drunk most of the time, and you know what happens to people who drink too much for to many years. I believe Philly, or whatever his name, died a long time ago. At one point—I don't remember having any involvement myself—someone decided to get even with him. While he was in the gas station, they took all four tires off his car, put it up on blocks, and left it there. They stole the tires right off the car. When Philly came out, obviously, he was very angry at whoever had done it. I am betting someone somewhere on Orchard Street was watching the scene unfold out a window, laughing hysterically. Philly was on fire over what had happened to his car as a group of us observed the situation and were laughing harder than that someone somewhere on Orchard Street looking out a window.

"Clearly, Philly failed to see the humor. Clearly, we didn't.

"We kept ourselves entertained every day mostly with sports. We would play baseball in the field across from North Side School on the east end of the street. From the southeast corner of the playground, which we used as home plate—I don't know if it was built or it was just the paths we made from running the bases—a baseball diamond developed. We would choose up teams. Then by using our closed fists one on top of the other wrapped around an upside-down bat, someone's fist would eventually reach the top, actually the bottom end of the bat. The fist that ended up on the top of the upside-down bat would get the first at bat for their team. We all paid close attention when my brother Ronnie came up to bat because he could hit a long ball like none of the rest of us could. Any point over the center-right fence was home run, and Ronnie was the person who could hit the most home runs. He didn't even hit high ones. He hit them like ropes out over the fence in right field or over everybody's head in left field because there was no fence in left, just grass stretching out toward the other end of the playground. Ronnie may have not been real fast, and he could hit the ball a long way, which made up for the lack of speed. Butch Spina was another good player. He hit the ball hard most times right up the middle, and he was fast. If when we choose up teams Butch and Ronnie got on the same team, that was pretty much the end of the game. With Ronnie hitting the home runs and Butch running the bases, they could score a lot of runs. I hear Butch doesn't live in Frankfort anymore. I think he lives in North Utica or maybe Deerfield. I'm not sure, but I understand he sold his house and moved. He's still in the area but not in Frankfort.

"We had another game we played, which was a version of Leapfrog, that I think you said your uncle John Iocovozzi recounted too. He didn't have a name for it, but we called it Peter Cabana. I have no idea where that name came from, but at least it wasn't macabre like Dead Man's Trail or ethnically inappropriate like spaghetti bender, and other local nomenclature that we can discuss later. We played Peter Cabana in a similar fashion as your uncle. One person would bend over and wrap his arms around a tree or a telephone pole with the second person bending over and wrapping their arms around the waist of the first person, then a third would do the same, a fourth, and so on until we had six or seven people linked together. Another team would form linking themselves to another tree or telephone pole in the same manner. Next, a lighter weight person would back up about ten yards and run toward the linked-together people to try to leapfrog from the back of the last person in the chain as far down the chain as possible. The other team would do the same, and we would compete to determine which team got farthest down the chain. There were times when we took the concept farther, and instead of linking together parallel to the ground, we decided to apply the same concept to go up a tree or telephone pole with the lighter people climbing up over those below to perch on the shoulders of what previously was the highest person in the tower of people that we were assembling. Again, competing against another team, doing the same thing to determine which team could get the highest up the tree. If the trees were close enough to each other as each guy tried to climber higher, he would pull the guy climbing over the lower people on the other team off of their column. The struggles got pretty intense at times with some real pulling and yanking to get the highest guy on the other team off his teammate's shoulders. We got up in the air some distance at times. If you were unlucky enough to get pulled off your team's spire, which could be quite high, it generally wasn't pretty, especially on the way down, and it certainly wasn't when you hit the ground. Thankfully, no one ever got hurt, but it did turn wild at times.

"We played a lot of tackle football, full-speed tackle football with no equipment, and we hit each other pretty good. It was like a rugby game with the hitting and tackling that we did. We played on the grass between the fence on the west end of the playground and the fence on the east end. As I said, the east end was our baseball diamond, and in between which was really the outfield of our diamond, we played football. My brother Ronnie was usually the one who organized the football games because he loved football. We would choose up teams. I don't think we ever had eleven players on each team, probably seven or eight, but we would line up and run plays. Anthony and John Spina were usually there too. John was the quarterback, and we would create plays drawn in the dirt. We would use running plays at times, but mostly it was passing. We would run pass patterns that had been drawn out a minute before in the dirt with a stick or even a finger if no stick was available. The beauty of it was we were a bunch of kids who really got along well, outside in the fresh air and sun, getting a lot of exercise. I don't think that we really appreciated at the time how much we were benefiting our health, social and physical. There was never any arguing or fighting. We simply wanted to compete to have fun and be in each other's company. We couldn't wait for school to get out in the summer so that we could live and play the way we wanted to. The lifelong benefits of those idyllic childhood days on Orchard Street are still alive today for me as they were way back then some seventy years ago. The difference is until now they were only memories, but by what you, I, and the rest of us are doing, those memories are alive again on an entirely different level for years to come.

"My high school years really put the icing on the cake for my younger days growing up on Orchard Street. Sports were still a big part of my life, but now they were organized interscholastic sports. Football was by far my favorite, although I did compete in basketball and baseball also. Football was a sport I enjoyed the most. I paid attention to school, but it was only to the level I needed that allowed me to participate in sports. If I were given a choice, I probably would have not spent a lot of time in the classroom, but to play sports, I had to have a certain level of grades. I did my best to learn, but it wasn't the driving force of me going to school every day. That position belonged to sports. As I mentioned before, Jim Alsante and I were very close friends. Jim weighed 145 pounds, and I weighed 143. Jimmy played linebacker, and I was always trying to get in the game to replace him. He was pretty good too, a little taller than me and faster. I wanted to replace him on every play. We both played for Coaches Joe Campo and John Moseley. Both were very good coaches and knew a lot about football. Campo's wrestling teams were the best around for a long time too.

To play basketball, we used to go around behind the gymnasium of the North Side School and wedge the door open with a pipe. There was a stairwell that went down a flight to the door that we had wedged open. We would wait for the school to empty out and then sneak back in to play basketball. There would be a few lights on for safety purposes, and I think at times we turned the lights off hoping that no one would notice us in the building. All we did was play basketball, but we weren't supposed to be in there anyway because it was after school. We didn't do any damage. We just wanted to play indoor basketball because it was winter and the court across the street was frozen. We never got caught, which gave us even more impetus to sneak in one or two nights a week. Again we didn't do any harm, break anything, or vandalize. We played basketball. When we were done, we would leave out of that same back door, push the door closed from the outside, walk up the stairs, and go home all in a matter of about two hours. Should we have been in there? No, but we didn't do any harm, and no one ever got hurt. We all went home after some fun competition and exercise. I bet half of the kids whom

I grew up with did the same thing at whatever school was in their part of the village, whether it be Frankfort High School or Reese Road. We made a situation and took advantage of it. No harm, no foul. The way I see it, it was good, clean fun.

"Jim Alsante and I also made sure we created a little mischief in the high school. I tried just hard enough to get decent grades. I was never an A student, but I did understand the value of education. My priority in school was, as I've said, sports. Education was at best the second priority and at worst my third. I bet you could make an accurate guess as to what my second was. In any case, I was happy to go to school every day. I did my homework, probably not as well as I should have or studied as hard as I could have, but I did good overall. In the end, I have a master's degree, so it worked out for me. I really can't complain about any of it.

"As we got to be seniors, Jim and I really didn't have much to do in school anymore. The entire afternoon was filled with study hall and gym classes. Nothing along the lines of academic subjects like English or Math. After our lunch, there was really no point in staying in school any longer, so Jimmy and I would sneak out the back door of the school by the chemistry lab to walk across Fifth Avenue and through a little clump of woods on the other side of Fifth Avenue from the high school. That walk brought us to Fourth Avenue where Jimmy lived. Many days we stayed for the lunch period in school, but once that was over, we left and went over to Mrs. Alsante's. The lunches in school were good, but Mrs. Alsante's were better. Once we were at her house, we would stay for the rest of the afternoon. I couldn't go home, because naturally my mother would ask me why I wasn't in school. We would stay at the Alsante's house most of the afternoon, hanging out, talking to Mrs. Alsante, and enjoying ourselves. If we had a sports practice after school, we would go back in time for that, but if we weren't participating in a sport, many times we would go back to school at dismissal to socialize. Then I would go home to prevent my mom from asking why I was out of school early. Other days I would walk home directly from Alsante's house to mine. By the time I walked back to Orchard Street, it was the usual time I got home, and my mother wouldn't ask me any questions. We did this for at least six months before anyone caught on. Eventually, I'm not sure if it was a teacher or another student, but someone turned us in. I don't know if you remember him, but Nick "Prof" Frank was the principal at the time. In any case, someone caught on that we were leaving the school and informed Mr. Frank. However, much time elapsed from when whoever informed Mr. Frank until he called us in his office. I'm not sure, but he did eventually call us in. When he asked us why we're leaving school, we were both honest. We told him we really didn't have anything to do in the afternoon, thus what was the point of sitting in school accomplishing nothing? He wanted to know where we went, and being fully honest, we told him that we went to Alsante's house. Then he wanted to know what we were doing there. Again, we were honest and told him not really much other than having lunch, visiting with Mrs. Alsante, or watching TV. We weren't getting in any trouble. We just weren't in school. Mr. Frank was not upset, but he told us he felt we had to be more productive than just sitting there watching TV all afternoon. If we could find something productive to do at the Alsante's house, he would overlook us not being in school. We promised to find out what we could do to make us productive, and he let it go at that. When we came back at some point, we had to inform him what exactly we were doing that he should consider productive. In light of his conditions, we started cutting the grass, cleaning out the garage at one point, and we even painted in Mrs. Alsante's dining room. Whatever we could do so that when we went back to school and Mr. Frank asked us, we could report to him that we had cut the grass, painted, or whatever, which was the truth. Those were the things we did, and he bought it. It got to the point that he was sending us over to his mother's house to cut the grass or whatever job she needed done around her house. Rake leaves, whatever. The point was Mr. Frank was happy, Jimmy and I were happy, but most importantly, we didn't sit in school wasting the whole afternoon doing nothing educational or otherwise. In the end, it all worked out. It's Aristotelian logic. You do the things the most that you like the most, and you do the things the best that you like the best. Prof Frank and the Frankfort Schools got what they wanted. Mrs. Alsante and Mrs. Frank got what they wanted. Jimmy and I got what we wanted. The perfect deal if you ask me.

"I vividly remember some of the colloquial names we used for specific locations. South of the village in the Frankfort Gorge, there was a favorite swimming hole we called the Merry Widow. It was covered by an old farm bridge with some deepwater holes that eons of water running through that gorge had carved out. We called it the Merry Widow, but I was never sure if it was spelled Merry Widow or Mary Widow, but it was one or the other. I have no idea where the name came from. I would think it probably came from the last name of the farmer who owned the land, and his wife was deceased, or maybe his wife was alive, just very happy, with Widow as the couple's last name. The Merry Widow, let's call it that, is directly behind Steve Zipko's house. Truly a very interesting name that I wish I knew more about. Another eerie name that comes to mind was Dead Man's Trail. As you move west up Hilltop Road by the former Frankfort Pool, which leads to Lehman Park, or as we called it the Hilltop, to the left of the road, there a footpath through the woods that also led up to the park. About halfway up the trail, there was another path that veered off to the left and went downhill to the bank of Moyer Creek. I was never clear which one was Dead Man's Trail, the one that went straight up the hill or the one that went off to the left? In any case, where that name came from I also have no idea. Merry Widow and Dead Man's Trail—two creepy, curious names if you ask me. Chances are they both got names from some real event. I wouldn't think there would be anybody alive who could fill in the blanks, but assuredly that info would be something to pursue for fun if nothing else. The Flats was another name you heard often in and around town. That name I can take a good guess at where it comes from because of the geography of the area. The Flats were the surrounding floodplains of the Mohawk River moving east and west along the banks of the river. In the spring, when there was a lot of rain and the snow melted, those areas would flood because they were flat, thus the name the Flats. The Flats were far enough away from homes or barns to prevent any damage other than fill up the empty fields with water from the overflowing Mohawk River. In the summer, when the area dried up, the water would go back into the actual bed of the Mohawk but leave all that thick, rich mud from the bottom of the river where it had flooded, creating the perfect field to plant corn, strawberries, or whatever the farmer was growing that year. That name makes geographic sense, but the Merry Widow and Dead Man's Trail are ghastly names for simple plots of real estate.

"The ethnic names that we used for each other were not very positive either, along the same lines as the not-very-positive names we used for various locations in the village. The ethnic names were more characterizations than colloquialisms, whereas the location names, to the best of my knowledge, were strictly colloquialisms. Unfortunately, we used characterizations based on ethnic backgrounds. Few, if any, came right out and used plainly derogatory terms, but the innuendo was obvious. For many years there was a conflict of sorts that took place between Frankfort and Ilion residents. Frankfort being mostly Italian American and Ilion being mostly Irish American, there tended to be competition. Usually in sports but other times between the various families or loosely organized groups that inhabited each village, real tribal stuff. The proximity of the two villages automatically lent itself to competitiveness, and that competitiveness morphed into different forms. The residents of Ilion generally referred to the residents of Frankfort as spaghetti benders. Clearly a derogatory slang term for an Italian American. Funny how that idea could be extended to almost any ethnic group. It would make sense then based on that concept to call Polish Americans kielbasa benders or Mexican Americans taco benders. The concept could be extended to any ethnic group, and it would certainly not be a polite extension. On the other hand, people in Frankfort called Ilion residents cake eaters. I think that idea stemmed from the fact that the mostly Irish residents of Ilion somehow inhabited a very white Caucasian-isolated world, and what they ate was generally colorless, bland-appearing, and tasteless food. Like the world Ilion residents inhabited. There was no diversity to speak of in Ilion, mostly a Caucasian-based Irish and Anglo-Saxon culture that existed around itself only. No one different, leading to any diversity, ever went in or out of the culture of the village. The way of life revolved around itself only. Cake eater is actually an old term for people who lived in a more affluent, comfortable backdrop. It stems from the fact that centuries ago, every day people ate bread because that's all they could afford, whereas wealthier people ate cake because it was more expensive and difficult to obtain. Now that I think of it perhaps the slang *cake eater* stemmed from the fact that people in Ilion may have been more affluent due to working at Remington Arms than those living in Frankfort working at the Union Fork and Hoe. Honestly, I don't recall that being the case, but I suppose it is a possibility. I think the two phrases were more based on one group maligning the other due to ethnicity. It did cause problems, as I said, particularly in sports but also in any type of competitive endeavor. Even years later, as we all got older, it continued to cause problems in terms of girlfriends and boyfriends being from one village or the other, crossing ethnic, physical, religious, and cultural bounds. That generational competitiveness caused fights mostly in bars between two guys who may have been interested in the same girl or two girls who may have been interested in the same guy with the participants each residing in their separate villages with their corresponding ethnic group. When there was such an incident, it was usually, as I said, in a bar when one person or the other or both had too much to drink and decided that was the time to resolve their differences.

"In Frankfort, especially in the vicinity of Orchard Street and Main Street, there was a number of what we used to call "watering holes" where on the weekends, crowds tended to gather from throughout the valley because those watering holes had the most action, so to speak. Places like Grippes', the Club Royale, Billis's Hotel, and Puzze's were usually packed every weekend, especially weekend nights, with young people doing what young males and females do. During the week most of the bars were pretty quiet with an older crowd, but on weekends they were filled with young people under the age of thirty. At night the bars were so full that the only way you could get in is when someone went out. Those were the days of go-go dancers in cages, and the bars got pretty wild. The whole bar scene sometimes led to problems many times in light of the cultural, ethnic, and geographic boundaries that separated the various groups living in the valley. Whatever the issue was, it caused problems that were not necessary. Obviously, nobody thought of those things at the time. In the end, it was mostly a bunch of young men and women trying to establish their territoriality and reputations for all intents and purposes in a dangerous, silly fashion. A consummate example of how youth can be a very unbecoming slice of life.

"Also, there was a guy who lived on Orchard Street whom we knew as John Peach. He was generally a good guy but certainly a vagrant. I never knew him to have a house or apartment, and he habitually slept under the milk plant on the west end of the street. I have no idea who he was or if that was his real name. My suspicion is that his name came about in a fashion similar to Merry Widow or Dead Man's Trail. Murky, I feel, is an apt description. I don't recall him getting into any trouble or causing any problems in the neighborhood, but he was always there. Moving in and out of different areas and blocks of the street all day long. Maybe he was an alcoholic, a drug addict, or something else. I was never sure how he got on Orchard Street or where he ended up after that. Maybe he had relatives in Frankfort, or maybe he just found an area he liked, so he stayed. He just existed in the neighborhood. A shadow if you will.

"My point is the validity of the names and how they came into existence. They had to be grounded in some degree of reality at some point. Yet I am guessing.

"Things that make you go, 'Hmm.'

"After those august years in high school and growing up on Orchard Street as I got older, I married, went to college, and started to raise a family. Whether it was consciously or unconsciously, I was still working to keep Orchard Street and the environment in the village of Frankfort the same as it was when I was growing up. Perhaps I tried to keep that atmosphere alive in more concrete ways than I realize, but in the end, exactly what I was doing was recreating a way of life. I was a member of the Frankfort Fire Department and refereed high school football games for many years. Now I see that my end game was an attempt to keep the village and the lifestyle that I grew in the same for my family and every family in that village.

"Beyond the village level, now with a long-term perspective in hand, I was recreating that Orchard Street lifestyle through my job too, but that fact was unbeknownst to me the time. I originally worked at Remington Arms but in the mid-1990s was hired by SLM Action Sports in Mayfield, New York, which had taken control of Coleco based in Amsterdam, New York. Coleco had a long and varied history beginning as a leather company in Connecticut in 1932, founded by Maurice Greenberg with the name the Connecticut Leather Company. By the 1980s Coleco had transformed into a successful toy company with its most famous product being the Cabbage Patch Kids. Coleco was also an early developer of video game consoles, specifically the Coleco Telstar and ColecoVision systems. In the late 1980s Coleco ceased operations as a result of a bankruptcy but was revived in 2005 and is still active to this day. Being a company that started out as a leather supplier and shoe repair business prior to World War II, with the onset of World War II, the demand for its products soared in light of the need to outfit the military. I believe how Coleco got into toys was their production of home-based leathercraft kits, which debuted at the 1954 New York Toy Fair and was awarded the prestigious Toy of the Year medal. The management, seeing an opportunity, quickly moved out of the leather business into toy manufacturing. The company's first foray into the toy business was manufacturing inflatable vinyl pools and swim toys. From there they moved into manufacturing aboveground pools and soon became the largest producer in America. With this ever-expanding market, Coleco operated ten manufacturing facilities. After many years in the recreation business, Coleco even moved into snowmobiles by way of an acquisition. After Atari released the Pong game and console, Coleco quickly released their Telstar console with a variety of games. Next came direct competition with Mattel and Atari in the handheld game business. Many arcade games like Donkey Kong, Pac-Man, and Frogger became big sellers still in arcade models but also in home console and handheld versions. In 1983 the most wildly successful of all Coleco products was introduced. I am sure you remember the Cabbage Patch Kids. Cabbage Patch Kids were an instant success. With all that success in hand, Coleco next tried board games like Aggravation and Perfection, which were accepted far and wide too. The Alf doll, based on a TV series, was also a huge hit in the United

States. Coleco even went so far as to produce a cassette that enabled Alf to tell a story using any cassette player. Alf was now a talking toy. A transformative point in the history of the toy industry.

"As the management of SLM became increasingly aware of the impending maturation of the toy business, a decision was made to evolve to the manufacturing of sports equipment. Being a company based in the northeast, mostly in New York and Connecticut, the obvious sport to connect to was hockey. The hockey division was successful to start with but slowly declined due to strong competition from other companies such as CCM, Bauer, Sherwood, and eventually bigger companies like Nike. The choice proved profitable but not for very long.

"As with anything else, the public's fascination with Cabbage Patch Kids eventually declined. That fact along with the disastrous introduction of Coleco's game console Adam led to Coleco's ultimate demise. In 1988 Coleco filed for bankruptcy. Its swimming pool and pool toy product division was purchased by a Canadian company along with Hasbro purchasing most of Coleco's remaining toy lines. SLM then acquired what endured of Coleco in June of 1989.

"While working for SLM, I still resided in Frankfort hoping to maintain for my family and any other residents of Frankfort the same lifestyle that I grew accustomed to. How this all connects between SLM and the life I wanted to maintain as a resident in the Village of Frankfort was based on a sense of altruism for my community and family. My intentions were based on the concept of SLM's community involvement. Anytime I was able to convince the management to make donations of Cabbage Patch Kids, toys, and sports equipment, which were in huge demand all over the United States, if they agreed, I would accept the donations and distribute them to Toys for Tots and the children on Orchard Street. It was equally as thrilling for me to donate such a wildly successful product as a Cabbage Patch doll as I bet it was for the children who received them as gifts from Santa Claus or for whatever reason. Again, securing these dolls in the retail market was very difficult. The dolls were so popular that they had to be preordered, and people would stand in line for hours at stores to purchase them. I was fortunate enough to have access to the toys free of charge and then have an opportunity to donate them to the most deserving situations I could find. It had to be a big thrill for some child on Orchard Street who wanted a Cabbage Patch doll, knowing how hard they were to get, that they had one. The best part being for free. I bet it made the child very happy and their family also, especially if the parents couldn't afford or find one. The Cabbage Patch dolls were cultural phenomenon like, in later years, the Yu-Gi-Oh! trading cards but bigger.

"Although hockey was never a big sport in Frankfort, I was also lucky enough when in the hockey business, to get donations that provided young hockey players with equipment usually free of charge. Most times the hockey equipment and the toys donated were free of any flaws, but at times there may have been a minor flaw, which prevented SLM from marketing the product. Maybe the paint ran, the foot of the doll was stained, or a hockey glove had a small stitch missing, but everything was fully functional, and of course, the price was right. You can never beat free. All of that seems to me now to be my personal attempt at keeping and preserving the lifestyle that I was raised in alive for the young residents of Frankfort and their families.

"Did it work? I think it did, yet more importantly, I think the children and families on the receiving end felt it worked too. Whether consciously or unconsciously, I cannot be sure, but I would bet my last dollar it worked for them.

"The names changed, families changed, and the residents changed, but in the end, I think it all prolonged, even if only for a short period of time, the strong, willful, family-oriented, accepting atmosphere that I was lucky enough to be raised in. I hope others, many times whose names I didn't know, experienced the same blessings that I did. Even if only temporally."

I have noticed on a number of occasions while obtaining the various King of Orchard Street reflections that time goes by rapidly. As is the case today with Richard and I discussing his younger years growing up on Orchard Street and in Frankfort. When I finally looked up at his kitchen clock, it seemed as if four hours had been compressed into a time warp of one. Richard seemed to be tired again due to the flu. He clearly needs rest, and I need contemplation. The message is focused and consistent for both of us. Although Richard worked in many cities or towns during his younger years while his job had him traveling all over the World to places in Asia, Europe, and South America, Frankfort and West Orchard Street, specifically, were always in his heart and will always be his home.

Just as they are today sitting in his kitchen only a few miles from "The World's Most Famous Beach."

The first blessing Rich and I received was the day we were born; the second was the families we are born into, and the third was those respective families resided on the one hundred block of West Orchard Street.

Blessings can take on many forms.

The King

Now that all the recollections have been documented, the many highs and few lows spelled out with the sheer strength of it all put on paper, the final task belongs to you, the reader. That task being to make the determination as to who, all considered, is the King of Orchard Street. My impression of the success of Orchard Street is practically a prototype of the long-term success of Sesame Street. As with Sesame Street and Orchard Street, there was a heartfelt formula applied daily to grow contentment. That formula was simple and dominant. We were all accepted, we were all kind, and we all helped each other all the time. A profound formula on numerous levels that has stayed with all of us every day of our natural lives and I hope always will. My final observation is one that all the King of Orchard Street participants, regardless of which one of us is fortunate enough to be deemed the king, the residents both living and deceased who inhabited Orchard Street from the late 1930s through the mid-1960s, along with everyone who reads this book, can agree on without reservation.

That all six of the potential King of Orchard Street contenders and all the residents of Orchard Street throughout the years were extremely lucky to have been born and raised in the locale we all called home—Orchard Street on the north side of the village in Frankfort, New York.

The End

About the Author

Vincent Palmieri was born in 1955 in the small upstate New York village of Frankfort. He resided on Orchard Street in the village with his parents and sister. After a thirty-four-year career as a middle school special education teacher in a small city school district, he began his long considered second career as a writer. His first book, *Ruthie Deeply*, was published in 2021. *The King of Orchard Street* is his second book, and he is currently considering numerous other options for future publications. Vincent continues to live in upstate New York with his wife of over thirty-five years and his two adult children.